Pythagoras and the 1
Transmigration

Continuum Studies in Ancient Philosophy
Series Editor: James Fieser, University of Tennessee at Martin, USA

Continuum Studies in Ancient Philosophy is a major monograph series from Continuum. The series features first-class scholarly research monographs across the field of Ancient Philosophy. Each work makes a major contribution to the field of philosophical research.

Aristotle and Rational Discovery, Russell Winslow
Aristotle's Metaphysics, Jeremy Kirby
Aristotle's Theory of Knowledge, Thomas Kiefer
The Enduring Significance of Parmenides, Raymond Tallis
Happiness and Greek Ethical Thought, M. Andrew Holowchak
The Ideas of Socrates, Matthew S. Linck
Parmenides and To Eon, Lisa Atwood Wilkinson
Plato, Metaphysics and the Forms, Francis A. Grabowski III
Plato's Stepping Stones, Michael Cormack
Pleasure in Aristotle's Ethics, Michael Weinman
Pythagoras and the Doctrine of Transmigration, James Luchte
The Socratic Method, Rebecca Bensen Cain
Stoic Ethics, William O. Stephens

Pythagoras and the Doctrine of Transmigration

Wandering Souls

James Luchte

continuum

Continuum International Publishing Group

The Tower Building	80 Maiden Lane
11 York Road	Suite 704
London SE1 7NX	New York NY 10038

www.continuumbooks.com

British Library Cataloguing-in-Publication Data
A catalogue record for this book is available from the British Library.

ISBN: 978-1-4411-3102-7

Library of Congress Cataloging-in-Publication Data
Luchte, James.
Pythagoras and the doctrine of transmigration : wandering souls / James Luchte.
     p. cm. – (Continuum studies in ancient philosophy)

ISBN-13: 978-1-4411-3102-7

1. Pythagoras. 2. Transmigration. I. Title.
B244.T73L83 2009
182'.2–dc22
2009001099

Typeset by Newgen Imaging Systems Pvt Ltd, Chennai, India
Printed and bound in Great Britain by the MPG Books Group

For my Mother, Judy

Contents

Acknowledgments

I would like to express my appreciation for the radical singularity of the late Reiner Schürmann (1941–1993), whose teachings of Plotinus, Meister Eckhart, Nicolas of Cusa, Nietzsche, Heidegger, and Foucault created a space that made possible unconventional retrievals of the many hidden events and junctures of the history of philosophy and thought.

I would like to thank Johannes Hoff for his comments upon the present work and for vigorous conversation and debate upon the relationship between philosophy and theology.

I would also like to thank Johannes Fritsche, Richard Bernstein, Dmitri Nikulin, Jonathan Wooding, and Alastair Walter for their comments on earlier drafts of this work.

Finally, I would like to express my thanks to my children Zoe, Soren, and Venus, and to my partner Tamara Al-Om, who provided welcome encouragement to bring this project to fruition.

Introduction

The Poetic *Topos* of the Doctrine of Transmigration

I made up rhymes in dark and scary places,
And like a lyre I plucked the tired laces
Of my worn-out shoes, one foot beneath my heart.[1]

(Rimbaud, "Wandering," Stanza 4)

Remind yourself that all men assert wisdom is the greatest good,
but that there are few, who, strenuously endeavor to obtain
this greatest good.[2]

(Attributed to Pythagoras by Stobaeus)

No, not yet, old seer!
No, from this good green earth my eye shall not
Depart without a tribute of late gladness.
And still I wish to dwell upon things past,
Recall once more the dear friend of my youth
Remote now in the happy towns of Hellas,
My brothers too, who cursed me—so it had
To be. Now leave me. When over there the light
Of day goes down, you'll see me once again.

(Empedocles, in Hölderlin, The Death of Empedocles*)*[3]

Pythagoras and the Recurrence of the Tragic

Nietzsche briefly refers to Pythagoras in *The Birth of Tragedy,* as one of the exemplars, prior to Aeschylus (himself attributed by Cicero in *Tusculanae Quaestiones* to be a follower of Pythagoras)[4] of tragic sixth-century Greece.[5] The pregnancy of this reference seems, however, to have been lost on Biebuyck, Praet, and Vanden Poel in their important essay, "Cults and Migrations: Nietzsche's Meditations on Orphism, Pythagoreanism, and the Greek Mysteries."[6] For, while it is clear that Nietzsche savagely castigates Pythagoras (and Orphicism) as a pre-cursor to Plato and as a proto-Christian, the Pythagorean doctrine of transmi-gration could, from the perspective of *The Birth of Tragedy*, be interpreted as a variant of tragic *pessimism*, which abides, at its heart, an affirmation of the eternal recurrence of the All.[7] In this light, the significance of Pythagorean phi-losophy could be seen under a radically different aspect, the basic features of which have not been questioned since W.K.C. Guthrie's monumental *History of Greek Philosophy* in the 1960s. The work of Guthrie, while he to a significant extent merely repeats the ascetic picture of Pythagoras, served to begin to undermine basic features of the dominant interpretation, such as that of Corn-ford (and of Nietzsche himself), which had sought to quarantine the mathe-matical, "scientific" aspects of Pythagorean philosophy from its dispensable and baroque "mystical" shell. Radicalizing the work of Guthrie, the present inter-pretation will seek to recontextualize the status and place of mathematics and science in Pythagorean philosophy (and philosophy *as such*), as aspects that participate (though do not dominate), alongside art, music, and practical tech-niques of the self, in the articulation and the *sheltering* of an esoteric teaching. In this instance, the teaching is that of the *tragic myth*—just as mathematical limit intimates and reflects the deeper ultimacy of tragic fate, of the mortal sin-gularity and limits of existence.

Others may counter this contention with the claim that Pythagoreanism was in fact a religious philosophy of optimism—or, in other words, that in the face of the devastation of temporal existence, they held that there were grounds for hope for an escape from *suffering* in the manner of Buddhism, Platonism, and Christianity. I will oppose this *traditional* account of Pythagoreanism through a return to the researches of the early twentieth century which served to consol-idate the picture of the Pythagoreans as a historically divided phenomenon, of, on the one hand, an older "mystical" and ascetic wing concerned primarily with ethical, religious, and political questions, and, on the other hand, a younger, *modernist* intellectual wing who were focused upon mathematical and scientific endeavors. It is precisely such an ideological and divisive portrayal of the Pythagorean community which will foreclose on any attempt to disclose a *unified* interpretation of the Pythagoreanism in the tragic sixth century. Such a portrayal would furthermore lead to the contention that Pythagorean philos-ophy was a *Holzweg*, a false path, or a dead end, and that, with the suppression of the existence of irrational numbers, this philosophy was merely a step along the path to the "true" philosophy of Plato and the "optimistic" theology of Christianity (and to its later secularized versions after the so-called Enlighten-ment). It would seem that, if we were to accept such an interpretive framework, it would be necessary to hold—rather anachronistically—that the Pythagorean view of the unity of the *Kosmos* was simply not true, that it neither acknowl-edged, nor reflected the reality of the irrational chaos—negativity—of the sen-sible world. In this way, it would be necessary to posit the existence of a *radical other*, an *elsewhere* characterized by an infinite mirror of all that the sensible world is not—eternity, unity, order, and beauty. From this perspective, as the story goes, a purified mathematics would intimate this other world, that of the invisible, and it was number and its study which was to lead the soul toward its eventual *escape* to the other world of a divine which is not identical with the All.

Such a scenario does not however ring true—nor does it even *make sense*—as the latter intellectualist path of liberation from the body, one undertaken through the study of mathematics and philosophy (mathematically conceived) does not accord with what we do know and what we can find out for ourselves (through *praxis*) about the early sixth-century Pythagoreans. Indeed, such an interpretation is fatally anachronistic, for, as we will see in the following pages, it is highly questionable whether we must routinely continue to attribute Platonic ascetic prejudices against the body and the sensible world to the Pythagoreans, not to mention any notion of transmigration that signifies the desire to flee from the embodied world of flux, from the unity of opposites.

At the same time, this conflict over the significance of Pythagorean philosophy is mirrored in the controversy over the extant evidence of two types of Pythagorean students. Both sides of this historical dispute agree that there were two types of students, *akousmatikoi* (hearers) and the *mathematikoi* (mathematicians). From one perspective, the former are esoteric students, who are the earliest Pythagoreans, and who gathered together in a community of *praxis*, cultivating an attunement with the *Kosmos*, as the orchestration of an indigenous unity in the world of the body. The latter, that of the *mathematikoi*, who emerged over time, were students who were trained in the general sciences and mathematics until they were permitted to become "hearers." The other perspective, however, which is widely current, and seems to be based upon a selective reading of Iamblichus, contends that the mathematical students were the highest and that the hearers (in the sense of auditors) were only allowed to listen from *outside the veil* and were thus not trained in the depths of the teaching.[8] Once again, however, this account is anachronistic, not only in light of the late emergence of the mathematical students in the formalization of the Pythagorean school, but also in light of the fact that our notion of auditor as a lesser student does not accord with its probable meaning for the Pythagoreans. Indeed, the conflation of auditor and hearer fails to comprehend the philosophical significance and primacy of the notion of *hearing* for a philosophy whose founder not only discovered the musical scale, but which was disseminated exclusively in the oral tradition. The importance of poetry and song (as tokens of remembrance) is, moreover, clearly in accord with our original indication of the tragic, that is of the Apollonian *and Dionysian*, aspect of the Pythagorean philosophy of transmigration.

This conflict over preeminence, mirrored in our own contemporary divisions and conflicts, eventually contributed to the dissolution of the Pythagorean community, which was effectively (though not entirely) destroyed in the Pythagorean riots. It is significant that there has occurred a repetition of a version of this division in our own era, not only in regard to the sectarianism in philosophy, such as those of the analytic/continental, materialist/idealist, realist/antirealist divides, but also due to the fact that our very understanding of our own past, in this case, that of the nature of the Pythagorean philosophy and community is orchestrated in terms of our own partisanship, by our own wills for preeminence. To the mathematician and scientist, it is the *mathematikoi* who were the true Pythagoreans. To the phenomenologist and post-structuralist, it is the *akousmatikoi* who were the truth or higher Pythagoreans. This investiture of the question in terms of power is no idle matter, however, due to the fact that in the twentieth century, in the wake of the so-called analytic revolution, Pythagoras too was placed under the spotlight of the eliminative strategy and was severed into mysticism and science. In a repetition of the original trauma, the latter aspect of the teaching was salvaged, while the former was placed in the museum of metaphysical ideas, ideas to be spoken with a smile. It is here that the *scientistic* and *logicistic* background of early Analytic philosophy shows itself in its dismissal of, on the one hand, esoteric and practical questions, those of ethics, and, on the other hand, cosmogonical, ontological, and existential questions, which it crassly labels as "metaphysics."

It is this eliminative strategy—and its comprehensive rejection by Continental philosophers—which has tragically lead to the Analytic-Continental divide, one which weakens philosophy in its depth and scope, especially in the face of a resurgent theology.[9] Such a mathematical, Platonizing strategy is, however, being played out again in the polemical interventions by the "last" and latest French philosophers, Badiou and Meillassoux.[10] Each of these has laid down the post-Analytic gauntlet to Continental philosophy advocating the centrality of mathematical universality for the discernment of truth in philosophy.[11] Of course, this is not a recurrence of Pythagoreanism, as they have already dismissed the mystical, idealist character of Pythagorean philosophy in line with the prejudices of a post-Analytic philosophy.[12] This "new" philosophy is, instead, concerned with a quasi-platonistic, *mathematicized* methodology as the predominant way to discover truth ("thing without me") within the labyrinth of utter flux and subjectivism in the sensible or apparent world. In this way, the original tragedy of the Analytic vivisection of Pythagorean philosophy has startlingly recurred, but, in tune with Marx's *Eighteenth Brumaire*, this time as a *farce*—and with the result that the house of philosophy has become ever more divided against itself. It is questionable whether such a divided house will have the strength to contend with a *timely* resurgence of theology which lies in wait for the house of reason to *collapse*.

The following exploration will resist the drive toward a logical, mathematical, or scientific philosophy, through a poetico-phenomenological exploration of the doctrine of transmigration as an intimate philosophical interpretation (hermeneutics) of tragic existence. I will resist, moreover, the uncritical equivocations that either identify the Pythagorean philosophy with that of Plato, or, which trace a genealogy of philosophy which seamlessly divines the development of Platonism out of Pythagoreanism. As will become clear in the following pages, the emphasis that is placed upon the body and *praxis* in the Pythagorean *bios* precludes a strong identification between Pythagorean and Platonic philosophy beyond anything more than a family resemblance. A poetics and *praxis* of transmigration will underscore not only the expressive and mnemopoetic aspect of the doctrine, but will also highlight the emergence of the Pythagorean philosophy contemporaneously with the philosophy of the tragic age. While the tragic destruction of the Pythagorean community erased from our awareness a more thorough account of their way of life, it is in their use of poetics and art that the significance of their teaching, in both its exoteric and esoteric dimensions, remains accessible to us through tokens of remembrance, poetic, artistic, and mathematical, each of which is united in their articulation of *philosophia*. It will be in the affirmation of the body and the *Kosmos* that the truly *pagan* dimension of transmigration will emerge which seeks not an eschatological escape from being, but an affirmation of the All in the manner of Empedocles and, jumping to the next mountain with very long legs, the early German Romantics such as Hölderlin and Schelling.

Transmigration and the Remembrance of Being

The mythical narrative of transmigration tells the story of myriad wandering souls, each migrating from body to body along a path of recurrence amid the *becoming* of the All. Yet, for the Pythagoreans, this story does not describe the passive revolution of a circle, but a pathway for an active exploration and return to the All. This endeavor, expressed in the exoteric narrative, is strenuous as it occurs amid a suspension within the double bind of nativity and fatality, repeatedly to be born and to die, and to be reborn as still another being.[13] The thread of the narrative, of reminiscence, is, with each demise, always severed amidst the tragic labyrinth of mortal existence. Yet, as the narrative is a rope of many threads, the persistent rearticulation of the narrative instigates a *mnemopoiesis* that transcends one's individual mortal life amid the broader community of a greater soul (the multiplicity of the self).

The Pythagoreans, along with others, cultivated an *ethos* of a divine soul, one thought to be capable of communion with the divine All. For Homer, such a desire would have been *hubris*, even if it was not, in the end, articulated outside of the horizons of his mythological ontology. Pythagoras, against the background of Homer's portrayal of the thirsting soul, maintained the requirement of a body, of a microcosm of the All, for its life and its expansion (but only during life, as the soul had its own integrity beyond each body). Pythagoras articulated a philosophy of return of the soul to its divine source through yet another—though forbidden—possibility in the Homeric constellation. He turned the necessity of body into a virtuous *topos* of return of the singular mortal to the cosmic All. Indeed, despite this "mingling of essences," Pythagoras remained true to the Homeric valorization of the life of the body, of this self that is remembered by the passive, imitative soul. Yet, as the shade can return to another body, and as the divine *is* the *Kosmos*, the body becomes the site from which the pursuit of the All commences and finds its way. The myriad bodies are the successive abodes of an *active, creative* soul amid its transmigration through each of the circuits of the All.

The Pythagorean transgression of Homeric limits casts into relief a different relation of the soul to body, which is, in the narrative of transmigration, only one body amid a succession of others. The body, here, is not an end in itself, but "plays its part" amidst a narrative that asserts a different destiny for the soul. Moreover, in contradistinction to the *metaschematism* of Leibniz, death is not the envelopment of body, but is the release of the soul into a transitionary *topos in-between* embodiments.[14] Even for Homer, the soul or shade dwells in Hades, and thus, survives the death of the body. Pythagoras is simply changing the path and the destination of the soul—it now has a capacity to move along through differing bodies, each being a microcosm of the All. Once the soul has seen the All, has been the All, as the story goes, it will be the All.

Transmigration distributes souls through the stirrings and strivings of beings; this soul migrates across body to body, flows through a labyrinth of instants, to chance upon the thread that keeps the fire of wisdom still burning. Each has been, and remains, to use Reiner Schürmann's phrase, a traveler throughout and toward the All, but an amnesiac traveler, a wanderer who desires to fathom and abide the multidimensional depths of oneself and the world. In this sense, truth, as the wisdom of the path, is the same as be-ing, as traveling upon the path, of remembering the truth of Being from out of a fog of oblivion, the intoxication of the waters of Lethe. Remembrance is drinking from the river of Mnemosyne. And yet, it is, strangely, the fog of forgetfulness which clears a space for novel disclosures, embodiments, for an expansion of wisdom arising amidst an attempt to become the All. Since we can conceive of an existence which is cultivated in an oral tradition, in which *truth is the same as being*, we will need to critically engage those bland caricatures of Pythagoras which set his mathematics over against his esoteric narratives of existence and the soul, or of an account which severs his theoretical from his practical philosophy.

Transmigration is a poetic *topos* which opens the space for a complex *indication*[15] of existence amid a *mnemotechnic*[16] dwelling for a philosophical questioning which seeks to be attuned to the All. This *topos* abides a "mythopoetic symbol" of the event and life of the All.[17] It is as an artwork, in the sense of Heidegger's essay, "The Origin of the Work of Art,"[18] that discloses truth as a *poetics of being.* The narrative houses and communicates a single teaching of *that which is* and *how one is to live.* Within its "symbolic nexus," in this way, transmigration abides the fundamental significance and specific regions of Pythagorean thought. It is a *cathexis* which articulates the myriad facets of inquiry, both esoteric, philosophy and poly-theology (the *tragic myth*), and exoteric, mathematics, cosmology, cosmogony, and musical theory. An attentive retelling of the tale of transmigration, from this perspective, would reveal all that which is tacitly assumed by such a "primitive narrative": conceptions of body, perspective, *praxis*, and of soul, souls, kinship, number, geometry, and music. These many strands come together in the Pythagorean philosophical movement, articulated in its narrative, the unity of which abides an *ethos* of the *bios*, or way of life, which encompasses not only the various facets and aspects, but also the destiny of lived existence. The *bios* is rooted in the cycles of recurrence which is an even more primary "unity." For the Pythagoreans, existence and eschatology are separated only by forgetfulness.[19]

Each of us belongs to the All, move with the All; still each is distinct, one from another, fallen away into mere forgetfulness. Within the horizons of the narrative, however, such wisdom may be discoverable within one's own self and world. Instigated by "truth events," life, then, is a learning, a remembering, but simultaneously, an unlearning of that which has been learned. This unlearning, forgetfulness, is not only a disintegration produced via the world of actions, slowly gnawing away at the immediacy of Memory, but is an active forgetting of older patterns of thought amid the birth of novel possibilities. With each life, we plunge into the rhythmic flux of the world only in the end to forget this world as it seemed to be when we had originally set out upon our pathway toward the All. A forgetful soul wanders into another body and finds itself in-between other bodies, lives. Forgetfulness, as it allows for an awakening into a new opening, serves in the eschatological attunement of the All, as the silence between two musical notes. This temporary forgetfulness sets free the soul to a different wandering; to become a bird, as Orpheus had wished for himself. Between each incarnation we must drink from the waters of Lethe.

Yet, such forgetfulness is not, for Pythagoras, absolute as he is said to have remembered and recounted his previous lives. It must be granted that forgetfulness does have its uses and status as the criteria for differentiation of one incarnation from another. But, as transmigration is oriented to an immanent understanding of the All, there must be the possibility of a remembrance not only of each previous transmigration, but also of transmigration itself. Indeed, it is this very possibility which grounds the philosophic a priori in Pythagorean (and Platonist) philosophy. It must be, in this way, much more than Dacier's mere "cure by lies" or Cornford's "primitive mysticism." For the Pythagoreans, it is only through the exploration of the All, and of becoming attuned with the All, that one may attain a return to the divine. As each incarnation discloses a facet of the All, and as the goal of the exploration is *true* enlightenment, these myriad instantiations are not to be regarded as undertaken for the sake of *punishment*, as with some strains of Platonism and Hinduism, but perhaps, as with the Buddhists and Taoists, as pathways of or along a way of learning, and of building a dwelling for wisdom in the mythical narrative, in this case, that of transmigration.

Such an aspiration of return is ceaselessly disrupted by the death of the body, of bodies. But, as the body is the *topos* of departure for such an aspiration, with each death and rebirth, there lies the possibility that the destination of return may be forgotten, ceaselessly postponed. It takes a work of cultivation to remember one's own *greater soul*, that synoptic memory of all of one's incarnations, or, in other words, of one's pathway from and to the divine. In this context, the wanderer of Rimbaud, finding himself in "dark and scary places," makes up rhymes, plucking his worn-out shoelaces as he would a lyre. He does not remember his aspiration, thrown into a world, happy to merely comfort his fear and mortal singularity with jests and mimicry. He is engulfed in the darkness of night and can only distract himself, lie to himself about his predicament. He has fallen away into a dream within a dream, into oblivion darker than the Homeric soul in Hades.

The doctrine of transmigration tells the story of a differing chance, it sets forth a novel possibility, one which suggests that even in this mimicry and distraction, as *poetic rhymes*, lie seeds of remembrance, perhaps of a playing of the lyre "one foot beneath my heart." The silent aspiration of a return to the divine remains harbored in the heart which sets above the static din of forgetfulness. This aspiration can be recaptured through a path of remembrance achieved through a movement away from the forgetfulness of the divine. For Pythagoras, this path of remembrance *is* philosophy, a step back away from the overwhelming involvements of the din, and to see that which is and what must be. It is in this context that it is a preparation for death, an event the tragic significance of which is limited within the affirmative horizons of an overriding task of a return to the All. Death discloses the fragility of a mortal self, and it is perhaps amid the truth event of anxiety before death that we are called to remember our source in the divine and thus seek to cultivate an attunement with the All through a way of life of ever deeper remembrance.

Method and Scope

Not only must we be aware that Pythagoras wrote nothing, but we must also remember that the Pythagoreans were suppressed, exterminated, and the thought of writing down their teaching came only amid the threatening horizons of this obliteration. Much is lost amidst such urgency, and consequently, we must keep close to their historical *context of emergence* and to that which is left behind by the Pythagoreans themselves, such as the monochord, the doctrine of transmigration, the musical scale. We must also gather testimony from related sources so as to set forth an interpretation with the sufficient depth to do "justice" to the Pythagorean teaching.[20]

At the same time, however, we will be forced to rely upon testimony, much of which has been deemed unreliable in a tidal wave of attempts to fill this void of evidence. This question becomes complex in that we are not only seeking an account of a sixth century BCE philosopher, but are at once obliged to consider the historical archive of interpretations and treatments of this subject. We have for instance the *Lives* of Iamblichus, Porphyry, and others, which are of questionable value, but also various "modern" interpretations, such as Cornford, Guthrie, Dillon, and Wertheim. Yet, although this procedure remains necessary, the procedure of evidential authority remains essentially arbitrary in this case. What is "evidence" in this case and how does our perspective on the development of Presocratic philosophy influence our interpretation of "evidence"? To whom shall we listen? Only those who are primarily scholars of Ancient Greece? What of those who are mathematicians, or musicians, or theologians? What of philosophers who are inspired by Pythagorean teachings? What of a Nietzschean, post-structuralist, or feminist reading of Pythagoras? Where do we, and, where can we draw the line? Are we in a circle? Or, should we, in some kind of Kierkegaardian leap, seek instead to remember the myriad lives of our own soul, as Pythagoras counsels his disciples?

It is clear that since Pythagoras wrote nothing, we must rely to some extent on extant records. We must consider these in order to familiarize ourselves with the various perspectives of the doctrine of transmigration and of Pythagoreanism as such. But, we must also be willing to engage practically and indeed imaginatively with the sources so as to retrieve a phenomenologically adequate reading of the formally indicative senses of the doctrine. We must attempt to create a *topos* of inclusivity with respect to sources of knowing, which will include references to hermeneutic practices or perspectives not treated or permitted in a Modern interpretation, one which operates amid the framework of a sharp, though duplicitous, distinction between science and religion.[21]

In light of this hermeneutical entanglement, I will open up the *topos* for the possible contributors to this project, according to a criterion of whether or not the various sources cast light upon the doctrine of transmigration. Of course, it remains our primary goal to unpack, as it were, the doctrine of transmigration in order to disclose the *unity* of Pythagorean philosophy—and this implies certain preliminary orienting decisions, such as the questioning of the received and echoed positivist reading. Opening up the field to differing voices will lend us some perspective and, in some cases, important "evidence." We will, in this light, to some extent, with Robert Frost, be "playing tennis with the net down," or, with Wittgenstein, attempting to understand the *grammar of use* and the *bedrock practices of existence* which are disclosed through the narrative of transmigration. Yet, we will still be playing tennis. In this way, I have included the contributions

from the extant fragments of the "Pythagoreans," such as Ocellus, Sextus
Empiricus, and Theon of Smyrna, despite questions as to their authenticity and
dating. I have also incorporated the insights of Marsilio Ficino, who, after all,
was the first translator and interpreter of Plato and Plotinus in the West, after a
millennium of eclipse, and has much to contribute, especially with respect to
the reconstruction of the Pythagorean *theoria* and *bios*, as suggested in his own
practical *ethos*.[22]

Such an interpretation which seeks to retrieve the *unity* of Pythagorean
thought goes against the grain of a long standing tradition which dismisses the
notion of transmigration as a "mere figure," or, as a "cure by lies," (Xenophanes,
Hierocles, Dacier, Cornford, and in his own way, Riedweg)[23], thus, separating
this doctrine from the status of "true wisdom," or, of genuine "science."
Following dutifully in these footsteps, Cornford asserts that the very presence
of the doctrine of transmigration in the Pythagorean corpus is a "symptom" of
a philosophy caught up in an inexorable web of contradictions, one which
seeks to contain within itself utterly incompatible axioms, such as Monism and
Dualism, "mysticism" and "science." In this way, Pythagoras became just another
victim of the eliminative strategy of the logical positivists, who had pointed out,
as they had done to almost every philosopher from Plato to Heidegger, a "confusion" in his thought which was at odds with the "Scientific Worldview." In the
following, I will argue against the interpretation of Pythagoras, which projects
with him the segregation of "mysticism" and "science." I will lay out an alternative
interpretation of Pythagorean philosophy as *magical* in the sense that it exhibits
an existential harmonization of *theoria* and *praxis* amidst a sacred pagan ethos[24] or
form of life. This harmony is most prominent in its interpretation of the body as a
microcosm of the All, as the conduit for the life of the All, and a place in which
one may seek to cultivate a *bios* of "attunement" amid and as the All. In this way,
a philosophical magic, occurring amid the horizons of an extended kinship of
the All, would be a cultivation of harmony via the memory of the event and the
bios of return.

Following the lead of Ficino, W.K.C. Guthrie, Dillon, and Burkert, I will interpret the notion of the transmigration of souls as a *complex symbola*, requiring for
its possibility a notion of extended kinship, "extended" as a transgression of the
limiting horizons of Homeric blood kinship. The *symbola* implies a transmigration of the mortal-immortal divide, as a kinship of the All, and thus, of the disclosure of mortality as an aspect of immortality. For Homer, again, such an
aspiration for mortals was *hubris*. Poseidon tells Odysseus that without gods,
man is nothing. With demise, for Homer, the mortal soul descends toward
Hades, a cave of deficient similarity, craving blood, breath and body, fated to
passively reflect upon a life that had been "completed" in death. Any claim of
a return to a divine source is undercut by Homer as mankind is a creation
of Prometheus, a Titan, who was censured by Zeus. For Pythagoras, on the
contrary, such a return is not a transgression, but a fulfillment of the soul amidst
an *ethos* of sacred *praxis* (*bios*) and thought (*theoria*).

I will begin, in Chapter 1: *Genealogy of the Doctrine of Transmigration* with a discussion of the selection of source materials that will come into play in the present study. There are many sources, ancient and modern, each of which will be assessed in terms of their capacity to contribute to a plausible interpretation of the *unity* of Pythagorean philosophy and its mythopoetic symbol, the doctrine of transmigration. I will place great emphasis upon the formative work of W.K.C. Guthrie, which, in juxtaposition to the division of mysticism and science asserted by Cornford, sets forth a unified interpretation that is guided by a notion of philosophical magic and an extended kinship of the All, allegorized in the *complex symbola* of the doctrine of transmigration. Such a unified interpretation will allow for a proper appraisal of the role and significance of the doctrine of transmigration. In Chapter 2: *Beyond Mysticism and Science: Symbolism and Philosophical Magic*, expanding on our prior consideration of Guthrie, I will argue that this symbol, if read in light of the Pythagorean oral tradition, serves as a mythopoetic *dwelling* for the Pythagorean philosophy as a whole: a doctrine of the soul, of body, music, number, and of a *bios* of *praxis* and attunement. In Chapter 3: *The Emergence of Mystic Cults and the Immortal Soul*, I will explore the mytho-historical context of the emergence of Pythagoreanism and give a description and assessment of what Cornford and Burkert regard as the "revolutionary" character of Pythagorean philosophy. I will tentatively follow this interpretation in terms of its displacement of Homeric blood kinship with extended kinship as friendship, yet, I will trace the significant continuity between Pythagoras and Homer with respect to the body. It will be in this context that we will most distinctly comprehend the radical difference between the *magical* and *mystical* interpretations of early Pythagorean movement. Indeed, the primary role that is played by the body in the narrative of transmigration gives much weight to Guthrie's *magical* interpretation over against one that would have little use for the body and which regards it as merely a prison house or punishment.

In Chapter 4: *Philolaus and the Character of Pythagorean Harmony*, taking up the insights of the previous chapter, I will explore the character of harmony in early Pythagorean philosophy through a juxtaposition of our Pythagoras with the fifth-century "Pythagorean" Philolaus who, contrary to the indigenous harmony of contraries (such as the musical opposition), advocated by the sixth-century Pythagoreans, set forth a position which required an external mediation of "warring opposites" (akin to Anaxagoras' *Nous*). Such a difference in perspective is significant in light of the fact that Plato is said to have borrowed a book about the Pythagoreans from Philolaus, and in this light, it will be argued that the latter, prior to Socrates, is perhaps, in a revision of Nietzsche, the first "theoretical man." In Chapter 5: *The Alleged Critique of Pythagoras by Parmenides*, I will return to Cornford in his contention that the subject of criticism of the Hexameter Poem of Parmenides was the Pythagorean containment within one "system" of the principles of monism and dualism. Again, as in the case of Philolaus, I will argue that the character of Pythagorean thought consists in a harmony of opposites, of contraries amid a unified All, and not contradiction, and would not have, in that way, been subject to the alleged critique of Parmenides. Moreover, taking the criticism of Cornford further, I will comment on *his* Parmenides, in contrast to the one of the Hexameter Poem who hears the goddess tell him that he should also learn the ways of mortal knowing. In Chapter 6: *Between the Earth and the Sky: On the Pythagorean Divine*, I will set forth a rough sketch of the Pythagorean divine through a consideration of the mythopoetic symbol of Apollo. I will argue that this symbol must be understood in its narrative context, which was that of pagan pantheistic polytheism. I will focus upon the ambiguity of Apollo, including questions of his gender, and upon his relationship with his half brother Dionysus, so as to cast into relief a tragic sense of divinity, related to the question of the mortality of the *Kosmos* and the necessity of its own rebirth a la Empedocles. In Chapter 7: *The Pythagorean* Bios *and the Doctrine of Transmigration*, I will make good on my earlier claim that the doctrine of transmigration is a mythopoetic dwelling for early Pythagoreanism by outlining the two pathways, or aspects, of the philosophy which are contained in the narrative. On the one hand, in *The Path of the Event*, I will provide a glimpse into what Cornford calls the *theoria* of the Pythagorean philosophy that includes the cosmology, cosmogony, number theory, the theory of body, musical theory, and the theory of the soul. On the other hand, in *The Path of Remembrance, or Return*, I will give a rough sketch of the *bios* in which the Pythagoreans, living communally, attempted to orchestrate an *ethos* or way of life that was attuned to the divine All. Again, the primary significance of this practical form of life underscores the significance of the body and of the magical interpretation of Pythagorean philosophy.

In Chapter 8: *The Platonic Rupture: Writing and Difference*, I will outline the Platonic interpretation of the doctrine of transmigration so as to more distinctly specify the uniqueness of the Pythagorean teaching. Using the critical insights of Nietzsche in such works as *The Birth of Tragedy, Beyond Good and Evil*, and the *Genealogy of Morals*—in light of my own contention of the merely intellectual significance of Philolaus—I will examine the doctrine of transmigration in a variety of Plato's dialogues, emphasizing the persistent devaluation of the body, the attitude that transmigration as a means of punishment, and the debasement of the sensual world as one of suffering. In Chapter 9: *Plotinus: The Ascent of the Soul toward the One*, as a further specification of the Pythagorean doctrine of transmigration and its relationship to the *bios*, I will explore the doctrine of Plotinus, who unlike Plato, was committed to a practical *ethos* of the body, but still gave allegiance to a pathway of *ascent* to divine. In Chapter 10: *Plotinus as Neoplatonic Mystic: Letter to Flaccus*, in a continuing exploration of Plotinus, I will set forth a critical reading of his doctrine of *ascent* against the backdrop of his *Letter to Flaccus*, a Roman Senator, in which he laments the *prison house of the body*. It will be in this context that the doctrine of transmigration would be set forth as a philosophy of attunement with the divine All, and not a doctrine of ascent, as this would imply a diminishment of the body. I will close, in Epilog: *The Fate of the Doctrine of Transmigration*, with a final juxtaposition of the magical and mystical interpretations of Pythagorean philosophy. It must be remembered that, in the 1920s, Cornford's charge of mysticism was enough to discredit the established pictures of Pythagorean philosophy and necessitate a program to isolate a "scientific" Pythagoreanism. It will be in this light that I will juxtapose what we have learned of the Pythagorean teaching to British Christian mystic, A.E. Waite, who, contemporary with the logical positivists, can be said to serve as an fatal example of the mystic in that era. In distinction from Waite's aspiration for *nihilation*, I will emphasize the primary desire of the Pythagoreans for an *attunement*[25] of the life of the body with the All, which is a magical and not a mystical desire, one attuned more with the philosophy of Empedocles, with its play of Love *and Strife*, and with the Jena Romantics, such as Hölderlin and Schelling, than with Plato and the Neo-Platonists.

Chapter 1

Genealogy of the Doctrine of Transmigration

Ever since the Diaspora of the Pythagoreans, there has been testimony and interpretations of Pythagoras and his teachings. It does not begin with the dry chalkboard of the Pythagorean Theorem, or with the ridicule and caricatures of the religious Sage. These are later developments, and are furthermore circumscribed by the post-Christian distinction between science and religion, or reason and faith. There are very early texts, even from his own contemporaries such as Heraclitus, however, which not only mention the Pythagoreans, but assume a casual knowledge of their philosophy. Indeed, for ancient writers, Pythagoreanism meant a belief in the immortality of the soul in that they held mortality to be ultimately a *topos* of transmigration, just as a snake does not die when it sheds it skin. Pythagoreanism indicates a body of doctrine which indicates a phenomenological genealogy of the world and a pathway of return to the divine (via successive transmigrations). It would be very safe to say that the Pythagoreans were a minority, who held their own beliefs amid and against the received narratives of a Homeric underworld, of Paradise, or, of Nothing. Yet, despite the wide agreement of early modern and ancient commentators, Pythagoras' religious and "mystical" preferences—his doctrine of immortality—are not taken seriously by late Modern scholarship, most notably that inaugurated by the so-called analytic revolution, and are never considered as intrinsically related, even in a symbolic sense, to his mathematical or scientific significance.

Resisting this prejudice, I will lay out a sketch of the narrative of transmigration as the mythopoetic *dwelling*[1] of the primary doctrines of the Pythagorean teaching. Transmigration is a *topos* which opens up an inclusive place for the myriad perspectives of souls amidst a "dys-eschatology" of return. Pythagoras sought to subvert the mortal-immortal divide of Homer and set forth a pathway of transcendence, but one that relied upon a transfiguration of the ontological presuppositions of Homer in his valorization of the body. This pathway entails a radical transformation of our thinking and being in light of our own post-Christian *topos*. We cannot assume that we can simply understand ancient sources immediately as if by analogy to our own network of meanings. We are in a labyrinth of hearsay, of gossip, reportage, sympathizers, re-creators, philologists, hoaxers, theologists, and philosophers. Let us only hope that in our wandering in the labyrinth, we will find Ariadne's thread.

Diogenes Laertius reports a testimony of Xenophanes about Pythagoras and his espousal of the doctrine of the transmigration of souls:

> Once they say that he was passing by when a puppy was being whipped, and he took pity and said: "Stop, do not beat it; for it is the soul of a friend that I recognized when I heard it giving tongue." [2]

This jest (if it is one), one of many against Pythagoras, is possibly the only testimony by one of his contemporaries which connects him directly to the doctrine of transmigration. Yet, if we are to accept Cornford on this issue, there may also be the poem of Parmenides which is said to focus its attack on the Pythagorean advocacy of the doctrine of transmigration and its "religious" containment of the contradictory principles of monism and dualism.[3] It is indeed possible that this poem does attack Pythagoras since it is known that Parmenides was a student, while not a follower, of Xenophanes, and that Parmenides was a younger contemporary of Pythagoras. At the same time, there are perhaps better reasons to reject Cornford's account of the relation of Pythagoras and Parmenides. We will return to this issue below.

Besides these sparse contemporaneous sources, however, there are only posthumous materials which refer to the doctrine of transmigration. Kirk describes our predicament as follows:

> Pythagoras wrote nothing. Hence a void was created which was to become filled by a huge body of literature, much of it worthless as historical evidence of Pythagoras' own teachings. It included accounts of Pythagorean physics, ethics and political theory as well as metaphysics; biographies of Pythagoras; and several dozen treatises (many still extant) whose authorship was ascribed to early Pythagoreans—although all of them (excepting some fragments of Philolaus and Archytas) are nowadays judged to be pseudonymous fictions of later origin.[4]

Kirk acknowledges that the several *Lives* of Pythagoras, written by Iamblichus, Photius, Porphyry, and Diogenes Laertius contain valuable information, but significantly describes these works as mere "scissors-and-paste compilations of the Christian era."[5] Excepting that preserved by Photius, dating from the ninth century A.D., these *Lives* were composed eight hundred years after the life of Pythagoras by Porphyry and Iamblichus who were direct successors of Plotinus in the Neoplatonic tradition, and Diogenes as a compiler of ancient philosophy. Each of these biographical works gives some prominence to the doctrine of transmigration.

In his work, *The Life of Pythagoras, or On the Pythagorean Life,* Iamblichus writes that death is a migration, one having a direction depending on the particular life that had been lived, and that there is a training of *ascent* which may overcome the descent to lower levels of being.[6] He also mentions the preexistences of Pythagoras, and how the latter made use of his remembrance of his past incarnations to induce others to discover their former existences as well. Iamblichus writes,

> For by the clearest and surest indications he would remind many of his intimates of the former life lived by their soul before it was bound to their body. He would demonstrate by indubitable arguments that he had once been Euphorbus, son of Panthus, conqueror of Patroclus.
>
> What Pythagoras, however, wished to indicate by all these particulars was that he knew the former lives he had lived, which enabled him to originate his providential attention to others, in which he reminded them of their former existences.[7]

Pythagoras, in this account, is distinctly connected to the doctrine of transmigration and this latter doctrine seems to provide a background for a pedagogical practice of regression, or recollection. It was in this context that Pythagoras was said to have had a "divine sign."

Porphyry, in his work, *The Life of Pythagoras*, writes:

> Many of his associates he reminded of the lives lived by their souls before they were bound to their present body, and by irrefutable arguments demonstrated that he had been Euphorbus, the son of Panothus.[8]

This account, surely the source for Iamblichus, also contains the following reference to the doctrine of transmigration:

> He taught that the soul is immortal, and that after death it transmigrates into other animated bodies. After certain specified periods, he said, the same events occur again, for nothing is entirely new; all animated beings are kin, he taught, and should be considered as belonging to one great family.[9]

These references provide specific information concerning the doctrine of transmigration as a practice of recollection, as a conception of the migration of the soul, and as a notion of the kinship of all life, "one great family," this having practical, ethical implications, such as vegetarian abstinence, etc.

A short anonymous biography of Pythagoras, "preserved" by Photius also refers to the doctrine of transmigration. In this account, it is written:

> The Pythagoreans abstained from eating animals on account of their foolish belief in transmigration, and also because flesh-food engages digestion too much, and is too fattening. Beans they also avoided, because they produce flatulency, over-satiety, and for other reasons.

And, in the next numbered statement:

> They affirm that man may improve in three ways: first by conversation with
> the Gods, for to them none can approach unless he abstain from all evil, imi-
> tating the divinity, even unto assimilation; second, by well-doing, which is
> a characteristic of the divinity; third by dying, for if the slight soul-separation
> from the body resulting from discipline improves the soul so that she begins
> to divine in dreams—and if the deliria of illness produces visions—then the
> soul must surely improve far more when entirely separated from the body by
> death.[10]

In this account, there is a statement of the viability of a total separation of the
soul from the body, one prefigured in dreams, and again, a connection between
the doctrine of transmigration and vegetarian abstinence. There is also reference to a discipline, a training of ascent which aspires to higher levels of being,
away from evil.

Diogenes Laertius, in his *The Life of Pythagoras*, in addition to his account of
Xenophanes' jest, portrays the incarnations of Pythagoras. He writes:

> Heracleides of Pontus says that he was accustomed to speak of himself in this
> manner: that he had formerly been Aethalides, and had been accounted to
> be the son of Hermes, and that Hermes had desired him to select any gift he
> pleased except immortality. Accordingly, he had requested that, whether liv-
> ing or dead, he might preserve the memory of what had happened to him.
> While, therefore, he was alive, he recalled everything, and when he was dead
> he retained the same memory. At a subsequent period he passed into Euphor-
> bus, and was wounded by Menelaus. While he was Euphorbus, he used to say
> that he had formerly been Aethalides; and that he had received as a gift from
> Hermes the perpetual transmigration of his soul, so that it was constantly
> transmigrating and passing into *whatever plants or animals it pleased*, and he
> had also received the gift of knowing and recollecting all that his soul had
> suffered in Hades, and what sufferings too are endured by the rest of the
> souls. (My italics)

> But after Euphorbus died, he said that his soul had passed into Hermotimus,
> and when he wished to convince people of this, he went into the territory of
> the Branchidae, and going into the temple of Apollo, he showed his shield
> which Menelaus had dedicated there as an offering. For he said that he, when
> he sailed from Troy, had offered up his shield which was already getting
> worn out, to Apollo, and that nothing remained but the ivory face which was
> on it. He said that when Hermotimus died he had become Pyrrhus, a fisher-
> man of Delos, and that he still recollected everything, how he had formerly
> been Aethalides, then Euphorbus, then Hermotimus, and then Pyrrhus.

When Pyrrhus died, he became Pythagoras, and still recollected all the circumstances I have been mentioning.[11]

In this account we have the explicit connection of the doctrine of transmigration and *memory*, this latter being the key not only to the hope of immortality, a thread out of the labyrinth of incarnations, of forgetfulness, but also to what we would call the philosophical *a priori*, the basis of knowledge. There is also reference to a bloodless sacrifice at the altar of Apollo, who is conceived as the giver of life. The bloodless sacrifice is important for the soul "revolving around the circle of necessity, is transformed and confined at different times in different bodies."[12] The soul is not simply immortal, but must inhabit the circle of necessity as the condition for its return to the divine. The habitation of the circle of necessity effectuates the existence and kinship of all life.

The accounts given in the various *Lives of Pythagoras* must be approached with some caution to the extent that they do not seem to rely on evidence which is contemporary to Pythagoras, except perhaps the jest of Xenophanes. These works also come long after Plato, Aristotle, and Plotinus, and betray their own concerns and historical attitudes as we can see, for instance, in the Neoplatonism of Porphyry and Iamblichus. This issue of originality and influence will come into clearer focus in our consideration of Plato below, where we will examine his displacement of a kinship of the body of the All via a kinship of only the soul and the divine. Yet, even with the transmutations and errancy of later philosophies, the works must not surely be disregarded in our search for source material. But, to the extent that our question is that of the status of the doctrine of transmigration in the Pythagorean philosophy, these are only hints and anecdotes for a preliminary rough sketch, and do not constitute an explicit interpretation of the doctrine—although the various references to memory, abstinence, kinship of life, and the immortality of the soul are significant and will be helpful in our interpretation. Kirk deems the evidence for Philolaus and Archytas, two sources among other later Pythagoreans and neo-Pythagoreans, to be reliable, but of a fragmentary and doxographical character. The fragments of Philolaus—who is said to have provided a written manuscript of Pythagorean philosophy to Plato—do not refer to transmigration explicitly, although it may be implied as a possible meaning of some of his various inscriptions concerning the nature of the soul and of its immortality. Philolaus casts the soul into relief in analogy to the motes in the air due to their constant state of motion. The soul is an attunement, a harmony of opposites, as with Heraclitus and Empedocles, self-moved in eternal motion. Having a character similar to that of the divine, moreover, it is through this movement, that it will come into relation with the divine as like will seek out like. Philolaus also reports that Alcmaeon contended that "men die for this reason, that they cannot join the beginning to the end."[13] It is further attributed to Philolaus that the soul cherishes its body, because without it the soul cannot feel; but when death has separated the soul therefrom, the soul lives an incorporeal existence in the cosmos.[14]

Even though each of these tenets is compatible with some form of the doctrine of transmigration, this does not necessitate that we attribute this tenet to Philolaus—and it compels us to attempt to become clear as to the specificity of the doctrine of transmigration for the early Pythagoreans (in distinction from the conception of Plato and Plotinus). Nevertheless, at this stage of our inquiry, this evidence from Philolaus does indicate an "eschatology" of the soul distinct from the narrative of Homer, a soul which is, for most of the fragments of Philolaus, in kinship with All, and is similar to All. And, thus, it could seek to return to the All. We will return to Philolaus in Chapter 4.

Archytas comes in the fourth century BCE and was a close friend of Plato. As we will see, this affiliation in itself will place a question mark of caution over his work with respect to its status as a source for our inquiry. As with Philolaus, his contribution consists of a series of fragments which are concerned with a hierarchy of knowledge and the means by which one would attain to true knowledge. It is recorded, with a striking resemblance to Plato:

> That is why thought must rise from things that are sensible, to the conjectur-able, and from these to the knowledge, and on to the intelligible; and he who wishes to know the truth about these objects, must in a harmonious grouping combine all the means and objects of knowledge.[15]

While this may be a Pythagorean goal, it is also a Platonic one, and this aspiration is expressed in a Platonic manner. And, despite Plato's treatment of the doctrine of transmigration in the *Phaedrus* and the eschatology of the soul in the *Phaedo*, there must again be caution exercised, if we are to interpret the status of the doctrine, specifically, for early Pythagorean philosophy. Such an interpretation will require that fine lines be drawn between positions which with deeper examination will be seen to be incompatible. We will return to this matter later.

There is no evidence in the fragments of Archytas which would lead us to assume that he accepted or taught the doctrine of transmigration. Yet, this does not mean that it is not contained in lost treatises, but this merely underscores the uncertainty of the evidence of these fragments. At the same time, if it is true that the microcosm is one with the macrocosm, then, each fragment will abide the signature trace of the philosophy as such. The significance, for instance, placed upon harmony by Archytas indicates his compatibility with many of the philosophical implications of the doctrine of transmigration. Yet, we may find that what he deems as harmony, as in the case of Philolaus, is not consistent with that of the Pythagoreans of the oral tradition. As we will see in the several fragments of Philolaus, the question to be explored will be that of the character of harmony and of its relation with the world—or whether "harmony" is an indigenous "unity" amidst the being of the world, of the *Kosmos*, as we may find in a pantheism, or if, the seat of "unity" resides outside the world and is thus imposed as an alien assertion of order. Archytas, in what seems to be an anachronistic, Aristotelian formulation, comes down upon the side of the latter, externalist conception of harmony:

> God is the artist, the mover; the substance is the matter, the moved; the essence is what you might call the art, and that to which the substance is brought by the mover. But since the mover contains forces which are self-contrary, those of simple bodies, and as the contraries are in need of a principle harmonizing and unifying them, it must necessarily receive it efficacious virtues and proportions from numbers, and all that is manifested in numbers and geometric forms, virtues and proportions capable of binding and uniting into form the contraries that exist in the substance of things. For, by itself, substance is formless; only after having been moved towards form does it become formed and receive the rational relations of order. Likewise, if movement exists, besides the thing moved, there must exist a prime mover; there must therefore be three principles: the substance of things, the form, and the principle that moves itself, and which by its power is the first; not only must this principle be an intelligence, it must be above intelligence, and we call it God.[16]

The proximity of Archytas to certain fragments of Philolaus and to the text of Plato immediately places a question mark over his severance of form from "formless substance," as if the body of the *Kosmos* did not have its own indigenous harmony in the unity of limit and the unlimited. This proximity will become clear in our consideration of Plato's treatment of the body in the context of the doctrine of transmigration, a doctrine, as I have suggested, that is susceptible to various and radically different interpretations. Anticipating Christianity, with Archytas, the body becomes the "other," of matter, evil; it does not belong with a Platonic Divine which is no longer of the All (the body of the *Kosmos*), but is recognized by its *flight* from the All. We will see in the following that it is clearly the pre-understanding and valorization of the body and the world which coordinates these respective interpretations of transmigration. To foreshadow this problem, Archytas writes:

> For an exact discernment of these goods, we should outline its proper part for the divine element, and for nature; yet some do not observe this relation of dignity from the better to the worse. But we do so when we say that if

the body is the organ of the soul, then reason is the guide of the entire soul, the mistress of the body, this tent of the soul, and that all the other physical advantages should serve only as instruments to the intellectual activity, if you wish it to be perfect in power, duration and wealth.[17]

This vision of Archytas complements Plato's own perspective of the respective status of the soul and the body, of eternity and time, a perspective which is organized by an overriding commitment to an interpretation of philosophy as a merely intellectual activity, as the lifeworld of the *theoretical* man. The importance of this point will become increasingly clear as we will increasingly focus upon the overriding practical aspect of Pythagorean philosophy and its relation to the poetics of transmigration. Suffice it to write that the doctrine of transmigration, as it relates in an essential way to the body, will be configured according to the status of the body and the world, each of which being constitutive of the divine All. The conception of philosophy as an intellectual activity stands at a distance from the Pythagorean insistence upon a *bios*, as a magic, a sacred *praxis* of the body. However, since we have little *direct* evidence, we will also consider the work of Plato below so as to set forth a specification of Pythagorean *praxis*. Kirk writes of our dilemma of interpretation:

> It is notorious that Plato's metaphysics is deeply imbued with ideas we recognize (even if he did not avow) to be Pythagorean. The *Phaedo*, for example, eloquently recreates an authentically Pythagorean blend of eschatological teaching about the fate of the soul with ethical and religious prescription, and sets it in the Pythagorean context of a philosophical discussion between friends. (Burnet felicitously suggested that "the *Phaedo* is dedicated, as it were, to the Pythagorean community at Phleious," EGP, 83 n.1.) But just because Plato is reworking Pythagorean materials, the historian of Presocratic philosophy has to be cautious in using the *Phaedo* as evidence even of early fourth-century Pythagoreanism, let alone Pythagoras' own philosophy. At the same time, it would be wrong and in any case impossible not to let the *Phaedo* and other dialogues influence our picture of early Pythagoreanism.[18]

We must always keep in mind the distance of Plato from the sixth-century Pythagoreans, and attempt to consider the possibility that, even if genuine Pythagorean teachings and manners of expression are preserved in the Platonic text, these phrases and ideas have been assimilated and put to work into a differing philosophical organization. This caution speaks not only of the distance of Plato from the Pythagoreans, but also the distance occupied by the suppression of the Pythagoreans, written Pythagoreanism a la Philolaus, and the Peloponnesian War, to name only a few indices. What I am also bringing into focus is the distance of the Platonic text from Plato himself, a point that concerns the question of any "modern" interpretation of the Ancient Greeks, a question which unavoidably brings philosophy and history into dialogue. Jacques Soustelle writes, in his *The Four Suns*:

> Plato's work . . . is separated from modern philosophy not only by a specific number of sidereal revolutions, which are nonhuman phenomena, but also, on the strictly human level, by the fact that we can trace the development of classical ideas and their successors up to our own ideas through the meditation of the thinkers and the schools of the ancient world, of Christianity, Judaism, and Islam.[19]

It is with these genealogies in mind that the ancient sources will be considered, as indicating a problem of interpretation which is irreducibly "modern," or, perhaps, "postmodern." As we consider the ancient sources that we do have and begin to move closer to the early Pythagoreans, we will have to draw some fine lines between the various ancient sources, and also the lines between the various "modern" interpretations.

This approach to sources implies, however, that other treatises and compilations, such as the *Golden Verses* and the Pythagorean sentences of Sextus Empiricus must stand on an equal footing, among others, including the post-Aristotelian text of Ocellus Lucanus, *On the Nature of the Universe*. Even those writings of pseudonymous or dubious authorship will have some usefulness in that these provide an inducement *to think for ourselves* through the contours of the doctrine of transmigration. And, in the light of a deficit of direct evidence, we must be able to draw upon our own resources to think through the implications of this plethora of indications, including those which pertain to issues of practice and action. Nevertheless, the question of the status of the doctrine of transmigration will remain of primary importance.

As far as our playing tennis with the net down, moreover, we must also, and unavoidably, pay heed to the various modern interpretations of the doctrine of transmigration. For although these will provide little new information concerning the doctrine, these interpretations not only *enframe* our own epochal perspective of Pythagorean philosophy and the doctrine of transmigration, but also, if read together with the ancient sources, allow for a fresh perspective on this matter to emerge.

The authority of modern "theories" of the doctrine of transmigration is due, to a great extent, not only to the paucity of indigenous evidence, but also to the lack of an explicit interpretation of the status of the doctrine of transmigration in posthumous ancient sources. Modern sources, however wrong they may be, enact precisely such an interpretation of this doctrine. In this way, they serve to "break the ice," if you will, they start the discussion in the near proximity of our peers. Yet, caution will be exercised to the extent that what is sought in this present work, as much as it is possible, is an interpretation of the doctrine transmigration vis-à-vis its status for the Pythagorean community, and not one which remains entangled in the modern distinction between "religion" and "science." In the following, there will be contributions to our discussion of the doctrine of transmigration by Marsilio Ficino, Giordano Bruno, M. Dacier, F.W. Cornford, Walter Burkert, and W.K.C. Guthrie. On the basis of this discussion, which is by no means exhaustive, I will set forth a tentative interpretation of the status of the doctrine of transmigration in Chapter 2: *Beyond Mysticism and Science: Symbolism and Philosophical Magic.*

Marsilio Ficino (1433–1499)

Marsilio Ficino, though now lost in forgetfulness, is said to have been the greatest philosopher of the Renaissance, teacher of Michelangelo, Botticelli, and Pico, and must therefore hold pride of place in this list of "modern" (after the recovery of ancient manuscripts) commentators. Under the auspices of patronage from the Medici family, Ficino, born in 1433, translated, by the time he died in 1499, almost everything that we know as Plato, Plotinus, Iamblichus, and Porphyry, not to mention his fruitful connections with the thinkers of the Islamic world. On this basis alone, we can consider Ficino to be highly important as a formidable commentator and translator, and indeed, as a *topos* for the survival of ancient Pagan philosophy in Christianized Europe. His indispensable translations and commentaries, not to mention his way of life, have opened up worlds previously hidden, and much of what is known of the Pythagoreans emerges with his work.

Ficino was also an important philosopher, doctor, and "dissident" Roman Catholic priest in his own right. He advocated and enacted a *bios* amid the mythopoetic horizons of cosmic magic, and composed symbolic treatises in which a way of life was to be lived, a way which promised health and longevity. The mythopoetic orientation of the way of life was of a work of attunement circumscribed within a theurgical excession of the world via emanations from a fruitful divinity, one so vast that the All, the eternal *Kosmos* in its plethora of cycles and each traveling star and planet, was its symbol. In his *Book of Life*, composed of three shorter books, *On Caring For The Health Of Students, How To Prolong Your Life, On Making Your Life Agree With The Heavens*, Ficino orchestrates a symbolic terrain of divination and *praxis*, which describes an astrological, magical, and mythopoetic matrix of signs coordinated with an affirmation of the presence of the divine in all things, that the world is the body of the divine. To this extent, he recommends, prior to the work of Jakob Boehme, a manifold of magics, medicines, potions, and tonics in order to bring the body into a condition of temperance. The first book gives a description of the problems that can beset students, such as the black bile of melancholy, and recommends various courses of practice and action not only to heal, but also to strengthen, the student. The second book focuses on the problems and concerns of the aged, and provides a detailed list of suggestions, such as massage, sunshine, certain colors and sights, odors, conversation, and once again various potions and tonics, regimens of working and reading, not to mention various metallic and talismanic images and amulets to bring vitality back to the life of an older person. As an example, Ficino writes concerning the tonic effect of music upon the soul:

> Mercurius, Pythagoras, and Plato claim that a dissonant soul, or a sad one, is helped by strumming a lyre and by constant singing and melodious playing. David, the holy poet, freed Saul from unhealthiness with his psaltery and psalms. I, too (if it is permitted the lowest to appose the highest things), have often found out at home how much the sweetness of the lyre and song avail against the bitterness of black bile.[20]

These books provide us with a vivid description of the interplay betwixt the body and the thoughts and actions of the self amidst a way of life devoted to making oneself "agree with the heavens." The self interacts within a *cathexis* of symbols and pathways, wandering through the labyrinth, guided by its intimate relation and kinship with the world and *Kosmos*. This one with "rage in the heart," the one who seeks to open the "poetic doors" must become aware of her way of being, in all of her intimacy, and seek to construct a *bios* appropriate to the ends desired, for the ends and the means, as Bakünin counsels, must be one and the same. Like is drawn only to, and through like.

The third book is more comprehensive than the first two and sets out a broader interpretation of the Kosmos, involving the project of making oneself attuned with the universal harmony of All. Once again it gives detailed recommendations concerning the powers of the stars and of the various rules for making talismanic images and amulets, rules regarding time, place, positions, and aspects of various celestial entities, the seven planets, the fixed stars. There is a strong astrological "semiotic" at work throughout the discourse, which contributes to a symbolic architecture coordinating various meanings of signification with respect to the attunement of the self with the All. Astrology harbors within itself a means of temporal designation amidst a mythopoetic horizon which is tangible and intelligible. It is, thus, one symbol system (along with others) which allows us to gain orientation amidst a tragic world, of life and death, in our pursuit of a return to the divine. Another symbol that we see in his work is that of music which acts as the conduit and complex symbol of the harmony of the "opposites" of the world. These various symbols and symbolic sites are neither ends in themselves, nor are they just disposable and ephemeral "images." They have an intrinsic significance to a way of life which is seeking to cultivate a harmony with the divine.

Ficino writes concerning this work of attunement:

Do this work so that you are turning in perpetual motion with these powers, avoiding fatigue, so that you will set the right motion against the external motions that are secretly harmful, and so that you will imitate the heavenly movement for the sake of its powers. But if you are able to go through very large spaces with these movements, you will be imitating the heavens even more and you will attain the many powers that the heavens have scattered here and there.[21]

In this context, we could think of the "music of the spheres," yet, a music that we could also see, taste, smell, and touch, one which made the body and the self "dance" along amidst a similar rhythm. Ficino makes many references to Pythagoras throughout the *Book of Life*, in which the Magus is referred to as an undisputed authority. In a similar way, he makes such references to Plato, Peter Abano, and to the Islamic philosophers, such as Averroes, among others. He holds also, as is unavoidable in this era, that the dubious Mecurius preceded Pythagoras.

In the *Book of Life*, Ficino does not explicitly mention transmigration, yet, as with most of the fragments of Philolaus, there need not be a conflict of his positions with the doctrine. Indeed, in his focus upon the care of the self, of the soul and body, and of his vision of the reciprocal mirroring of the microcosm and the macrocosm, in his affirmation of the All, we will see, is fully in accord with what we know to be Pythagorean tenets and practices. However, we must keep in mind his status as a priest of the Roman Church, and of his experience of the ceaseless harassments by the Orthodoxy. Despite the possibility of self-censorship, Ficino opens our eyes to not only a symbolic interpretation of actuality, but also to the intimate care of the self which is the accomplice of the desire for return.

It is in this sense that Ficino will mainly contribute to our portrayal, in the chapter, "The Path of Remembrance, or Return," of the elements of a way of life seeking attunement of the self amidst the All, and thus, of a return to the divine via the pathway of transmigration. He gives us an intricate and proactive description of an *ethos*, a way of being, which, in its ancient philosophical orientation, can serve as an example of the "synchroncity" of *theoria* and *bios*—of better, perhaps, of the rootedness of the former in the latter as a self-interpreting, self-organizing way of life, bound up with the doctrine of transmigration. It will be, in this way, that Ficino's symbolic orientation and exquisite practical sense and imagination will provide us with a plethora of clues toward a deeper insight into the early Pythagoreans.

Giordano Bruno (1548–1600)

While it will be impossible to give an adequate treatment of the life, thought and creative work of the heretical priest Bruno that truly reflects his significance for

Western philosophy and science, it must suffice to give some account of his sophisticated appropriation of Greek learning, especially that deemed Pythagorean, in post-Renaissance Italy. Burned at the stake in Rome in the year 1600, Bruno suffered the fate that Galileo escaped, though both had accepted the Copernican Revolution in Astronomy, a conception, we must remember, derived originally from the fourth century BCE Pythagorean philosopher, Aristarchus.

It is clear, however, that Bruno went beyond Copernicus and Galileo with his contention that the center is everywhere, or that there is indeed no fixed framework from which we can construct a system to describe an infinite, pantheistic universe. In his many philosophical works, such as *The Expulsion of the Triumphant Beast*, which is staged as a dialogue between the gods and goddesses in a council in which they will decide whether or not to flee the world, Bruno elaborated narratives of philosophical and theological significance within a labyrinth of esoteric and magical methods, qualitative mathematics and geometry, and memory and mnemotechnic systems. After refusing to fully recant his heretical theological opinions, which concerned his acceptance of the doctrine of transmigration (metempsychosis) and his questioning of the divinity of Jesus and the virginity of Mary, he was burned in 1600. At his sentencing, it is said that he responded to the clerical judges with the following ominous words: "Perhaps you, my judges, pronounce this sentence against me with greater fear than I receive it."[22] Bruno will serve, in the present work, as a prime example and an indication, contrary to Nietzsche's warning against being a martyr of truth,[23] of the seriousness of one's decisions with respect to fundamental, philosophical, and theological questions.

Andre Dacier (1651–1722)

The lack of direct evidence concerning the relationship between Pythagoras and the doctrine of transmigration lead Dacier, writing in 1707 in his *Life of Pythagoras*, containing the *Commentary on the Golden Verses* by Hierocles, to repudiate any essential association of Pythagoras with the doctrine of transmigration. He contends that there is no mention of the doctrine in any of the extant texts, including the *Golden Verses*, a claim that is debatable. He further maintains that Pythagoras, even if he is portrayed as its advocate by Xenophanes, was not the author of the doctrine.[24] Following Herodotus, he claims that the doctrine is Egyptian and that some Greeks had taken it over dishonestly, claiming it to be their own.

Furthermore, Dacier reconciles his insistence that Pythagoras did not nor could not believe in the doctrine of transmigration by citing Hierocles in his position that transmigration is a fiction. The human soul, for Dacier, is *singular* in its eternal essence, returning to the divine with the death of the body, once. It is incompatible with other bodies due to this singularity and preeminence of form.[25] In this light, Dacier characterizes the doctrine as simply a figure to communicate the truth that a "good man" will, with the occurrence of death, be set free to a being of eternal felicity in the Christian Heaven. To further buttress his position, he cites Timaeus of Locri, in a document that has itself been dated to the period of Middle Platonism,[26] where it is stated that one must "cure by lies" if a "patient" does not acquiesce to the truth by reason.[27] In this account, therefore, the doctrine of transmigration is simply a figure taken over from the Egyptians and is just a "lie," deployed as a medico-pedagogical technique; it, in other words, has only a negative, or constraining, significance. In this way, it is not an essential aspect of the Pythagorean teaching.

Dacier's impetus for writing, he admits in a highly indicative "confession," is a dire situation in which some of his contemporaries, who as "poets and thought-less philosophers" teach the doctrine of transmigration as if it were a literal truth, as did some of the Orphics, who sought to cross over into the body of a bird, or, as some other living being. Since they have embarked upon this irre-sponsible and unproductive path, Dacier charges that these preachers do not understand the significance of this figure, and thus, have no understanding of the "true" teaching of Pythagoras. Dacier contends abruptly that transmigra-tion is not relevant; it is simply a hangover from an intoxicated Pagan "past."

For Dacier, the doctrine of transmigration must be understood by means of the distinction between fable and science. It may be a useful figure in the edu-cation of the irrational or young, but since the goal of this education is truth, eventually this figure must be seen as a fiction, and thus, as inessential, be cast aside.[28] In many ways, this position set forth by Dacier can be seen as a guarded response to the jest of Xenophanes. Dacier would admit that this doctrine is laughable, if one merely regards it as a literal truth, or, ultimately, even as a symbol. Yet, as Dacier has already asserted that the doctrine cannot be literally true, the laughter is not ultimately merited, for like the tale of Hades, transmi-gration is a potent medicine for the disease and division of the soul. In this way, although just one figure among many, the doctrine of transmigration is of the utmost seriousness. Yet, despite this correction to Xenophanes, Dacier in fact agrees with the latter that the doctrine of transmigration is in essence false, despite its brief pedagogical usefulness.

F.M. Cornford (1874–1943)

In essential respects, Cornford, in two of his essays, 'Mysticism and Science in Pythagorean Philosophy' and 'Divisions of the Soul', simply repeats this time-honored distinction between fable and science. In the former essay, he casts into relief two distinct systems in the Pythagorean tradition—a "mystical system" of the sixth century and a "scientific system" of the fifth century, which he also calls number-atomism. That which separates the two "systems" is the critique of

Pythagoreanism allegedly set forth by Parmenides in his hexameter poem. By means of this event of demarcation, the doctrine of transmigration is quarantined from the "scientific" regions of inquiry. In this view, the doctrine, if it is still expressed at all, is simply a fable surrounding outdated ethical practices.

For Cornford, Parmenides, in his delineation of the two paths, is criticizing Pythagoreanism for its containment of the axioms of monism and dualism, expressed most forcefully in the doctrine of transmigration. Cornford writes, betraying his *logicist* credentials,

> Both the axiom of Monism and the axiom of Dualism are implicit in the doctrine of transmigration, which was certainly taught by Pythagoras. All souls come from one divine source and circulate in a continuous series of all the forms of life. Each soul involved in the conflict of good and evil, seeks escape from the purgatorial round of lives and deaths into a better world of unity and rest. Any philosophy that arises from a religion of this type is threatened with internal inconsistency. On the one hand, it will set the highest value on the idea of unity and, at this stage and long afterwards, the notions of value and reality coincide. Unity is good; reality must be one. On the other hand, Nature will be construed in terms of the inward conflict of good and evil, appearing in the external world of light and darkness. Light is the medium of truth and knowledge; it reveals the knowledge aspect of nature—the forms, surfaces, limits of objects that are confounded in the unlimited darkness of night. But it is hard to deny reality to the antagonistic power of darkness and evil. Hence, the tendency to dualism—to recognize not the One only, but two opposite principles.[29]

Cornford lays out the contradiction: on the one hand, the doctrine wishes to say that All is Unity, One (Monism), in its statement of a universal kinship of all, and of the communion of the soul with the divine. On the other hand, it also wishes to assert a second principle (Dualism), that the soul has come to be in the world and that there is the necessity of a change, of a movement of ascent to return to the divine, a position in seeming conflict with the first proposition. For Cornford, accepting and reciprocally influencing the program of the logical positivists, contradiction cannot be interpreted in any other way than as that which must be eliminated. But, what of other possibilities, of the dialectics of Hegel (a student of Parmenides and Heraclitus) or the eternal recurrence of the Same of Nietzsche (a student of Heraclitus and Empedocles)? Is it still necessary, after Wittgenstein, Heidegger, and Derrida, to bow down to the laws of formal logic? Ignoring other possibilities, however, Cornford sets forth his reading of Parmenides and of his supposed segregation of the realms, as the only criteria available to decipher the early Pythagoreans. This is his Archimedean point; he must make a strict separation of rest and motion, eternity and world; he must separate the ways, even if such a method irretrievably erases or distorts that which is sought in the inquiry. The Byzantine, Egyptian, Greek or indigenous fashion of mingling the spheres does not meet the modern criteria of truth. Cornford simply waves his hand and asserts that this conflict of realms is typical of religious philosophies or of philosophies which have a religious dimension as their basis.

From this perspective, and without any historical basis for such a portrayal, the "mystical system" is asserted to contain within itself a mingling of religious elements and those inquiries, such as number theory, which will, in the fifth century, be separated from the former in the formation of a "scientific system." It is with this alleged transformation that the two systems are segregated, and it is with this that the doctrine of transmigration becomes, in this markedly questionable portrayal, merely of religious, or, "mystical," significance and will begin to acquire its prejudicial connotations.

In his essay, 'Divisions of the Soul', Cornford details his "religious" or mystical interpretation of the doctrine of the transmigration of souls. The religious aspect or dimension is intimated with his unexplored mention of a possible diffusion from the Buddha to Pythagoras of their shared belief in transmigration. He allows this question to remain unanswered, but writes that this belief "in more or less crude forms, exists among barbarous peoples."[30] In other words, questionably, he contends that this belief diffuses from "barbarous" peoples, a prejudice to which I will return below. With regard to the belief in transmigration in Greece, Cornford gives the following psychologizing opinion:

> In Greece, at any rate, we have here an instance of a belief adopted from a lower strata of culture by a certain section of a highly civilized people. In such a case, the belief is cut loose from its original roots. Only the part of its primitive content is taken over, which responds to some unsatisfied need already felt by the people who adopt it; its previous history and associations are left behind.[31]

The unsatisfied need that compels the absorption of "primitive" belief, Cornford claims to have found expressed in the poetry of "Orphic religion." Without providing any textual references or detailing the connection between Pythagoras and the Orphics, he contends that the supposed need for this belief in transmigration emerges from an experience of a "divided self." This divided experience comes with the awakening of the soul amidst the dimension of phenomenal, mortal life.

He contrasts this conception of the soul as transmigrating, and thus, as immortal, with the Homeric soul-shadow of *eidolon*. In this context, transmigration is the pathway from the mortal realm to that of the immortal. The soul comes from the divine and returns to the divine; it is not a shadow of passive recollection. In effect, he situates the experience of a "divided self" in the context of the self-realization that there is a soul which "possesses powers of its own, superior to the bodily function."[32] The soul finds itself amidst the phenomenal world, but it is divine "by origin and nature."[33] The soul is the divine amidst nature, and it is more enduring and of greater value than the ephemeral world. Cornford describes this quasi-Platonic conception of the soul:

> It is a *daimon*, a spirit, endowed with supernormal powers of cognition in vision and ecstasy and with a moral nature intrinsically good.[34]

Yet, despite its divine source and nature, the soul has found itself with body in the experience of the divided self. In this way, its divinity must in some way be compromised. Cornford writes in phrases reminiscent of Plato's *Myth of Er*:

> On the other hand, during its round of incarnations, it is called "impure," tainted with prenatal guilt, to be expiated by the sufferings of terrestrial life and of purgatory. Of the origin of this evil taint only a mythical account can be given, in the story of some primal sin.[35]

In a rhetorical amplification of his religious interpretation, he writes that he does not wish to imply a distinction between body and soul, but, one of spirit and flesh. This distinction parallels his previous discussion in 'Mysticism and Science' in that the terrain of the divided self becomes one of desire and asceticism. He writes, in a passage that echoes the unrequited lust of Augustine:

> Here, in the concept of a divine but impure spirit, we have, not the old contrast of soul and body, but an opposition of higher and baser desires within the soul itself. The lower desires are rooted in the Flesh with its senses, its feelings of physical pleasure and pain, its hopes and fears, loves and hatreds. This cluster of functions we may call the animal soul, whose central aim is the preservation of the mortal life in a material world. So man conceives himself as a divine spirit imprisoned in the Flesh—for we may adopt a religious name for the body with its animal soul.[36]

One can clearly hear the Platonic and Christian overtones of this passage, which are inescapably wedded, as Nietzsche suggests, to a hierarchy of value rooted in the propagation of an ascetic ideal. Such a perspective asserts an exclusive hierarchy between world (flesh) and divine (spirit), grounded upon the distance between matter and the divine (form), and upon a radical devaluation of the sensuous phenomena and life. The animal soul is not the "real" soul, and, thus, is cast into Tartarus. The world is not the truth; thus, it does not matter. As I will detail in the succeeding chapters, it is certainly not clear if such an interpretation can facilitate any understanding of the perspective of the early Pythagoreans. Not only is there an implication of nihilism in Cornford's portrayal of the higher soul, but there is also another positing of hierarchy between science and religion, the most important aspect of this hierarchy being the segregation itself (and the reduction of knowledge to this dualism).

In his deployment of "Orphic texts" (without, however, reading any of them) for his speculative realist interpretation of Pythagorean philosophy, Cornford assumes that all religious experience is in essence the same, and thus, the mystical doctrine of transmigration, in that it has been deemed to be of religious character, must also be a participant in this naturalized sameness. In this architectonic, since transmigration cannot ever be proper science, it must be religion. Cornford writes:

> The religious antithesis of the Spirit and the Flesh is perpetuated in the earlier of our two philosophic divisions of the soul—the twofold (as opposed to the three-fold). We observe that the believers in transmigration are so deeply penetrated by the consciousness of this division that they carry the idea of separation to its furthest point. The Spirit and the Flesh may be called *parts* of our nature in the fullest sense. They are actually separated at death, when the Spirit passes into another form, while the animal soul is extinguished; and even during life they remain not only distinct but antagonistic. The Flesh is no more than an "alien garment," a "prison" or a "tomb."[37]

The need for, or, the therapy of a disposable belief such as the doctrine of transmigration comes about, for Cornford, through the experience of the "divided self," and of an intense awareness of this division. The "self in conflict" is the designation of an experience of the divine flickering amidst the terrestrial, mortal abyss, a situation in which the Spirit and Flesh do battle for the duration of this life. Under this *schizophrenic pretext*, as Deleuze might join in, it is the duty of the self to differentiate, to divide itself between higher and baser potentialities, betwixt selves. Cornford illuminates:

> When man thus divides his nature into a divine and an animal part, disowning the lower part as alien and hostile, it means that he identifies himself with the higher and considers this to be his "true self."[38]

Cornford designates this prioritization of the "true" self as indicative of a pessimistic philosophy, which is "in love with death." This 'pessimism' denotes the realm of sense as incompatible with the aspiration of immortality. For, in the release of the divine spirit from its captivity, death is an event which, if the soul has undergone adequate preparation, qua asceticism, will allow the soul to radically transcend the *punishing* rounds of incessant incarnations. In his view, the realization of the divided self is an invitation for the soul to choose that aspect of itself for a cultivation which will lead to its eventual, and peculiar, return to the divine. Cornford does not even mention, however, the *bios* of the Pythagoreans, the primordial status of the creative body as a symbol of the All and *topos* of return,[39] nor, the possibility that Pythagoreanism was an affirmative pantheism. Moreover, Cornford flatly contradicts himself when he writes in his *Plato and Parmenides*:

> As a religious philosophy, Pythagoreanism unquestionably attached central importance to the idea of unity, in particular the unity of all life, divine, human, and animal, implied in the scheme of transmigration.[40]

It is here where we can detect some initial problems with his interpretation of Pythagoreanism as a "religious" philosophy, a problem of an intrinsic ambiguity in the text, one which we will also witness in our consideration of Philolaus. In 'Divisions of the Soul', Cornford constructs a psychological notion of the "religious as such," *stylized* as an irreconcilable conflict between the disparate realms of spirit and flesh. Yet, his clear recognition of the central importance of an already prevailing "unity," encompassing the All, seems to be at odds with his notion of division. Cornford also writes in *Plato and Parmenides*:

> The world itself is a living creature. The element that makes it "divine" will be the principle of beauty and goodness which is manifest in the perfection of its completed order (κοσμος).[41]

For, as will be discussed below in a discussion of harmony, there seems to be a contradiction between the attribution of the body as a "prison" or "tomb" of the soul, when, in this philosophy, there is such a vivid affirmation of "nature," expressed not only in a contemplative interest in its workings, but also in the importance of considerations of the body with respect to health and practical living, these being the necessary conditions of a *bios* and *theoria* which aspires and works for a return to the divine. In this way, Cornford's perspective is guilty of the same contradiction which he claims to beset religious philosophies, such as that of Pythagoras.

Walter Burkert (1931–)

Walter Burkert provides a description of the Pythagorean movement which, although sharing certain assumptions with respect to the distinction between logical and a-logical modes of thought, not only points to the unity at the basis of the teaching, but also, despite his nod to Cornford in the title of his *Lore and Science*, clearly and significantly contradicts the division made by Cornford between the sixth- and fifth-century Pythagoreans:

> Ecstatic experiences of a Bacchic, Shamanistic, or Yoga type may stand in the background. Furthermore, what appears in the fifth century is not a complete and consistent doctrine of metempsychosis, but rather experimental

speculations with contradictory principles of ritual and morality, and a grop-
ing for natural laws: the soul comes from the gods and after repeated trials
returns to them, or else it runs forever in a circle through all spheres of the
cosmos; sheer chance decides on the reincarnation, or else a judgment of
the dead; it is morally blameless conduct that guarantees the better lot or else
the bare fact of ritual initiation that frees from guilt. The idea finally that the
soul is some light, heavenly substance and that man's soul will therefore eventually ascend to heaven set the stage for a momentous synthesis of cosmology
and salvation religion. Since these contradictory motifs are assimilated at
a pre-philosophical level; at the level of free *mythoi* and not as dogmas, the
contradiction with the existing traditions were not found disquieting.[42]

In this interpretation, the doctrine of transmigration exists at an experimental
stage, but yet, in the lifeworld of Paganism, the diversity of perspectives upon the
narrative and its meaning was analogous to the treatment of other narratives,
such as Homer, Hesiod, and Orpheus. Nevertheless, it is clearly intimated in this
passage that transmigration served as an inclusive poetic *topos* for the philosophical practices and explorations that were being undertaken by the Pythagoreans.
Such an inclusivity was destroyed with the Pythagorean community, well before
the emergence of the Platonic academy and its "divided line." The exclusivity or
hierarchy of truth which emerges with Christianity, moreover, has as its condition
the nexus of beliefs which achieved completion with the philosophy of Plato.[43]

What is problematic is Burkert's reference to a "momentous synthesis of
cosmology and salvation religion" in the Pythagorean teaching. This interpretation begins with the prior separation of these terms, consistent with the
modern severance of science and religion. This throws doubt upon Burkert's
picture and upon his reliance upon Philolaus who also severed form from matter, limit and the unlimited. There is instead the necessity to trace the common
rooting of the various aspects of early Pythagoreanism to its lifeworld, which
though temporal, was a community, and in this sense, a "unity" or "gathering."
The notion of a "pre-philosophical" existential unity, in the sense of an extended
kinship amidst harmony, must guide us in our navigation of the myriad sources
of interpretation. For it seems that this is the most unproblematic attribute of
the Pythagorean philosophy. In the notions of kinship and friendship, there
is little to be detected of the *agonistic* divisions which are sought by Cornford.
Any attentive interpretation must be sensitive to this holistic sense of community which grounds and understands distinctions as aspects of the All.

W.K.C. Guthrie (1906–1981)

W.K.C. Guthrie, in his monumental *A History of Greek Philosophy*, also mentions this
"religious-philosophical synthesis," but contrary to other modern interpreters,

he seeks to display a "unifying" core, not dependent upon the methodology which radically segregates these realms of "religion" and "science." He undertakes what he calls a cautious inquiry of the sources for early Pythagoreans, concluding from his investigation:

> The religious doctrines of immortality and transmigration are assigned to Pythagoras on incontrovertible evidence.[44]

And he writes:

> We have seen that Pythagoras himself taught transmigration, and may also be safely credited with the complex of ideas with which transmigration is bound up: the doctrine that the human soul is immortal, that it owes its immortality to its essential kinship with the divine, universal soul, and that it may hope to return to its divine source when purified.[45]

Guthrie agrees with both Cornford and Dacier that Pythagoras is not the author of the doctrine of transmigration. With the former, he traces the origination of this doctrine, or at least its source for Pythagoras, to a "noncivilized" culture. He holds that there is no evidence that the source for the belief is Ancient Egypt and thus disagrees with both Dacier and Herodotus.[46] Guthrie does, however, agree with Cornford's thesis that transmigration implies a scenario of the purification of the soul from the body, despite his consistent emphasis upon the body and upon magic. Nevertheless, despite his being a child of his time, Gurthrie's interpretation, with its emphasis on the notion of an "extended kinship," is quite different from that of Dacier and Cornford to the extent he does not insist that the doctrine of transmigration be "cut off at the root." He seeks instead to learn from these peoples, who are labeled "noncivilized" since they remember and cultivate the beliefs and practices of sympathetic magic in its relation to the doctrine of transmigration. Guthrie distills his perspective:

> The general belief in the possibility of transference, which underlies all the taboos of sympathetic magic, rests in turn on an extended notion of kinship or relationship which is foreign to civilized thought. It appears again in the beliefs associated with a totemic organization of society where the tribe is conscious of a kinship, even an identity between itself and a non-human species of animal.[47]

He continues:

> [T]he kinship of nature provides the general world view within which alone the transmigration of souls is a tenable belief. Only the fact that the souls of

men and of animals are of the same family could make it possible for the same soul to enter now a man's body and now that of a beast or a bird.[48]

A universal notion of kinship thus underlies the possibility of transference, which in turn underlies sympathetic magic. Moreover, this selfsame kinship underlies the doctrine of transmigration. Is Guthrie seeking to make a connection betwixt sympathetic magic and the doctrine of transmigration? We find that this is indeed the case. Guthrie writes concerning the Pythagorean teaching:

> The essentially magical conception of universal kinship or sympathy, in a more or less refined and rationalized form, permeates its central doctrines of the nature of the universe and the relationship of its parts. To be aware of this will assist an understanding of its mathematical conception of the natural world, as well as of its religious beliefs concerning the fate of the human soul.[49]

Guthrie would therefore disagree with the strict separation between the religious and the scientific asserted by Cornford.[50] Guthrie instead offers an interpretation which, while nominally recognizing different arenas of inquiry, instead seeks to disclose the kinship of these pursuits, as these latter are contained within the horizon of a magical conception of the universe. In this way, far from being an expedient fiction or a well-intentioned lie, the doctrine of transmigration acquires an undeniable and essential significance for the teaching *as a whole*. Guthrie writes:

> The Greek ideal of *philosophia* and *theoria* was at a fairly early date annexed by the Pythagoreans for their master and linked with the doctrine of transmigration.[51]

And, echoing his earlier cautious approach to Pythagorean sources, especially those pertaining to the doctrine of transmigration, he writes:

> The importance of even these scanty items of information becomes evident when we remember that for Plato the problem of the possibility of knowledge was central, and that he solved it by the supposition that since the world of experience is strictly unknowable, such awareness of truth as we acquire in this life must consist of the recollection of what we discovered before birth, i.e., it depends on the doctrine of reincarnation.[52]

The acquisition of knowledge *as such*, the philosophic *a priori*, is grounded upon the doctrine of transmigration or remembrance. This interpretation stands in direct conflict with that of Cornford. For the latter, there are distinct principles which underlie the contradictory domains of mysticism, or religion in his interpretation, and science. For Guthrie, on the contrary, it is sympathetic magic, expressed in the doctrine of transmigration, which underlies each of these regions of knowledge. This suggests, therefore, a distinction not between mysticism and science, as elaborated by Cornford, but one between mysticism and magic.

There is, of course, some similarity between these in that both seek to effectuate an explicit return to the divine; which divine we do not know. Yet, what distinguishes these is their respective comportments amidst the phenomenal world, a "sensible" world which Parmenides allegedly rejects as inherently false, of merely mortal knowing. The doctrine of mysticism shares with Parmenides a suspension of belief with regard to the visible world, while magic, as suggested by Guthrie, unites in its perspective the domains of the visible and the unseen on the way to a harmonious self. In other words, there is thus a thread which links the "shades of opinion" with the "light of truth," a link which is conceived as a pathway from the former to the latter.

In this way, we can ascertain from this interpretation the vital importance for *philosophia* of the doctrine of transmigration, together with the conceptions of sympathetic magic and the kinship of nature upon which it rests. To be sure, Guthrie is not seeking to identify the Pythagorean *bios* with the totemic and tribal collocations of human existence. He writes that the magical conception of the universe has undergone an "Apollonization" through its association with the Greek philosophic ideal and with the worship of Apollo. Yet, as with tragedy, the magical essence remains intact as indicated through the prominence of the idea of kinship and doctrine of transmigration.

Not only is Guthrie's position distinct from interpreters such as Dacier and Cornford, but it is also distinct from those which interpret the doctrine of transmigration as literal truth. In this camp, I include, perhaps unjustly, those writers, such as Iamblichus and Proclus who, as true believers, do not attempt to "investigate" the significance of the doctrine for accounting for the philosophic *a priori* and as being a dwelling for the philosophy in its various regions and aspects. Instead, and this indicates the tutelage of a tradition of antiquarian history, these writers "couch" their articulation in the anecdotes of the successive incarnations of Pythagoras without much, if any, further elaboration. In this way, these accounts, if we get caught up in Cornford's scenario, are merely the "other side of the coin" of those which regard transmigration as a fiction. Entangled in this vicious cycle, the transmigration of the soul, whether fiction or fundamentalist truth, is to be regarded by the late modern philosopher as a lie; it is "religious" and is thus differentiated from the so-called scientific Pythagoreanism.

In the wake of the antithesis between these oppositional, though secretly incestuous, camps, the interpretation that the doctrine of transmigration accounts for the possibility of knowledge as such is left unexamined. Contrary to Cornford, and in distinction from the religious interpretation of the doctrine of transmigration (as literal truth or as a fiction for the regulation of behavior), the doctrine of transmigration can be conceived as a *complex symbola*, a variant of the *tragic myth* serving as the poetic ground of Pythagorean *philosophia*, incorporating *theoria* and *bios* amid a mythopoetic lifeworld.

Chapter 2

Beyond Mysticism and Science: Symbolism and Philosophical Magic

Guthrie provides us, in a way disallowed by the *scientistic* interpretations of Pythagoras, with a clue to an interpretation of the doctrine of transmigration which seeks to understand the teaching from out of the context of its own "historicity." For it cannot be overemphasized in this regard that even the so-called materialist philosophers of this era referred to what would be deemed in modern analysis as the "religious," mythical, or sacred. And, it is clear from the evidence of this period that there was a consensual, albeit myriad, array of "religious" and spiritual affiliations which not only encompassed the various temples, cult societies, and poets, such as Sappho, but also interspersed the *polis* and its political occupants. In this way, if we are to attempt to grasp the doctrine of transmigration outside of the late modern antithesis, we must seek to understand how the Pythagorean teaching presented a unified account of body, world, soul, and the divine.

In this context, the notion of magic will allow us to grasp a symbolic interpretation of the Pythagorean teaching as a philosophy of an unbroken harmony, one that maintains a nuanced continuity with so-called primitive cultures, and with Homer, with regard to the terrestrial horizon and the specificity of the event of life. As the *Golden Verses* begin, one must honor the self, for in and amidst the self, from this perspective, a world coalesces, pointing toward the divine. Magic, as a sacred *praxis*, enters into this realm of the self; it is the self in its harmony and in its thoughtful action or *praxis*. This actual circumstance of the self, its environment, is its condition, and through the action of the self, the world becomes a symbol of aspiration for and distance from/to harmony. Frankfort writes in his important, though virtually forgotten, work *Before Philosophy*,

> We understand phenomena, not by what makes them peculiar, but by what makes them manifestations of general laws. But, a general law cannot do justice to the individual character of each event. And, the individual character of the event is precisely what early man experiences most strongly.[1]

We, who as yet live in the "age of science," usually understand "phenomena" through recourse to the conceptual logic of schematic explanation. Yet, in the present inquiry, we will have to embrace the unusual, for the usual will not suffice. The attempted application of a conceptual totalization to the event will not transcend the horizon into the "essence" since what is occurring is singular, and cannot be conceptualized. The "event" cannot be totalized into a conceptual-logical system since being, as Kant and Heidegger have pointed out, is not a real predicate. The event may be indicated, but only as indigenous self-expression. As Gödel once warned, a completed system is impossible. We must begin to fathom a different way or *ethos* of knowing in order to do "justice" to the event.

The "system," whether it is calculus or technical philosophy, no matter how much it claims to achieve its own systematic perfection, will always remain only at the surface of the event. It always waits for the flight of Minerva at dusk. It cannot transgress the horizon of limit, it cannot be this event—will not be attuned with the event. Deaf to the spirit of this music, its modus operandi is impossible in principle, and thus it acts through violence, it displaces, replaces, contains this event. In this way, the fabric of reality is portrayed as infinitely ruptured in the artifices of the pure scientist, a portrait of rupture that is also shared by the mystic, who after all is the other in this hegemonic artifice. Through the violence of this rupture, the event is erased into the oblivion of forgetfulness.

An indication of the alternative approach which seeks to trace the memory of a harmony of All, as symbolized in the doctrine of transmigration, comes from Alphonse Louis Constant (Eliphas Levi)**,** a nineteenth century French occult philosopher, who writes in his *History of Magic*:

> Magic combines in a single science that which is most certain in philosophy with that which is eternal and infallible in religion. It reconciles perfectly and incontestably those two terms so opposed on the first view—faith and reason, science and belief, authority and liberty. It furnishes the human mind with an instrument of philosophical and religious certainty, as exact as mathematics, and even accounting for the infallibility of mathematics themselves.[2]

It is important that this reference to a philosophical magic will lead to reflection upon the precise roles of *theoria* and *bios* in the dissemination of the Pythagorean teaching. These latter terms, however, are only distinguished after the event, and refer to differing aspects of an originary, though forgotten, attunement. Magic is a remembrance of the All, as the symbolic configuration of these memories in practical life, as knowledge, and as an act which opens a sacred space with a desired destination. For this is philosophy with a *goal* and a thoughtful *praxis* designed to obtain this goal. The Apollonian focus upon a future that is prophesied and attained via *praxis* is a sublimation of the random field of chance, an *ethos* for a *bios* which is attuned under the figure of harmony. Guthrie writes in his *The Greek Philosophers*,[3]

> Magic is a primitive form of applied science. Whether or not spirits or gods are thought to enter at some stage into the process, their actions are compelled by the man in possession of the proper magical technique no less than if they were inanimate objects. The sorcerer sets in train a certain sequence of events, and cause and effect then follow with the same certainty as if one took good aim with a rifle and pulled the trigger.[4]

If we substitute the metaphor of the bow and arrow for that of the rifle, then we can ascertain that magic is a *bios* of a terrestrial life which aspires to a harmony of All. Such an eschatology of the soul is intimated by the God Apollo, the inventor of archery, shooting from afar. With the arrow, we have the pathway to transmigrate toward the perspective of the sky. We will see that this magical interpretation of the early Pythagoreans may cast into relief the raison d'etre of the *bios*, the importance of numbers, geometry, and music, not to mention the visible analogue of the divine in the sky, as Heidegger muses, or, and most intimately, the analogue which is my body, as the place of this aspiration is the whole self.[5]

In this way, I will focus upon the unifying and grounding character of magic with respect to the doctrine of transmigration. This notion of sympathetic magic will be regarded as a Apollonized terrestrial, symbolical *bios*, as opposed to ritual or ceremonial magic, and also distinct from that magic which is prayer, celestial magic. It is a "constructivist" magic, which, on its way to its return to the divine source, builds a world in which such a harmony manifestly resounds.

"Primitivism," Magic and the Philosophical *a priori*

In order to answer the question of the status of the doctrine of transmigration, we must examine its function of accounting for the *a priori* as such and of articulating a magical conception of the universe. As will become clear, the function of the *a priori*, expressed in the doctrine of transmigration, must be grasped within the context of a philosophical notion of magical kinship. It would be inaccurate to conceive this sublimation as a transition from magic to philosophy in that, contrary to the Analytic rendition of the history of philosophy, the Pythagoreans maintained a "magic core." At the heart of their articulation of the "Greek ideal" of *philosophia*, lay their commitment to remembrance and magical *praxis*. Neither, in this way, is the transmigration of souls to be considered a primitive or infantile doctrine, nor, in its use, as one that could be distinguished from some alleged "primitive" cultural narrative, as Bertholet (1909) has made his premise.[6]

Guthrie, as quoted above, writes that the "possibility of transference, which underlies all the taboos of sympathetic magic, rests in turn on an extended notion of kinship . . . "[7] As we can gather from Guthrie's text, the "primitive" notion of sympathetic magic is the activity of effectuating some intention within a field of resemblance.[8] Soustelle, in his illuminating work, *The Four Suns*, describes an Otomi and Mazahua magical practice focused upon an instrument called the *Chicauaztli*, or, the "ringing stick," which is "both a farming implement and a magical device."[9] The stick which has tiny bells tied to one end is used in a performance of music and dance, in which the stick is for a long duration struck against the ground, making holes, with the bells ringing. It is observed by Soustelle that the ringing bells resemble the sound of rain. He writes:

> It is easy to understand what the basic gesture here means: striking the floor with the digging stick imitates the sowing of maize, while the little bells are calling to the rain. At all times, the farming peoples of Mexico have relied upon the magic of sound to obtain water from the sky.[10]

The dance is performed at the commencement of the planting of the crops before the onset of the rainy season. The striking of the stick by the women of the tribe is a symbol of the fertility of the goddess in this mythopoetic narrative of two major deities, a pair of gods, Tsitanhmou, the "venerable great Lord," of fire and the sun, and Tsinana, the "moon mother and earth mother." The performance parallels the actual planting of the seeds, in which the woman makes a hole with her ringing stick and places a seed into the hole. The ringing of bells is meant to attract the attention of the rain god, Tlaloc; as like of like, resemblance.

In this example, we are shown a practical and magical activity which occurs as a temporal symbol amidst a field of resemblance. This is also a symbol within a teaching, which like the early Pythagoreans, is disseminated and preserved through an oral tradition of stories, song, dance, and *praxis*, abiding an ancient lattice of memory, one that has been preserved despite the premeditated extermination of 23 of the 24 million indigenous inhabitants by the Spanish. Such a capacity to act as a dwelling, as I have already indicated, was a central feature of the doctrine of transmigration.

Frazer, whose work is questionable for other reasons,[11] but who had an influence upon early-twentieth-century interpretations of Pythagoras, mentions two such "superstitions" of the Pythagorean teaching, *symbola* amidst an oral tradition:

> In ancient Greece superstitions of the same sort seemed to have been current, for it was thought that if a horse stepped on the track of a wolf he was seized with numbness; and a maxim ascribed to Pythagoras forbade people to pierce a man's footprints with a nail or a knife.[12]

And he writes:

> We can understand why it was a maxim with the Pythagoreans that in rising
> from bed you should smooth away the impression left by your body on the
> bed-clothes. The rule was simply an old precaution against magic, forming
> part of a whole code of superstitious maxims which antiquity fathered on
> Pythagoras, though doubtless they were familiar to the barbarous forefathers
> of the Greeks long before the time of the Philosopher.[13]

The notion of transference indicated by Guthrie suggests that these various
maxims, or *symbola*, are more significant and sophisticated than the derogative
label "superstition" allows them. As with the rites of spring performed by
the indigenous tribes of Mexico, it may be suggested that these *symbola* have
a practical and magical, or, at least an expressive,[14] significance in the life of
the Pythagorean community, a subject which will be considered in greater
depth in Chapter 7, "The Path of Remembrance, or Return."

Yet, at the same time, while these references suggest a continuity between
the "indigenous" notion of kinship and sympathetic magic and that of the
Pythagoreans, we can also detect significant differences which arise from the
transformation of the former to the latter. And, in this way, we will be compelled to distinguish the former notion and practice of sympathetic magic of
indigenous tribes from the philosophical magic of the Pythagoreans. Through
this distinction, we can specify the meaning of this magic, one which would
become the basis for all subsequent knowledge.

The basic notions bound up with the indigenous practices of magic, if we
can schematize them so formally, would be first, that all is kindred; second, that
within this web of kinship, resemblance implies connection; and third, that
there is action at a distance between similars. However, for the doctrine of transmigration to contain not only this magical conception of the *Kosmos*, but also
to provide an account of the philosophical *a priori*, what must be disclosed is
a *repetition* which moves beyond this immanent novelty of kinship and resemblance, a character that is beyond the immediate interplay amidst the *physis* of
terrestrial life. A repetition would serve to ground a theoretical-reflective and
indeed a "prophetic" orientation.[15]

The characteristics of the transformation effected by the Pythagoreans can
be discerned through a consideration of their primary philosophical doctrines.
Guthrie writes:

> What he said to his disciples no man can tell for certain, since they preserved
> such an exceptional silence. However, the following facts in particular became
> universally known: first, that he held the soul to be immortal, next that it
> migrates into other kinds of animals, further that past events repeat them-
> selves in a cyclic process and nothing is new in an absolute sense, and finally

that one must regard all living things as kindred. These are the beliefs which Pythagoras is said to have been the first to introduce into Greece.[16]

What distinguishes the Pythagorean notion of magical sympathy from that of the "primitive," is the notion of an immortal soul which, although it has a kinship, or communion of nature, with the All, must embark upon a path of return to the All, conceived as the Divine. This is what must, above all, be remembered by the initiate: each comes from All, and thus, within each, there endures a signature trace of the All, the thread which leads one back to the divine source.

In the "primitive" doctrine, we could envision an immanence in which a field of resemblance unfolds as a ceaselessly novel array of singulars, while preserving itself as the generative fountain of a phenomenal world existing in an extended kinship. In such a perspective, one could imagine the belief, as in Shinto, of spirits which reside along with the living. For in this belief, there is no question of a return, as one is already there-here. As the result of the transformation of the notion of magical kinship into the Apollonian symbolic *bios*, however, this eruption of novelty becomes contained by the additional directive of a kinship of the soul with a divinity transcending the proximate field of resemblance. This is an invitation to transmigration, this nuanced pseudo-alterity which is a possible *beyond* of our present state. Amid the particular body, we sense that there is more to being amidst the All, the event. This is only one incarnation, there is more to learn. And, that which is not there for us here remains invisible, concealed. The propositions that "past events recur" and "nothing is absolutely new" reiterate the original excession of the divine into a soul with body, an event recapitulated each instance a soul, leaving a corpse, wanders about and around, to be born anew. With the Apollonian sublimation, it is the "immortal" soul existing in kinship with the divine that transcends the situated dimension of perspective, and it is the ability of the music of the soul to disembark from the corpse which provides for the possibility of the philosophical *a priori*. Within the context of this extended kinship, the soul persists at a distance from the divine, but, it may return to the divine through the effectuation of a transference, conceived as an Apollonized sympathetic magic. The magical element remains in that there is no simple rejection of the phenomenal world, which is the chief characteristic of not only Eastern Buddhism, but also, Western, especially Christian mysticism, but an affirmation of the All which is wed to a specific configuration of *praxis*.

The path of return to the All must disembark from the phenomenal world, the soul taking its cues from the dimension of resemblance and continuity which surrounds its life as an animated body. The notion of a soul which enters a succession of bodies, human or animal, and circulates through all the elements of the universe underscores a *Kosmos* which is a manifestation of the divine and contains within itself more than the mere traces of the divinity.

As I will discuss in more detail below, the Apollonian form of transference is designated for Pythagoras as *philosophy*. Through this activity, one can return to the divine, in general, through an attunement with the divine. Guthrie writes:

> In this way the doctrine that all life was homogenes not only united men in the ties of kinship with animals, but most important of all, it taught them that their best nature was identical with something higher. It gave them an aim in life, namely to cultivate the soul, shake off the taint of the body, and rejoin the universal soul of which their individual souls were in essence parts. So long as the soul was condemned to remain in the wheel of transmigration— so long that is to say, as it had to enter a new body of man or animal after the death of the one which had previously teneted—so long was it still impure. By living the best and highest type of human life it might ultimately shake off the body altogether, escape from the wheel of rebirth, and attain the final bliss of losing itself in the universal, eternal, and divine soul to which by its own nature it belongs.[17]

Despite this disparaging portrayal of the body and the questionable imperative of purity,[18] Guthrie is expressing the central aspect of the Apollonization of sympathetic magic. The essential point is that there is a destination for a soul which will and has dwelt in a succession of bodies, amid an extended kinship. The philosophical notion of magic does not lend itself to a strict primary separation of the body and soul, nor, given the sense of kinship, does it seem congruent with the Pythagorean teaching that the body must be deprecated. This is demonstrated in the importance of the *bios* within the Pythagorean teaching. However, there is still an assignment of priority and significance between these "opposites," that of this singular body, and the extended self articulated as a succession of bodies. It can be discerned in this way that the problematic of the body, as this self, arises in that it dies and decays—or, in other words, that the body is the tragic individuation of the Dionysian All. Guthrie reports the utter disregard which Socrates had for life, a symptom of philosophy in his era:

> Philosophy in this sense is the subject-matter of Plato's *Phaedo*, where Pythagorean influence is obviously strong and seems to be acknowledged by reference to Philolaus. "I want to give you my reasons," says Socrates, "for thinking that the man who has truly dedicated his life to *philosophia* is of good courage when death approaches and strong in hope that the greatest of good things will fall to his lot on the other side when he dies."[19]

Although this represents, once again, a distortion of authentic Pythagorean teachings, philosophy, conceived as a practice of attunement with the divine, is a preparation for a death conceived as a necessary event within the scenario expressed in the doctrine of transmigration. Death is an event through which the soul is released from its abidance with this particular body. The direction taken by the soul depends upon its work of cultivation, or, more generally, its way of life. It may be transferred to the divine, if, that is, the self has "dedicated his life to *philosophia*," so says Socrates. Or, it may enter into another body amidst a succession of lives, a bird for instance, or it may become wind, a planet, etc. Many poets, such as Orpheus, were derided by Socrates for seeking to become various animals. Whatever may occur, the soul remains "intact," and, thus, has broader significance than the experience of a particular body, since it concerns a nomadic, broader self, that is a circuit of many bodies-selves. Yet, if the soul is to achieve its purpose amidst the myriad cycles of bodies, *this* body remains necessary as its point of departure and the place of its work of cultivation and attunement. We will see in our discussions of Plato that what is at stake in the interpretation of the doctrine of transmigration is the ability to distinguish the various, and often contradictory, mythopoetic scenarios that become invested in this doctrine. And, in this way, we may begin to understand why some poets wished to become birds, or the Pythagoreans to become All, distinct from Plato's deployment of transmigration as punishment and eventual purification and release.

The transformation from a "primitive" to a philosophical notion of sympathetic magic could be interpreted, with Frazer and Cornford, as a transformation from magic to religion. Yet, as we have seen, Guthrie writes that magic persists at the core of Pythagorean philosophy, even as this fact is forgotten via the erasure of historical displacement and suppression. Moreover, if we were to attempt to designate the doctrine of transmigration as merely religious, we would again clearly forget that this doctrine is the basis for the *a priori*, or as the narrative unfolding of knowledge, as it was, for instance, with Parmenides. This brings to the forefront an originary harmony which is suggested in Guthrie's reference to a "religious-philosophical" synthesis in the Pythagorean teaching. This synthesis, despite the modernist implication once again of a prior distinction between science and religion, would be the articulation and enactment of a teaching which gathered into a single opening the concerns for *physis* and *praxis*, as a *bios* which cultivated an *ethos* of harmony.

The Symbol of Transmigration and the Pythagorean Community

What is being accounted for here is a body of knowledge which dealt with both an exoteric conception of nature and an esoteric conception of the self amidst a divine *physis*. Both of these scenarios are gathered in the doctrine of transmigration in its providing for the possibility for knowledge as such, and as an operation and emanation of knowledge conceived as an Apollonized sympathetic magic. This distinction is analogous, as we have already suggested, to the exoteric and esoteric paths of knowledge in the Pythagorean distinction of *akousmatikoi* and the *mathematikoi*. Yet, again, there is some confusion in the evidence with respect to the meaning of these terms. Guthrie seems to suggest that the former, meaning "things heard" refers to those who were more advanced and participated in a rigorous *bios*, the first five years of which was conducted in silence. These pupils were guided into the esoteric dimensions of the teaching, a teaching which was synchronous with the *bios* conceived as attunement with the divine. The other division of the "school," the *mathematikoi*, did not undergo the initiation and commitment to a *bios*, or were not yet initiated, but underwent a "mathematical education and other rational enquiries." Yet, this portrayal seems to be contradicted both by Iamblichus and Porphyry in their *Lives*, in which the *akousmatikoi* are only hearers and are of a lesser depth in their discipleship than the *mathematikoi*, or students, who are also called by Iamblichus *esoterics*.

This distinction becomes even more problematic, however, in a different work by Iamblichus, where he reports a division in Italian philosophy between the followers of Pythagoras and Hippasus, the latter said to have been assassinated by the Pythagoreans for revealing the secret of irrational numbers. It is written that the *akousmatikoi* were considered by some to be the true Pythagoreans, while the *mathematikoi* considered the *akousmatikoi* to be Pythagoreans, but considered themselves "so in still greater degree . . . "[20] Kirk writes moreover of an account that there was "from the very first a distinction" in the teaching between "the older men, active in politics," who followed a *bios* and made the *akousmatikoi* their guide, and "the younger men" who had more leisure and aptitude for study."[21] It seems plausible that the confusion arises since the term *akousmatikoi* could, as I have intimated in the Introduction, refer to different phenomena.

Kirk suggests that there are two alternative descriptions of *akousmatikoi*, one as things heard, which might suggest the notion of Hearers or auditors as presented in the *Lives*. Yet, the other, more relevant description is "passwords" which seems to insinuate an esoteric interpretation, as tokens of remembrance used in the *bios*. On this basis, we could refrain from giving our complete consent to Iamblichus as a source. That which is "clear" is that there seems to have been some distinction in the teaching, one implying that some who conducted researches in science were not necessarily part of the *bios*. But, this question may be ultimately lost in the mire of history for we do not know *how* this movement was organized. The notion of a "school" must strike us as questionable on the grounds of anachronism, as this notion presupposes a specific economy of scale and division of labor, or in other words, of institutionalization. We must not be convinced by notions which merely reflect our own state of intellectual and political hierarchies, but must attempt to think through what can be thought of as a symbolist teaching of synergistic theory and practice. What can be suggested for our purposes is that the teaching had four dimensions: the auditors, the mathematical exoterics, the *bios* esoterics (hearers of passwords), and the teacher himself. Yet, this cannot be decided absolutely on the basis of the evidence.[22]

Despite this ambiguity, we can fathom that those who partook of the esoteric dimensions were seen as delving deeper into the teaching than those concerned only with "natural philosophy." In this way, an array of circles became established in the Pythagorean movement which corresponded to the distinction in the teaching between exoteric and esoteric. And, it seems that each of these circles contained aspects of *akousmatikoi* and *mathematikoi*. With regard to the organization of the Pythagorean *community*, we can consider the possibility of a path of thought and its corresponding practice in light of the temporal *reproduction* and life of a diverse community—which we must remember included men, women, and children. We can, for instance, consider the statement that magic permeates the teaching, illuminating the mathematical conception of the world as a protocol of education leading from memorization of propositions to exoteric mathematical knowledge of the world, and finally to an esoteric comprehension of this knowledge, symbolized by a nexus of passwords. Not higher or lower, but surface and depth; it is not an ascent which leads to the remembrance or return, but an uncovering of a certain depth of thought and practice. In this way, the esoteric significance has priority over the exoteric *eidos*, and, originally grounds the dimensions of any so-called rational inquiry.[23]

In order to cast light upon this pathway, I will turn to John Dillon, in his work, *The Golden Chain*, where he writes that Pythagoras rejected "images of God" in either human or bestial form, as a divinity of the All must not be particularized, for this would be to negate the life of the All in its unfolding betwixt these dimensions of macrocosm and microcosm. This is quite similar to his teacher Anaximander's criticism of Thales and Anaximenes, who each made an individual thing, water and air, respectively, the ground of all things. For the former, as well as his student Pythagoras—not to mention the similarity with the doctrine of Being of Parmenides—it is the *unlimited* which is the source. It is a nothing, which is the source and condition of things.

Such an indication of the source in the *unlimited* will provide a distinct clue to the meaning and practice of a philosophical magic in the Pythagorean context. As we have seen in Chapter 1, many ancient sources alleged that the origin of the doctrine of transmigration can be traced to the ancient Egyptians, and such an affiliation would cast a particular light of a discussion of sympathetic magic. However, it is important to remember that the Pythagoreans, as with the Jews and Muslims, forbade images of the divine, and such a prohibition would cast doubt on the testimony or even the relevance of some—admittedly late—ancient sources. A brief juxtaposition of Pythagorean and Egyptian magic will illuminate the problem. On the one hand, each of these magical practices has an affinity to philosophy in the law of sympathy, that like is of like, and that there is an action at a distance between similars. On the other hand, however, the *interpretation* of this sympathy and action of a distance differs with respect to the use of an image which resembles that which is sought. In the former, it is a mythopoetic indication, or rule, for a thinking practice; in the latter, the magical practice utilized images with a "resemblance" to the divinity, for instance the sun disc or the green shaded human (Osiris). In this way, that which distinguishes the Pythagoreans is the construction of a *bios* which actuated their notion of sympathy not merely in a ritual image, but as *praxis* situated in the community. Dillon describes the Pythagorean community:

> But generally, Pythagoreanism simply means, besides a personal devotion to Pythagoras and particular enthusiasm for number mysticism and a mathematical model; for the universe, a more austere stance in ethics and the observance of a certain bios, or way of life, involving abstention from meat and beans and the adoption of the other Pythagorean rules, or *symbola*.[24]

The Pythagorean movement cultivated a harmony of *bios* and *theoria*, as the intentional *praxis* of philosophical magic, as a way of practical, symbolic life, the horizons of which being an extended opening of kinship. The ends are achieved, not through the static practices of ritual or ceremonial magic, or recitative prayer (although this need not be excluded if it acted as a token of remembrance), but through an active *bios* which explicitly and thoughtfully cultivates an expansive participation amid the lives of those ever more complete and enduring spheres of actuality, in order to eventually become the All.

The distinction which is suggested betwixt the esoteric and the exoteric can be conceived as a retrospective contrast which has meaning in that an existential distance has been traversed. This is not the assertion of an abstract hierarchy, a plan that must be met despite singular specificity. Instead, giving deference to chance and contingency, a pathway of education and life is a way of memory for a community and the necessary preparation on the way toward a more encompassing disclosure of truth, as and when the initiate is prepared for such a disclosure of its predicament.

The pedagogy of the Pythagorean community consisted in the instillation of an awareness of that which is concealed at the limit of the seen, as the unseen which plays in our midst. One could state that the exoteric dimension of the teaching had an explicit reliance on the *seen* (theorein), and thus, ultimately upon the image. Mathematics, in its *seen* presentation, is a simple reduction of the phenomenal within the confines of the metaphoricity of sight, which gives access to an understanding of the natural world. However, an intimation of, to use its own metaphor, the invisible is also present, for as this activity is thought, it must be possible to conceive of the mathematical objects of point, line, etc. as somehow invisible or, perhaps, ideal or paradigmatic. In other words, it is not necessary for there to be a perfect, visible line for there to be a notion of one. Yet, this aspect of the invisible, as thought restricted to the natural world, will remain tied to visibility, and thus, will remain exoteric. However, there is another side to this natural world, that of the nonvisible which draws the initiate toward a deeper wisdom, beyond inscribed, imagistic equations. This "element," if we can use this word, is an indication that the All that is suggested in the doctrine of transmigration cannot be reduced to the meta-distinction of the visible and the invisible, at least as it has been deployed, in which is posited the same discordant opposition laid down by Cornford's interpretation. In this interpretation, the visible is used as a generic concept for all phenomenality as such. The invisible is beyond the phenomenon, beyond the world.

In this distinction, we can see the metaphorical seeds of the notion of the body as a "prison," a "tomb," for if the essence of truth lies in the invisible, and if this invisible is utterly distinct from the visible, then, the visible world would be only an impediment for the realization of an invisible truth. However, once again utilizing this metaphor of light, we can grasp that the esoteric dimensions of the teaching possess an inherent tendency to fathom amidst the visible "face," the trace of the invisible, hidden "spirit" of the divine. Yet, in this way, the invisible is not a beyond, of some distant essence, but is that which exceeds our immediate perspectival awareness. It is "still there," intimately involved in this ineffable event of the world. We could give as an example the case of music.

An image, an amulet, if worshipped in itself only, torn from the delicate fabric of symbolical life, can only be symptomatic of a pernicious form of forgetfulness. And, the same could be said for any similar metaphorical matrix such as that of light and dark, or of the visible and the invisible which is severed from an ethical commitment to the All. For this All encompasses smell, sound, taste, touch, in addition to the capacity of sight. The inclusion of these "other" senses suggests the possible rationales of their traditional exclusions. Each of these senses occurs as *unseen* amidst its event of being. While the seen "naturally" suggests an unseen, the traditional stratagem, in its exclusion of the unseen sense, shifts the focus of the search for substance not to the other senses, but to the dimension of the unseen as an *occult quality*, that is, to that which transcends the All as a external principle of possible mediation or form.

It could be suggested that a commitment to the All, and to a notion of an extended kinship and magical perspective of the event of existence would preclude such a reduction of the All to either an "image" or to a single "analogy" as an act of forgetful captivation to a fixed grammar of interpretation.[25] This commitment to a path of the All, to a way of life which embraces all and each of the senses is enacted as a *bios* amidst the world, as the necessary context for any use of static images or amulets. Yet, such trinkets were not preferred by the Pythagoreans, who instead engaged in practices involving herbs, gymnastics, music, and spoken tokens of remembrance. Beyond the image, the seen, we are guided to the living depth that is life, apprehended as a unity of sensation, where sight, the seen, takes on a differing, lived aspect. The *bios* is an act of participation in the event of the All; it is an attunement which effectuates a tuning of ever increasing concordance.

Dillon describes this transition from the exoteric to the esoteric in education:

> [F]or the Pythagoreans had the habit of placing before their scientific instruction the revelation of the subject under inquiry through similitudes and images, and after this of introducing the secret revelations of the same subjects through symbols, and then in this way, after the reactivation of the soul's ability to comprehend the intelligible realm and the purging of its vision, to bring in the completed knowledge of the subjects laid down for investigation. And here too the relating in summary of *The Republic* before the inquiry into Nature prepares us to understand the orderly creation of the Universe *through the medium of an image*, while the story of Atlantis acts as a symbol; for indeed myths in general tend to reveal the principles of reality through symbols. So the discussion of Nature in fact runs through the whole dialogue, but appears in different forms according to the different methods of revelations.[26]

We see that the transition from the exoteric to the esoteric is inherent in a process of education, of remembrance, which is seeking for its goal a transference from the site of the perspective of the body to the life of the All, of a possibility of return to the divine. We begin in a labyrinth of images, but the ultimate goal is to move through the image into a *bios* of attunement with the All. Dillon writes:

> For these *symbola* have obviously no resemblance to the essential nature of the Gods. But myths must surely, if they are not to fall short of resemblance to the nature of things, the contemplation of which they are attempting to conceal by means of the screens of appearance.[27]

Symbol has its genealogy in the Greek notion of a tally—two halves of one object, one held by each of the parties to a deal. In this light, the symbol intimates an interpenetration betwixt visible and invisible dimensions, a capillary bridge between these, each longing for its other half, abide via a *bios* of extended kinship. In this way, the doctrine is similar to the Myth of the Cave or of Atlantis in the Platonic teaching. Within this doctrine are encoded various regions of inquiry and the methods of their divination. The doctrine of transmigration is such a screen of appearance, not a fiction, but a nexus of symbola which, to borrow from Cornford, coordinates "a construction of the 'seen-order' (ορατος κοσμος) capable of providing for the needs of the unseen."[28] The screen of appearance conceals, as a riddle, the truth which is being sought in contemplation and action. Yet, it is not a mere barrier, but a paradigm, which contains within itself the entire teaching, if one only contemplates and enacts its implications. The doctrine is sheltered within a myth, but as a teaching which is only meaningful if composed as an active *bios* and *theoria*, amid a shelter in which the community can, with Hölderlin, poetically dwell.

The doctrine of transmigration is a mythopoetic expression of a teaching which contains symbolically an elaborate nexus of nodal references which describe a path of opening or elaboration of the *Kosmos*, and the wandering of souls upon a path of return to the source. The myth symbolizes the music and the life of this specific terrestrial collocation of mortal beings such as we are, *on the way*. The path of the seen to the unseen, from the partial to the All, finds its site of departure in a self, as a body with soul, but which like the image, realizes that its prevailing eruption into the open contains the seeds of its own dissolution, of its closing, and will be *transfigured* with the attainment of the goal. But, unlike the use of static images, which must be thrown away, or thrown down like a ladder, the *bios* is not thrown away, but simply converges in the life of the All. In the path of birth, life, death, and rebirth is contained the infrastructure of two primary migrations amidst the overall scenario of continuous transference. In birth, or the entrance of the soul into a body, there is implied a myth of opening which articulates the unfolding of the *Kosmos*, and of the emergence of the soul. As a doctrine which incorporates the event of death as a release of the soul into another body, or into a final return, however, it harbors a tacit overcoming of itself (unless we are to conceive of this return in the sense of eternal recurrence).[29]

The doctrine of transmigration must, therefore, be examined in three aspects: first, as a unique mythopoetic symbol which intimates a broad array of manifestations or happenings, including the elaboration of "world," of the event; second, as a "moment of vision" (Augenblick) in which the soul amidst body realizes its divine nature; and finally, as a soul which seeks and embarks upon the path of return to the source, but not as the annihilation of the world, but as its recurring fulfillment. In many ways, the return will be the obverse of the opening, yet, there will be a disjunction between the paths in that the phenomenal location of departure for the initiate will be one of remembrance, and thus, the methods of return, or the "training of ascent" will begin amidst the phenomenal with the body in its terrestrial habitat. For from a divine gaze, all may always already be One and eternal, but from the perspective of the phenomenal, this completion remains only a possibility, and perhaps, in a state of poetic irony. Yet, this last clue will show us, as we will see elsewhere, that it is language, "our way of speaking" which seduces us to, as Wittgenstein warned regarding Augustine, to find a substance for a substantive, a seduction that must be resisted by the philosopher.

Transmigration and the Oral Tradition

The foregoing may be better grasped through a discussion of the terrestrial dimension of this departure, and of its relation to the doctrine of transmigration. Again, Pythagoras wrote nothing. And as Kirk has warned us, a huge volume of mostly spurious literature continues to fill the void of this textual absence.

But, I would like to suggest that this lack of textual evidence may provide for our inquiry an important clue for any interpretation of the status of the doctrine of transmigration. For the *symbola*, often expressed in the form of the spoken word, were aspects of an oral dissemination and maintenance of the Pythagorean teaching and community. Such a dimension is suggested if we consider that the esoteric truth of the teaching was intimated via the *akousmatikoi* , conceived in this case, as "passwords" which harbored a remembrance. In this way, one way to gain perspective upon the status of the doctrine of transmigration is to take heed of the *praxis* of the Pythagorean community within the oral tradition. Albright writes concerning the introduction of writing in Greece:

> In the Greek world, especially in its cultural center, Attica, new life was stirring. Though a rarely endowed people, the Greeks had not emerged from the age of barbarism that followed the collapse of the aristocratic culture of the Mycenaean Age until the eighth century B.C. Then they awoke with startling suddenness and reacted to the advanced civilization of their Near-Eastern neighbors, among whom the Canaanite Phoenicians undoubtedly played the most important role. The Greeks of Ionia and the Islands led the way by shifting from piracy to commerce and colonization, by imitating Phoenecian artistic models, by borrowing the Phoenecian alphabet and adapting it to Hellenic use. About 776 B.C. national events began to be systematically recorded in writing and a century later arose Hesiod, the first Greek writer whose work and personality are at all tangible. It is very significant that the literary aspect of higher culture preceded the artistic aspects in its development.[30]

It is significant that the early Pythagoreans maintained their philosophy within the oral tradition, despite their late emergence in the sixth century BCE. This not only reiterates the importance of the *akousmatikoi*, which were an oral expression harboring a memory of the teaching, but also provides an insight into the continuity of the Pythagorean teaching with the cultures which preceded writing, such as a Pelasgians. It also provides a sense of the intimacy of their thoughts, words, and practices in the dissemination of their community. Furthermore, Albright writes concerning the status of writing for those who employed it:

> As has often been emphasized by scholars, writing was used in antiquity largely as an aid or guide to memory, not as a substitute for it.[31]

In this way, one could contend that the Pythagoreans did employ—though as a secondary phenomena—a form of "writing" in the sense of a visible sign or symbolic construction, which was utilized in the transition from exoteric to esoteric education. For instance, the monochord abides and expresses the relations of musical and mathematical harmony. Yet, the monochord, if it sets unplayed, as an exhibition, is ultimately dependent upon the visible form, even if it can point toward the invisible, that is, it succumbs to the metaphor of light, of sight. The monochord casts into relief the relation between sight and sound, with a priority of the latter as closer to the All than the former. The same relationship is symbolized between writing and speaking.[32]

As the transmission of writing remains within the horizons of the visible, it cannot prefigure the divine, which cannot, for the Pythagoreans, be represented in image, even in written language. The Oral pathway of transmission is a speaking through breath, and in this vocal way, is analogous to the soul as breath, and therefore allows for the expression of esoteric truths in the unseen and heard of speech and music.[33] In this way, we can attempt to fathom the sacred dimensions of dialogue, of song, of music, the spoken word; not to mention, of smell, taste, and touch.

Albright writes concerning the modes of oral transmission, which must be read in explicit connection to the status of the doctrine of transmigration as a *complex symbola*:

> A clear distinction must be made between different forms of oral composition since the ease and success of transmission without the aid of writing depends largely upon the stylistic medium. Here it is generally recognized that the verse form is much better adapted for oral transmission that is any kind of prose. The ease with which Children learn poetry is well known; lists and recipes were formerly put into verse for mnemotechnic purposes.[34]

Albright suggests for us the idea of a story motif which forms a pattern for the transmission of a notion in an oral manner. Within this story motif there is an articulated array of guides and prescriptions and other items of knowledge which, exhibited by the doctrine of transmigration and the monochord, displays a style of composition suited to a *bios* which gave priority to the oral transmission of an esoteric wisdom and way of life.

In this way, the doctrine of transmigration is itself a story motif, but unlike the *Golden Verses* and the monochord, it explicitly exhibits a mythopoetic destination for the wanderer as such, of the love and strife of the one seeking "truth." The doctrine, therefore, has a specific mnemotechnic purpose, in addition to its grounding of the *a priori*, and, one which serves to poetically *shelter* the entire Pythagorean philosophy. As it is grounded in the extended kinship of all, philosophy may be conceived as an Apollonized sympathetic magic which responds to the implications of the finitude of tragic existence. In this way, philosophy, for the Pythagoreans, has no other meaning and context than the narrative of transmigration. All the efforts of philosophy, as a thoughtful *bios* are the handmaiden to the fulfillment of the meta-narrative of the migrations and eventual attainment of All. This attainment is the migrating across myriad perspectives until one attains the "perspective" and life of the All.

Chapter 3

The Emergence of Mystic Cults and
the Immortal Soul

If we are to attempt to comprehend the implications and significance of such a magical philosophy, we must seek to understand the context of emergence for the teaching of Pythagoras. In this spirit, Burkert describes the initiation of Pythagoras:

> Pythagoras is said to have undergone initiation to the Idaen Dactyl in a quite different manner: he was purified with a lightning stone—a double axe?— and had to lie all day long by the sea and at night on the fleece of a black ram by the river; then he was admitted to the cave, dressed in black wool, made fire sacrifice and saw the throne which is prepared for Zeus every year.[1]

The soul of Pythagoras recurred into a world ripe with "mystical" cults and other esoteric movements. He himself was initiated into an "order" and is comparable to Orpheus in that both were founders of communities which sought a "return" to the divine.

Each name, Orpheus, a poet and musician, Pythagoras, a philosopher and magician, is implicated within the accounts of significant sacerdotal transfigurations and revolutions which erupted in the sixth century BCE. These transformations were also associated with the name of Buddha, the Druids, and with the seizure and dissemination of the Egyptian archives by Darius of Persia after his conquest of Egypt. Much was happening; moreover, there were voices coming from other places, from the Asian kingdoms, notably, that of Zoroaster. Burkert suggests the possible influences upon Pythagoras:

> That an Ionian of the sixth century should assimilate elements of Babylonian mathematics, Iranian religion, and even Indian metempsychosis doctrine is intrinsically possible.[2]

The character of this transformation, coinciding as the myriad situation of influence just described, was that of a breaking free from traditional constraints, such as the parochial kinship arrangements, indicated in Homer, in order to set free a vision of an explicit extended kinship betwixt differing collocations of *homo terra*. There is a break within mythological affiliation, and a break with the terrestrial cultural regime of governance of which the myths of Homer were a phantasmagoric idealization. Burkert specifies the central feature of this new teaching within Olympian Greece:

> What is most important is the transformation in the concept of the soul, psyche, which takes place in these circles. The doctrine of transmigration presupposes that in the living being, man as animal, there is an individual constant something, an ego that preserves its identity by force of its own essence independent of the body which passes away. Thus a new general concept of a living being is created, empsychon: "a *psyche* is within." This *psyche* is obviously not the powerless, unconscious image of recollection in a gloomy Hades, as in Homer's *Nekyia*; it is not affected by death: the soul is immortal, *athanatos*. That the epithet which since Homer had characterized the gods in distinction from men now becomes the essential mark of the human person is indeed a revolution.[3]

Burkert continues with this leitmotif of revolution, despite the propensity of this term to deny individual variations:

> This revolution, however, was brought about in stages with the result that the break could even be overlooked. At first this constant something is quite distinct from man's empirical waking consciousness: Pindar describes it as the very opposite of this, sleeping when the limbs are active, but revealing its essence in dreams and finally in death.[4]

The revolution is one that is long and is elaborated across the extended unfolding of a terrestrial culture in flux. It asserts a novel conception of the soul amidst a culture which must consider this notion as an insurgency of *hubris*. Burkert describes the essential implications of this revolution:

> Thus Orphic and Pythagorean purity can be interpreted as a protest movement against the established *polis*. The dietary taboos impeach the most elemental form of community, the community of the table; they reject the central ritual of traditional religion, the sacrificial meal.[5]

The rejection of the sacrificial meal amounted to, within the horizons of an extended kinship, a rejection of cannibalism. For the *polis*, it was a rejection of the gods and law, a transgression that would need to be interdicted if the wrath of the gods was to be avoided.

Whether or not we are prepared to accept this "revolutionary" interpretation, we can suggest for the present, that the primary tendency of the Pythagoreans, in distinction from the Orphics, was a movement against ritual toward a *bios* conceived as a work of harmony, one that is orchestrated in a community according to a specific organization and practice. Moreover, implied in this orchestration of the *bios* is a displacement of the interpretation which emphasizes a purification of the soul for one which discloses the primacy of a bodily *praxis* of attunement. Cornford gives his description of the early Pythagoreans:

> The beliefs of a religious community in its earliest stages are externalized in its rule of life, and of the Pythagorean fraternity we know enough to guide us. It was modeled on the mystical cult-society, to which admission was gained by initiation—that is, by purification followed by the revelation of truth. To the Pythagorean, "purification" partly consisted in the observance of ascetic rules of abstinence from certain kinds of food and dress, and partly was reinterpreted intellectually to mean the purification of the soul by *theoria*, the contemplation of the divine order of the world. Revelation consisted in certain truths delivered by the prophet-founder and progressively elaborated by his followers under his inspiration.[6]

Indeed, the body of the revelation consisted in the *bios* of practices of affirmations and prohibitions which elaborated the rule and principle of the challenging form of life. As suggested before, this rule of life revealed to the initiate by the prophet-founder came into direct conflict with the rule of life then established. Transmigration was the symbol of this revelation. Cornford writes:

> It was assumed, moreover, in sharp contradiction to orthodox religion, that there was no inseparable gulf between God and the soul, but a fundamental community of nature.[7]

The contestation of basic doctrines and practices arose, as I have suggested, amid the disintegration of a traditional web of blood kin relationships, which were based upon the "theory or fact of blood kinship." Cornford sets forth an interpretation which emphasizes the psychological dimension of this revolution in the "deepening and quickening of religious experience—the revival associated with the name of Orpheus."[8] He provides a description of the transformation of the psychology of the initiate amid this spiritual revolution as one leading to an emphasis on individual responsibility for action:

> The solidarity of the blood group has entailed the diffusion of responsibility for the actions of any one member among all the other members which still survive in the vendetta. When collective responsibility goes, individual responsibility is left. The guilt of any action must now attain personally to its author. It cannot be expiated by another or by the blood group as a whole.

The punishment must fall upon the individual, if not in this life, then in the next, or perhaps in a series of lives in this world. When the Pythagoreans reduced justice to the *lex talionis*, the effect was that it applied to the guilty person only, not to his family. The doctrine of transmigration completes the scheme of justice for the individual soul.[9]

The Pythagorean community arose amidst a breaking up of an ancient order which strictly separated mortality and immortality. Yet, in contradistinction to Cornford, there is not a shred of evidence which connect their teaching to the notions of purification, guilt, or punishment. Nor are there any indications that the Pythagoreans held an individualistic notion of responsibility, in light of their orchestration of a collective *bios* and of the multiplicity of the self implied by the "greater" soul of the doctrine of transmigration. Cornford, in that he virtually ignores the existence of a *bios*, except to merely use this fact as evidence of *mysticism* and *asceticism*, makes no effort to either document arguments or to distinguish the Pythagoreans from the Orphics.

For Cornford, following the alleged critique by Parmenides, this constitutes the religious cohabitation of monism and dualism in a contradictory, nonscientific corpus, a state of affairs which is, for the logicist, unacceptable. The new conception of the soul not only admits the opening into the realm of temporal mortality, but also asserts the presence of the divine within this temporal realm as soul. Cornford writes of the implications of this transformation:

The appearance of new religious groups, transcending the limits and ignoring the ties of kinship, is attended by consequences of great importance. On the social side, at least the seed is sown of the doctrine that all men are brothers; the sense of solidarity set free from the old limits can spread to include all mankind, and even beyond that to embrace all living things. φιλία (blood-kin) ceases to mean kinship in the ordinary sense, and begins to mean love. At the same time the social basis of polytheism is undermined. Whether monotheism in some form must take its place, or at least the belief (essentially true) that the mystery gods, worshipped by different groups, whether called Dionysus or Adonis or Attis, are really the same god—one form with many names. There emerges the axiom of Monism: All life is one and God is one.[10]

Despite the questionable assertion that such a rejection of polytheism could be attributed to the early Pythagoreans, it is this universalization of love and strife within the context of the All which subverts the blood kinship of traditional communities and the notion of a soul which remains tied to the blood community as an ancestral spirit. At the same time, Cornford contends that the novel conception of the soul as a mirror of the All is linked with the antithetical axiom of duality. He writes concerning the mixture of soul and body, revealing his Platonist bias:

> So long as it is imprisoned in the bodily tomb it is impure, tainted by the evil substance of the body. Psychologically—in terms of actual experience—this means that the soul is profoundly conscious of an internal conflict of good and evil, the war in the members. This conflict dominates religious experience. In philosophical expression, it gives rise to the axiom of dualism: "In the world as in the soul there is a real conflict, or two opposite powers—good and evil, light and darkness." [11]

Cornford makes much of the Platonic severing of the body and the soul, this severance as a clearing of a distance for the identity of the soul, conceived as detachment. Yet, it would seem that the early Pythagoreans were on a completely different trajectory, one that was not "revolutionary" in the sense of the mystical cult, but was, perhaps, *subversive* of the Homeric notion of blood kinship, of φιλια (love) in favor of the extended kinship of *philosophia*, a proposal dependent upon the tragic vision of the soul as transmigrating, as nomadic betwixt the strife of bodies of even these entrenched rivalries of blood kinship.

Cornford, as we have seen, despite the fact that he does not link his discussion to Empedocles, posits a contradictory, discordant "opposition" between the "principles" of spirit and flesh, one which allows him to interpret the doctrine of transmigration as exclusively religious. Cornford presumes:

> The fact is that in dealing with the doctrine of the soul in philosophies of the religious type, we are dealing with a thing that exists, as it were, upon two different planes—the spiritual plane and the natural. On the natural plane the soul acts as a vital principle, distinguishing organic living things from mere casual inorganic masses of matter. In that aspect it is conceived in Pythagorean mathematico-musical terms as a *harmony* or ratio, expressible in numbers. It is the element of proportion in an ordered compound. But, on the spiritual plane, it is itself a compound of good and evil parts—of the element of limit, order, proportion, reason, and the disorderly unlimited element of irrational passion. So considered, it is a permanent immortal thing. [12]

This strict opposition will be confronted by the evidence suggested in the interpretation of the soul as a harmony amidst other strata of harmonies, distinct the ideology of a soul unity which is imprisoned in a radical, chaotic other. As suggested, the goal of the doctrine of transmigration is an attunement with the divine, or a becoming of an embracing of the soul as the All, a harmony, conceived as a unity of opposites, as a composite nexus of noncontradictory oppositions. As will become clear, it was not possible for the Pythagoreans to make a radical distinction between "oppositions," such as Limit and the Unlimited, as both issue forth from the divine All. These participate as principles of a world, conceived as a "living, breathing creature" that itself is said to breath in the Void, and thus, in a world in which the distinction between "organic living things" and "casual inorganic masses of matter" does not have any primary significance; this distinction is merely the *flatus vocis* of forgetfulness.

It must be stated that Cornford's interpretation displays an overreliance upon Orphic texts, or at least upon the clichés of Orphic coloring (since he provides no examples), and, thus does not take heed of the manifold differences between Orphic and Pythagorean teachings. For although there are similarities between these movements with respect to the doctrine of transmigration and of the *ethos* of abstinence that are implied in this doctrine, we must remember the earlier testimony given by Guthrie of the distinction held by the Pythagoreans in that these latter had a "method of their own," which was *philosophy*. Kirk lays out these differences:

> There were no doubt differences between Orphics and Pythagoreans. For example, it was on books that the Orphics rested the authority of their teaching, whereas Pythagoreans eschewed the written word. The Pythagoreans undoubtedly formed a sect (or sects), whereas the expression "Orphics" seems usually to designate individual practitioners of techniques of purification. Nor are Orphics and Pythagoreans in general identified or closely associated with each other in the fifth and fourth century evidence.[13]

What is significant in this testimony is the distinction which exists between these movements with respect to not only their respective modes of transmission, the Orphics deploying the written word, the Pythagoreans, the spoken word, but also by the fact that the former were individual practitioners and the latter existed in a community. As has been indicated, the oral mode of dissemination was synchronous with the Pythagorean emphasis upon the esoteric symbolism of the body, an emphasis that indicates a distance from ritual, but, instead, advocated cultivating the life of a collective *bios*. Kirk writes concerning the Orphics:

> However, Orpheus was then beginning to be treated as the patron saint of rites and ritual ways of life—and death; and his name, like that of his legendary disciple Musaeus, became attached to theogonical literature of the period.[14]

We can see distinct and important differences, ones which Cornford does not call into account in his interpretation of the early or later Pythagoreans. This is significant since there is such an extreme lack of evidence concerning the actual teachings of the early Pythagoreans. And, the lack of focus, or even mention of, the oral character of the teaching, and thus of its distance from the individual Orphic practitioners, merely blurs the only distinctive clues for an interpretation of Pythagoras and of the doctrine of transmigration that we do possess.

The doctrine of the immortal soul for Pythagorean philosophy follows from their novel interpretation of the nature of an extended kinship. This notion of kinship, as suggested above, included a kinship between the soul and the divine and one between the soul and the *Kosmos*, conceived as a living, breathing creature. As we will discuss below, the metaphor of imprisonment, frequently applied to the Pythagoreans, seems to be in conflict with this notion of kinship. With the latter, the soul as immortal exists in kinship with its source and goal, and vis-à-vis the notion of the *Kosmos* as a living, breathing creature, it could be suggested that, if the soul is properly cultivated, it can return to its source through the activity of philosophy, conceived as an activity which discloses and effectuates a radical affinity with the divine All.

As mentioned, this assertion of the immortality of the soul and of a primary divinity (in the sense of the All or One) came into direct conflict with the established Homeric order. This took the specific form of a conflict concerning the nature of the soul: the immortality of the insurgent cults and the mortal *shadow* of Homer and the nativist religion. Guthrie describes the Homeric notion of the soul as that of a shadow of the body, this latter being the true self, one to be remembered eternally. And, in his description of the significance of the Pythagorean postulation of the immortality of the soul: the soul is not co-terminus with the body. It is the soul which "joins the end of the circle to its beginning" and thus survives the death of the body. Guthrie writes:

> Since soul is immortal, it evidently outlasts physical death and if men die "because they cannot join the beginning to the end," it follows that the soul, which is immortal, does join them. Thus we have already implicit and for all we know explicit in Alcmaeon's philosophy the doctrine that the soul imitates the divine stars and heavens not only in self-caused motion, but in circular motion.[15]

The soul moves naturally in and of its self in a circular motion. In its imitation of the divine, we see that the notion of kinship is specified as a coincidence of the microcosm and the macrocosm. To suggest that the human soul is immortal in the sense of returning to the divine, was *hubris* and blasphemy for it must be cast off as a shadow, mythically descending into Hades. This is an existence which is eternally separated from the divine. In this way, the assertion of an immortal soul not only attacked the established order of myth and political theology, but also challenged the essence of the community and the conception of authority.

The truth of the self, this which is to be honored as the first duty (*Golden Verses*), is not merely its phenomenal self and its temporal life—although these are necessary aspects of the *complete self*. For Pythagoras, this soul is not a shadow which is doomed to passively recollect a single life in Hades. It is, instead, the self that is recognized amidst the body as the immortal soul, a divine spark with essential kinship to the divine, as it lives a plethora of lives, and harbors the potentiality of remembrance of each of its singular incarnations. Opposed to the shadowy, nostalgic soul in Homer, we have a soul, "possessed of powers of its own," as the "true" self, and, the possibility of a return to the divine source through soul-attunement, accomplished in the *bios*.

The Pythagorean Soul and the Question of Harmony

To display the significance of these claims for the present interpretation of the doctrine of transmigration, I will turn to the controversy surrounding the notion of the soul as an harmony, which concerns the seat of harmony vis-à-vis the body and soul; it concerns the character of harmony as conceived in the Platonic and Aristotelian corpus, the site of this debate upon "harmony." The guiding question in the controversy is as follows:

> If, like Simmias, we think of the soul as strictly analogous to the *armonia* (tuning) of a lyre, the last thing that is added after the framework of the lyre has been put together, it will be the first thing to perish when the lyre is broken. But did the Pythagoreans think of it so? [16]

Cornford draws out the implications of this controversy, which may even deny a connection of the harmony theory to Pythagoras, in that it may conflict with the latter's assertion of immortality:

> Does the doctrine that the soul itself is a harmony go back to Pythagoras? This is commonly denied on the ground that, if the soul is a *harmony* or *crasis* of the bodily opposites, it cannot survive the dissolution of the body: the doctrine is inconsistent with transmigration or any form of survival. [17]

This objection to the harmony theory of the soul is brought out in a discussion of Plato's *Phaedo*, in which Simmias is indicating a seeming inconsistency in the teaching of Philolaus; or that the harmony of bodily opposites could give rise to a destination of immortality, as harmony of the All. The inconsistency revolves essentially upon the meaning of the term "opposition" and of kinship betwixt such "opposites." And, as we will see in the chapter on Philolaus below, the "price" of immortality in this controversy is a sacrifice of the body, and the assertion of an external harmony that is not conditioned by *physis*. It is in light of this severance that the notion of "revolution" has sense. Yet, this sense may be of Philolaus and other writers of the fifth century written tradition, who knew little of Pythagoras.

Cornford delineates, in the absence again of any references, the meaning of harmony, as the "formation of identical structure" applied to the soul as a "tuneful adjustment." Harmony, in this way, is (1) a mixture of opposites, (2) order, (3) proportion, and (4) measure. He suggests, with this definition, a notion of harmony which is abstract, external, providing for an illustration, the example of musical harmony. He writes:

> A *harmony*, as we have seen, is a system of numbers linked by ratios and numbers and are the ultimate reality of things that embody them. Numbers themselves were not according to our conception, immaterial. The system of numbers which is the soul-*harmony* could be conceived as an organizing principle, which would, in Anaximenes' phrase, "hold together" (συγκρατειν) the body. A system of numbers and ratios would not cease to exist when the body is dissolved, any more than a musical scale perishes when a lyre is broken. This invisible and bodiless thing, altogether lovely and divine, as Simmias calls it, of the same nature as the divine and immortal, could be imagined (vaguely, it is true) as the principle that would survive the destruction of any particular instrument or body, and perhaps organizing a series of bodies, consistent with transmigration.[18]

The soul, as a spark of the divine, is separable from the body since it itself is a more complete harmony. The body, in its turn, exhibits a harmony and operates according to the same matrix of opposition, yet, it is only a living harmony in its particular instantiation as long as the soul is present with it. The body in its mortality is thus interpreted as a state of opposites which receives harmony from the "outside," from a nomadic soul. This sets forth harmony as an external seat of sympathy, kinship, of the "holding together." These *flatus vocis* stand apart at a distance, the causal inorganic mass is fleetingly animated via soul, but has no intimacy of nature with the divine.

The body, on the contrary, even though it dies with the departure of the soul, is itself a product of number, as we see in the fragments of Theon of Smyrna, and thus, is of a common nature. Guthrie writes:

> The ultimate elements of everything are numbers, and the whole cosmos owes its character as something perfect, divine and permanent to the fact that the numbers of which it is made up are combined in the best possible manner according to the rules of mathematical proportion as Pythagoras' students had revealed them. In short the cosmos owes all these desirable qualities to that fact that it *is* a *harmonia* and this *harmonia* is therefore found

above all in the majestic movements on a cosmic scale of the sun, moon, planets and fixed stars. The heavens do not *declare* the glory of god, for the cosmos is a living god, welded into a single divine unity by the marvelous power of mathematical and musical harmony.[19]

In that the ultimate elements of the body have been regarded as those which, it is said, 'supervene' upon body, it would seem necessary to put into question the logical notion of an external form which would "supervene" upon matter *as such*. Instead, there would have to be a self-determination of basic elements in their various configurations and temporalities. In this way, the body has a kinship with the soul, as a necessary, albeit temporary, dwelling of the soul in its aspiration to return to the divine. It is thus a question of attunement of being and not of purification of the soul from body or matter. However, as we have seen, Guthrie himself does not seem to give the body the same status as the other cosmic entities amid this All, despite his statement that the cosmos is a "living god." In many ways, he repeats the theme of conflict between the soul and matter, or body. This attitude is manifested in his consideration of the effect of embodiment on the soul. He writes:

If then our individual souls are essentially of the same nature, though separated by impurity in our incarnate state, then purely our identity with the divine must consist essentially of numbers in harmony, and in so far as we are still in need of the purification of philosophy it must be right to call the element of impurity, in other terms, an element of discord—a jarring note caused by the flow in the number of our souls—or, to put it in yet another Pythagorean way, an element of the Unlimited as yet unsubdued by the good principle of limit.[20]

Guthrie also writes:

In a human being, whose soul is essentially of the same nature as the world's soul though of inferior quality, the circuits of the immortal soul are confined "within the flowing and ebbing tide of the body." The shock of submitting to the exigencies of bodily nourishment and rapid growth distorts the circles of the souls, which were originally constructed by the Creator according to the strict laws of geometrical and musical proportion. But the assaults of matter they were "twisted in all manners of ways, and all possible infractions and deformations of the circles were caused so that they barely held together."[21]

There is no evidence that the Pythagoreans held the soul to be "impure" amid the body, or that the soul is "twisted" by the assaults of matter. This whole field of content, of examples and "facts," taken from Orphic and Platonic writings, distorts the very possibility of an interpretation of the Pythagoreans.

Implied in the example of the lyre and musical harmony, the soul is only recognized as soul amid body, even if that is only the body of a song, of music. Whatever event may have set up the distance between the soul and the divine, the soul requires the body, a temporal entity to which it is ultimately in kinship. The strict opposition between Spirit and Flesh, to use Cornford's jargon, does not make any sense for a philosophy which not only sought to tear apart the barrier erected between mortal and immortal, but one which also made so much of the body as a necessary dwelling and aspect of the self, and as a living symbol of the divine All.[22]

It is true the soul outlasts the body, but the divine also outlasts the soul; that is, if we continue to insist upon these terms, or formal indicators, as radically distinct. Even if we do continue for the sake of communicative meaning, as terms which are ubiquitous in the literature, this need not imply that the so-called lower must cause "infractions" and "deformations" to the so-called higher, especially if all of these participate in one divine process, tied together by number into a common nature.

A metaphor to suggest the relation between the soul and the body, taken from the corpus surrounding Apollo, the patron of the Pythagoreans, could be that of the bow and arrow, where the arrow is the soul and the body is the bow. In the symbol, both are of the same nature and each is required to accomplish the return. It is only their near-term destinations which are distinct, as one is "mortal," the other "immortal," but both are of a similar nature with respect to number and being; nothing of the All is consigned to forgetfulness. In this way, a metaphorical matrix of purity/impurity implies too radical a separation and deafens us to the overriding "magical" notion of kinship, or sympathy, which permeates the entire teaching of the Pythagoreans. The better term is, as I have suggested, one of attunement, for even discordance, if it is present, is of the same vibrational nature. It may be tuned without changing its essential nature. This is analogous to the nature that is shared by the body and the soul. For if the soul and body were not "like of like" there could be no bringing together of these into life. For as we will see, even Limit and Unlimited share a bond in their issuing forth from the divine, and this bond is displayed as the universal kinship of the All. In this scenario, there cannot be any radical separation, but only the recollection of how this world of fragmentation and chaos is in truth the out flashing of the divine.

In this light, however, the soul is neither co-terminus with the body, as its harmony is not one of bodily opposites, but of a wider circuit of movement, one which itself projects the existence of the body. The body is also a harmony, but one which is of necessity strictly temporal. But, if as the Pythagoreans held, past events recur, it is indeed possible that this same body will once again emerge as the memory of it cannot be extinguished. The seeming mystery that soul and body are ultimately of the same nature can be explained by considering harmony in the sense of the musical proportion. If we consider the musical scale, we can fathom a sense of opposition which is markedly distinct from that suggested by Guthrie in the previous quotations. The musical 6th and the 12th are "opposites," but not in an exclusive sense, but as positions which require each other for there to be an opening of a vibrational dimension, such as harmony. In this way, harmony is symptomatic of the existence of these "opposites," not as an external mediation of a "third," but as an originary and indigenous coalescence of All. In this sense, this term "opposition" can illuminate the way the Pythagoreans may have considered the distinction between divine and world or soul and body. In other words, a discordancy would be out of tune, but not impure, as it still is of the same nature, still of the same divine source.

The ultimate resolution of these oppositions only comes when and if there is a completion of the cycles of incarnation, and thus, as stated above, the disappearance of the soul from the perspective of world to the All of the divine. Only then do our distinctions between soul and body, divine and world, become superfluous, but in the mean time, it is necessary to keep in mind that these apparent oppositions are positions within a distantiated field of kinship, with a specific "musical structure." These opposites require each other in that they are the constitutive principles of reality, and moreover, the purpose of this reality is not as yet complete. For if these "opposites" persist in an exclusive battle, why not state that the only kinship is the divine with the soul, that Dacier is correct to say that the doctrine of transmigration is merely a lie, that the prospect of becoming an animal is a hollow threat, and that there is no real kinship of nature, for nature as ruled by the material principle, is nothing but a lie, a destroyer, a sadistic punisher of the soul? These statements cannot be made in that they do not apply to the Pythagorean teaching. And, it seems that "opposition," in the sense of an exclusive conflict, does not apply either.

The kinship of the body and the soul can be considered concretely with an examination of the monochord. In its configuration, it gives voice to the unseen musical spirit amidst the phenomenal world, displays the measure of musical harmony in its organization and operation. The body, like the monochord, incorporates and expresses the basic principles of the soul, and there is thus an affinity of the body and soul in the phenomenal world. The monochord is an intricate construction fabricated for the initiate to experience a specific reality amidst all else. It is a conduit for the expression of an unseen musical experience, demonstrating an "application of a *logos* to the tonal flux," a composition of number and space. But, the monochord is constructed with attentiveness to the fluctuations of tonality, its *logos* is spoken from out of this "tonal flux." In this way, an "application," if we indeed wish to continue using these various words implicated in the metaphysic of Cornford and others, is not violent for its *praxis* is and must be attuned with that from which it originally arose.

The monochord contains within its design and operation the entire Pythagorean teaching with regard to musical harmony. This is analogous to the doctrine of transmigration since it contains within itself, as a *complex symbola,* the Pythagorean teaching of the All. As a doctrine it is a body, whose purpose is to aid and guide in the recollection of the divine source of All. It thus contains an account of being, a delineation of this order, and a pathway initiated to fulfill the purpose of the "original" event. In other words, it contains in one curriculum what has been separated as "religion" and "science."

To get a better hold upon this philosophy of the All, and of its differing with the interpretations of Cornford, I will return to our earlier reference to Homer and to the alleged "revolution" in the vision of the soul, an extended transformation associated with the names of various mystical cults, etc. It is suggested that Pythagoras came into conflict with the Homeric restrictions of the mortal and the immortal, and thus, he came into conflict with the Homeric *nomos*, orchestrated as the Olympian *polis*. Yet, it would be incorrect to portray Pythagoras as a "revolutionary" in the sense of erecting a "breach" with the world of Homer. It is possible the Pythagoreans were simply attempting to absorb the radical innovations of the sixth century into a philosophy which did not simply "throw the baby out with the bathwater."

It must be remembered that Homer, although he may have not given much esteem to the soul, did deem it to be everlasting, as an indefinite state of nostalgia after death, as a shadow. It is the body and terrestrial life of *homo terra* that gains the esteem of Homer, and, it is this singular life of the body that the soul nostalgically ruminates upon, "forever" in Hades. From this site of departure, it is possible to envision Pythagoras as operating within the mythopoetic horizons of Homer, but, with a significant transfiguration of the "rules of the game." The differing of a mortal and an immortal is maintained, but not as an impassable barrier, but as a description of the specific situation of a soul amidst the perspectival horizons of the body.

The esteem for the body of Homer is maintained, but, it is the soul, as that which persists away from the body, as Homer himself maintained, which is given a destination that is not one of passive nostalgia, but one of an active remembrance of each of many lives, as an active becoming of and belonging to the All. This is the primary sense of the "extended kinship" of All. To juxtapose an affirmation of the kinship of All, extended from the blood kinship of Homer, suggests an ultimacy in the All, as the seat of kinship as such. But, to a great extent, this is the same All as Homer, with many of the same signposts and significant names. If we recall the speculation of Burkert of the influences of Pythagoras, such as Babylonian mathematics, Iranian religion, and Indian metempsychosis, we could suggest that Pythagoras exhibits a continuity that extends beyond even Homer, an unbroken lineage from not only his antecedents but also with his contemporaries in Asia, and, to a certain extent, with Africa. Soustelle intimates, in his work, *The Four Suns*, this sense of continuity through a suggestion that the appearance of a breach with the world of antecedents and contemporaries, of the African and Asian influences constituents of the Ancient World is only possible from the perspective of a post-Christian obliteration of almost every trace of this world:

> It cannot be denied that Greece and Asia shared a whole set of beliefs and representations which were perpetuated as long as the Hellenic and Roman civilizations lasted. An optical illusion, as it were, makes us believe that what occurred was a radical innovation or even the involuntary leap of a stifled civilization when the religions of salvation took hold of the whole Mediterranean world and when one such religion was finally triumphant, through Constantine and his Christian successors.[23]

Contrary to the representations of Cornford and Burkert, which lump Pythagoras uncritically together with mystic Orphicism, Pythagoras "merely" proposes an extension of the horizons of kinship through a novel interpretation of the meaning of the soul. Yet, such a project in itself is a serious challenge to and alteration of the Homeric genealogy, and, the "merely" is posed only to highlight those more destructive attempts to displace the world of Homer via the mysticisms described by Cornford and Burkert, which transgress the Homeric limits of mortal and immortal, as with Pythagoras, but, in addition, insist upon a devaluation of the status of the body and world. One could suggest that Pythagoras sought to *expand* the status of the body, as not only the dwelling of a mortal life, but also as a symbol of the nature of the All, as an active and living similar of the macrocosm. The body is thus divine in its life in the All.

Perhaps, the writers of the fifth century, living in the wake of the Pythagorean "riots," had a certain "forgetfulness," which is indicative of the crisis-intervention of the written word, amidst the after-shocks of the suppression of the Pythagorean *bios*, and one suggested to Plotinus by Porphyry in the wake of the ominous agitations of Christianity. The lacerations of this erasure still exhibit scars, traces amidst a mutilation ritually repeated by the inscriptions of the pen of the scribbler, writing in haste. The emphasis upon writing, as we see in Derrida, symptomatizes a tradition in crisis, as there is no "time" for the "luxury" of a *bios*. Perhaps this crisis-mode regime latched onto the notion and practice of philosophy as such, displacing its orientational horizons from *bios* to *academos*.

Chapter 4

Philolaus and the Character of
Pythagorean Harmony

Kirk, who does suggest Philolaus as a reliable source for a glimpse into the Pythagorean teaching, writes that he is "early associated with a written form of Pythagorean teaching; and the existence of a book by him is confirmed by Menon's report of his biological theories."[1] Kirk, following Burkert, in his *Lore and Science*, repeats the following account of the influence of Philolaus:

(a) that Philolaus' book is the main source of Aristotle's account of Pythagoreanism in 430 and elsewhere, and (b) that Philolaus actually *created* "the philosophy of Limit and Unlimited and their harmony is achieved through number," in its abstract form, in an effort "to formulate anew, with the help of fifth-century Φυσιολογα, a view of the world that came to him, somehow, from Pythagoras."[2]

There is also testimony that Plato borrowed certain "Pythagorean" books from Philolaus in order to write the *Timaeus* (DK 44, A1)[3] and we also have an explicit connection of Philolaus with Aristotle. Much is made of this fact by Burkert in his *Lore and Science in Ancient Pythagoreanism*,[4] in which he deploys Philolaus as a source for fifth-century Pythagoreanism. To this extent, Philolaus becomes a source of great importance for the subsequent development of Greek (and Western) philosophy as a whole, especially with regard to its attitude and comprehension of the Pythagorean teaching as such. That he is "associated" with a written form of Pythagoreanism must immediately present a signal to us that his work had to have been *written* at some distance from the originative "event" of the Pythagorean community with its participation in the oral tradition. This distance is also underscored by his attempt to create the Pythagorean philosophy "anew," via the construction of a syncretic joining of abstract number theory and physiology.

This distinction betwixt an oral and a written philosophy may seem trivial. Yet, not only does this difference serve to index the distance of the fragments of Philolaus from the event of the Pythagorean *bios*, but, may also indicate a transformation in the "essence" of philosophy itself. Perhaps the transition to a written philosophy may have had more significance than a mere historical accident, coincident with the suppression of the sixth-century Pythagoreans. This is a question of the compatibility of a culture of writing amid a symbolic *bios* that places great esteem in the *praxis* of the body, as a microcosm of the All.

No lesser figure than Plato, in his dialogue, *Phaedrus*, underlines this distinction, giving priority, ironically in his written text, to the "living word," one which is closer to the life of the All, and not caught up in the peculiar choreography of the movements of the body which a life of the scribe entails. Plato writes that the written word, once it enters the soul, sows the seeds of forgetfulness; memory is an active art, it needs to be exercised, to be vigilantly cultivated and strengthened.[5] We have already heard about the prohibition of images of divinity among the Pythagoreans, and also of the symbolic nature of education, of symbols which point to the phenomenal world as an *excession* from the divine and an active domain for the *praxis* of attunement amid the body-soul.

With writing, all of this changes in that what becomes primary is the activity of reading, writing, and the maintenance of texts, and not the phenomenal world as such. Or, in this brave new world, writing, reading, and the bodily *praxis* that such a world entails displace the activities of a *bios* in the oral tradition. Through this strangulation, a *bios* is forgotten, and, eventually dies. Yet, we will defer this question, turning instead to the more tangible problem of Philolaus as a source for our interpretation of the Pythagorean philosophy. The Pythagoreans were exterminated; in the very last times, it is reported, some had tried to write down their oral teachings. But, this is speculation as we do not have any of these texts, and all of the texts which had for some time been deemed as being these "last testaments," have since been rated as late forgeries. Yet, we could agree that they may have sought to insure some traces of remembrance, in a similar way as the Aztec priests hid sacred seeds, cacti, and other tokens of remembrance in the wake of the Inquisition.

Philolaus is a latecomer, he can only attempt to begin anew a philosophy from which he stands at a great distance. His project of projecting a conception of a principle of harmony which mediates the conflicts of *physis*, is proclaimed as the written "rebirth" of an alleged Pythagorean philosophy. Yet, Kirk writes:

> Examination of Aristotle's principal account of Pythagorean doctrine (430) will support the judgment that limiter (or limit) and unlimited, in particular, were not viewed by Pythagoreans in general as the master concepts of their system. They assume that role only in Philolaus—and perhaps, in another (anonymous) Pythagorean tradition reported by Aristotle.[6]

If Philolaus did create, in its abstract form, a philosophy of "external mediation," enacted via a detached harmony, or, if he is, at least, responsible for an extreme emphasis upon the notions of limit and unlimited and of their antipathy, then, we must exercise caution and consider the possibility that these fragments have no *essential* relation to the teachings of Pythagoras, nor, indeed, to the doctrine of transmigration itself.[7]

A distance from the domain of originality has overgrown and entrenched itself into the foreground of the interpretation of the doctrine of transmigration. This distance has been occupied by a tradition of interpretation which describes the world as one of a conflict of "warring opposites," a notion of inherent enmity *to the death* of wholly dissimilar "natures." Such a notion, as we will examine, is found in Philolaus, and, as we will apprehend, it is found in the philosophies of Plato and Aristotle, who after all received their information in varying degrees from the latter. In order to close-in on this distance, we must investigate the fragments of Philolaus to ascertain if they are compatible with the notion of the kinship of All, and thus, to the doctrine of transmigration as it occurs in Pythagorean philosophy. As mentioned earlier, there are no references to transmigration in any of these fragments. This does not mean that they are incompatible with the doctrine. Yet, we will find that several of the fragments are in conflict with the interpretation of transmigration which was set forward by Guthrie, emphasizing an extended, magical kinship. A suggestion could be made that this notion of a magical philosophy of harmony may describe the horizons of the biotic philosophy which preceded the later attempts to revive a philosophy that "in some way" was connected to Pythagoras.

In the previous chapters a good deal of time was given to Cornford's characterization of the soul and body, and his overtly "religious" severance of spirit and flesh into a predicament of "warring opposites". Limit and the Unlimited meet in the battlefield of the body, requiring an intervention of harmony via the intelligible unity of the soul. The body itself is described as an insatiable tension that is harnessed by the animal soul in order to secure a site of durable life. This conception of a state of "warring opposites" was rejected in that it was deemed to be out of tune with the notion of an extended kinship, and also that it, if taken to its "mystical" conclusions, excludes the role of the Pythagorean *bios* as a specific attuning practice of the body in its immersion in the tones and rhythms of the *Kosmos*.

The alternative idea, which is "equally" justified from a study of the doxographical sources, is that of a harmony, the elements of which are not different in type, but, in degree, or, in position, as within the field of distantiation opened with an excession of the divine into world – an event from out of a "primal source," as the Cosmic All.[8] The example of musical harmony was set forth as that which demonstrated not only the fruitfulness of the primal vibrations issued forth with the divine excession of the elements of number, *apeiron* and *peras*, but also the *symmachia*, or alliance, between these, and thus, betwixt other apparent antipathies such as the body and the soul. Each is a gift bestowed from the same divine saturnalia, each travels its own pathway, and performs with necessity its allotted task. In this context, the example of the monochord becomes prominent. Harmony opens as the network which animates a single life of All, which upon reflection, becomes exhibited through a symbolism, deploying an antithetical matrix of oppositions (in the sense of musical oppositions, of places amidst event). To aggrandize the significance of conflict per se, to take in a vulgar "literalist" or "fundamentalist" manner the "oppositions" of "mythical" narratives for "actual forces" in "conflict," erases the notion of a divinity, as the All, which is slippery with regard to our transcendental labels. Contrary to the notion of a divine excession into world, as a process which is still *on its way*, we see in Cornford a limited divinity which remains utterly detached from the world, the only link remaining is a discontented "higher" soul suffocating in the claustrophobia of a bodily tomb. While the fragments of Philolaus are of a doxographical nature, the first four fragments do intimate a logical order giving rise to a coherent thought and position with respect to questions that presently face us. The fragments read:

(I)
The world's nature is a harmonious compound of Limited and Unlimited elements; similar is the totality of the world in itself, and of all it contains. (DK 1)

(1B)
All beings are necessarily Limited or Unlimited, or simultaneously Limited and Unlimited; but they could not all be Unlimited only. (DK 1)

(II)
Now, since it is clear that the beings cannot be formed either of elements that are all Unlimited, it is evident that the world in its totality, and its included beings are a harmonious compound of Limited and Unlimited elements. That can be seen in existing things. Those that are composed of Limiting elements, are Limited themselves; those that are composed of both Limiting and Unlimited elements, are both Limited and Unlimited; and those composed of Unlimited elements are Unlimited. (DK 2)

(II B)
All things, at least those we know, contain Number; for it is evident that nothing whatever can either be thought or known, without Number. (DK 4) Number has two distinct kinds: the odd, and the even, and a third, derived from a mingling of the other two kinds, the even-odd. Each of its subspecies is susceptible to many very numerous varieties, which each manifests individually. (DK 5)

(III)
Harmony is generally the result of contraries; for it is the unity of multiplicity, and the agreement of discordances. (DK 10)

(IV)

This is the state of affairs concerning Nature and Harmony. The Being of things is eternal; it is a unique and divine nature, the knowledge of which does not belong to man. Still it would not be possible that any of the things that exist, and that are known by us, should arrive to our knowledge if this Being was not the internal foundation of principles of which the world was founded—that is, of the Limited and Unlimited elements. Now since these principles are not mutually similar, nor of similar nature, it would be impossible that the order of the world should have been formed by them in any manner whatever unless harmony had intervened. Of course, the things that were similar, and of similar nature, did not need harmony; but the dissimilar things, which have neither a similar nature, nor an equivalent function, must be organized by the harmony, if they are to take their place in the connected totality of the world.[9]

In this scenario, the world is a harmonious compound of Limited and Unlimited elements. Yet, according to (IV) these principles are exclusive in that they are dissimilar in nature, a severance which thus justifies the external intervention of a mediating harmony. It is this dissimilarity of nature that must be questioned in light of the notion of a divine unity at the heart of the Pythagorean doctrine of transmigration. Indeed, it could be argued that the limited and unlimited are of a similar nature as each is internally founded by the Being of all things, the All. Each can trace a common rooting in the divine, a unity that already is, and not one that would need to occur by an intervention. Disregarding this objection of an originary unity, Philolaus contends that an actual world order would necessitate something other than Being and the principles which it *founds*. There must be a "third thing," an act of intervention, via an alterior Harmony, configured as number to mediate these "warring opposites" of Being. It is in this "third thing" that the seat of value becomes detached from the divine All, and begins to reside in a supervenient, monotheistic "God." There are two other fragments which are akin to that which segregates Limit from the Unlimited:

Philolaus says that all things are by God kept in captivity, and thereby implies that he is single and superior to matter.[10]

And:

It will help us to remember the Pythagorean Philolaus' utterance that the ancient theologians and divines claimed that the soul is bound to the body as a punishment, and is buried in it as in a tomb. (DK 14)[11]

The divine, for Philolaus, superior to Matter, to Evil, keeps All in captivity, one that is a containment and a distancing from this supremely detached divinity, aloof from the All, the body and life of the world, which remains in captivity. The incarceration of the soul, or these, each—soul entombed, entrapped, "bound to the body as a punishment" is the expulsion of the soul from its source, thrown into the world, imprisoned in the body. This defamation of the body, almost inexplicable if juxtaposed to the Homeric tradition, is disseminated in these texts to further buttress the assertion that there is a primordial distance betwixt Being and Divinity, one between "warring opposites," a discordance that begs the question of an external intervention from that which is the "farthest." Number, in this view, is the farthest.

Utter matter (evil) itself is, in this view, outside the grasp of this divinity, there is only a temporary animation of a limited, finite domain. Moreover, this divinity itself in its relative detachment does not have any direct role to play in the pursuit by a mortal for a return to the divine. Life is accursed and the only example worth emanating, the only clue, thread out of the labyrinth of this dire captivity is the example of *that* God: a bodiless, abstract intelligence, permanent, silent, and One. Thus, the pathway suggested by this conception of God and of the possibility of return is that of the "mystic," one who castigates and constrains the *bodily*, one that seeks purification through purgation and rituals of cleansing. This world is a prison, and thus, the most agreeable occurrence would be its utter destruction. The cultivation, as it occurs in a "state of war" seeks to cleanse itself of foreignness, to eradicate that which is alien to that which is deemed the higher soul. This is a process of purification, cleansing, a program which bases its criteria on a strict separation of the bodily, as later with Mani, (including the so-called animal soul) and the higher soul. The latter as the seed and bringer of harmony is allowed to fly away at death, the body, falling, crushed by the opposition and the lack of the buttress provided by the soul, drifts and seeps back into the crust of the earth.

These notions of discordant conflict at the heart of Being, so often emphasized by Cornford, are however contradicted, indeed displaced, by the preponderance of the fragments in the doxography of Philolaus. For instance:

> The world is single and it came into being from the center outwards. Starting from this center, the top is entirely identical to the base; still you might say that which is above the center is opposed to what is below it; for the base, lowest point would be the center, as for the top, the highest point would still be the center; and likewise for the other parts; in fact, in respect of the center, each one of the opposite points is identical, unless the whole be moved. (DK 17)[12]

The world was born from the "center," it exceeds as a single living, breathing creature. "You might say that which is above is opposed to what is below it," yet, *you need not* for these are in truth "identical," of a similar nature in that these persist within a singular event of life. All that exists is also its own center, but amidst the divine excession, it is All. Such a possibility is further enhanced if we also consider, as will be discussed in Chapter 7 in the section "The Path of the Event," where we will ascertain the derivation of number itself from its elements, Limit and Unlimited. There is no need for an intervention of harmony for harmony issues from the divine and thus is not distinct from the All. Yet, according to this present account, this quotation also accords with "Philolaus," the supposed prophet of "discord" and "intervention," How can this be, as we have already digested his testimony that there is a situation of "alien" principles, each a distinct nature, a discordance which requires intervention?

Most of the fragments could be regarded as consistent with the notion of the *Kosmos* as a kinship of All. Yet, simultaneously, the fragments could be deemed as consistent with those several which we held out from the rest. What is at stake is the determination of the meaning of these technical terms, of Limit, Unlimited, world, soul, body, and divinity. In other words, there is lacking in the mention of these terms the mythopoetic horizons which send them in a unique direction of significance. It is those fragments which I have set out from the rest which abide amidst this mythopoetic dimension of a determination of meaning, or sense. And, it is these specific mythopoetic horizons which are in conflict with another mythopoetic horizon which gives much esteem to the body, to the *bios*, and to an originary harmony.

In this way, we are inclined to suggest either that the text of fragments which is given the name of "Philolaus" is ambiguous, if not in contradiction (as a sloppy assemblage of references), or, that it has only a negative significance for an interpretation of the doctrine of transmigration. For the evidence is clear that the fragments as such are at a distance from that which they purport to address; moreover, when we examine their content, we comprehend the distance from what we can fathom of the Pythagorean teaching of the oral tradition. Philolaus would thus be a questionable source. If there is any doubt about this suggestion, we can consider yet another example of the discrepancies between Philolaus and the early Pythagoreans. Our example is the "Table of Opposites":

Table of Opposites

Limit	Unlimited
Odd	Even
One	Plurality
Right	Left
Male	Female
At Rest	Moving
Straight	Crooked
Light	Darkness
Good	Bad
Square	Oblong

This table is often pointed to verify the assertion that the Pythagoreans had organized their teaching around a schema of oppositions, thus begging the question of a unifying principle which must come from outside of this nexus of extremes. This would be the interpretation of Philolaus which we have seen in Cornford, and that we will see most dramatically in Plato. Yet, as suggested, this probably is not the view of the early Pythagoreans, as the divine event *is* in its synchronicity with the world and the self. The Divine All as a root of the world was the "touchstone" of their philosophy. In addition to these considerations, Kirk throws into question whether there was any intrinsic affinity of this "Table of Opposites" with the teaching of the early Pythagoreans. He writes of the table:

> It looks like the work of someone who has been impressed by Parmenides' cosmological dualism and by the figures referred to in 437, which he has then attempted to connect under the Pythagorean principles of limit and unlimited and odd and even. The table has very little internal structure, but it is tempting to infer that limit and unlimited are intended to be the basic opposites which in some sense underlies all the others, odd and even included.[13]

This is tempting since the interplay of these notions is always given first place in accounts of ancient cosmology, as Limit draws in, begins to set definite boundaries for the Unlimited. However, considered from a symbolic perspective, any of these opposites could be transposed to portray this elusive cosmological event. What we must keep in mind is the distance of this tableau from the early Pythagoreans of the oral tradition. It would be reasonable to admit such a table if we insist upon the symbolic horizons of an education whose purpose was the cultivation of a *bios* that seeks to become attuned to the All. Yet, it would be quite problematic to give any of these opposites any essential significance as a *tabla* is a surface for writing, a writing which is not in evidence.

The positing of opposites is only for the benefit of the narrow horizons of our point of departure. In this sense, this "interaction" of any perspective-dependent opposition is merely the working of the All, spoken to the mortal in words he or she can grasp, as a "symbolic nexus" which merely indicates an "event," but remains always at the horizon of the event. As symbols, the body and soul have an interplay which tells a story: they work together before death for the same end, although each has a differing trajectory in the near term; yet, both have an ultimate actuality in the All, just as Love and Strife exist in a modulating harmony for Empedocles. Simultaneously, body and soul, these symbols of differing trajectories can be described as temporal in their own ways, and eternal, as an unfolding of the All. Both are generated from number, this itself emerging from the absorption and organization by Limit of the Unlimited, after these latter issued forth from/as the divine.

Apeiron and *peras*, contrary to the specified fragments of Philolaus, are not of a different nature, natures, but are of the same essence, as moments amidst a simultaneous All, as the life of the divine, of its growth and recurrence. It is only the retrospective reflections of reason which seek to hold aesthetical nuances and analyzed constituents as the truth itself, and forget the mythological strategy which sets apart that which is *in truth* of the Same—only to satisfy the limitations of language, especially the latter in its static, written form, this form in which *we* are embedded at the moment.

The difference of the two conceptions of harmony is indeed striking: (1) that which is presented in the current study, of a divine issuance from which springs many presences, but each of which participating amid and as a singular becoming and being; (2) a condition of chaotic separation betwixt a condition of inexorable discordance and an alterior hand of intervention and mediation, a conflict apparent and in need of overcoming, due to an exemplification of opposites.

In the first, All is Divine in a procession which aspires to everlastingness; in the second, there is the discord of Φυσιολογια, a conspicuous absence of indigenous divinity for All and Each, and a desire to arbitrate this seeming divide, one that is never overcome, only temporarily contained. This latter scenario lays a basic question over the value of this bodily, terrestrial existence. The body is a tomb, the basic character of our deep nature is conflict: it is only the soul as a gift from an external God which redeems us from this prison of mortal combat and suffering. This "suspicion" of the mortal body lay at the heart of a mystical cult of violent purification, with the hegemonic intervention of mediation/separation for any conflict of warring opposites. The mediation of soul is only temporary, but, in this view, without this mediation there would only be interminable conflict. In this way, the presence of soul, while in this scenario never complete (as there exists a section of Unlimited chaos inaccessible to the light) is a sign of grace, as a gentle reprieve amid this raging storm of violence.

With our working conception of a philosophical magic of kinship, there is a "symphonic" harmony of "apparent" opposites amidst an "opening" of dimensional possibility, inhabiting and exhibiting in this kinship an already existing All-ness of which any harmony is primarily derived, or engendered. Harmony is dispensed as a flashing out of the divine, this which has become other than itself and as itself, as a *topos*, bestows a world of each for us to dwell. It must be remembered that the *Kosmos* is the divinity, as the All; our perspective bound habits of making distinctions are always of secondary significance.

An extended kinship intimates the horizons which will allow for an adequate comprehension of transmigration, as a teaching of the All, spoken from the terrain of bodies; without it, if there is a radical breach amidst Being, there could be no transmigration of the All. We will see another possibility with our examination of Plato. It is the forgetting of the intimacy of body, of the self amidst this opening, which we live, that casts us adrift throughout the All to eventual return to the Same place that we are now, to sit wondering why we are here and if there is something beyond. Philolaus sets forth the position (in only three of the fragments) that the principles of Limit and Unlimited are inexorably exclusive, that they are not of a similar nature, that the persistence of opposites at war was a "natural" fact which justified the intervention of a third party. He begins in the everyday world with its tables of opposites and its physiological explanation of the world. What he recommends is an independent adjudicator to negotiate a containment of *this* conflict. He does not recognize the possibility of an original Same expressed as a mythical overcoming of this difference for, in his *post facto* mediation, these opposites are made into abstract, nonsymbolic principles; the differences become more real than that which they were the nominal differences of, and this latter becomes a process of mediation, when originally it was/is the simply itself in an act of opening, happening, and return.

The contrast of life and death, one which points to the All, to the Divine, becomes for the writers a *mathesis* of conflict, differences, a game of dissection, of a problem that promises to be solved, contained, absorbed, marketed, via the intervention from an alleged third party, from a detached, "objective" agent. Since there seems to be a case for ambiguity in the doxography of Philolaus and to admit that *what* philosophy may be implied by the fragments is uncertain as such, we can investigate what is at stake in these seemingly minute and obscure arguments. What is at stake is the meaning of the doctrine of transmigration per se – our interpretation is confronted with differing, and incompatible notions of "harmony" which present discordant associations and affinities with respect to the notion of transmigration.

In that the evidence is so paltry, we must allow ourselves to be guided by the notion of a transmigration of souls with an extended kinship of All. That is, we must conceive of a possible "reality" in which a singular soul has inhabited these differing bodies of many life-forms through a process of continual life. What this implies is that this soul is brilliantly suited to the life in the body; it is adaptable and eager to inhabit "its" next body. It does not simply just fly off into some cosmos, in some ethereal state, contrary to Philolaus and Hierocles. It, the soul, inhabits body after body, entering this or that body *dependent* on the initial conditions of attunement gained from the previous embodiment, for the purposes of discovery and attunement amidst All.

This "soul" learns from these diverse embodiments and remembers what it has learned, although it may not always be able to recollect what it knows. This dispersal symbolizes the paths which the soul must trek to truly comprehend an extended kinship of All. For this soul to be able to enter into the All, to become All via being each, each body of this *diaspora* which lives amidst a single breathing creature, there must be a coincidence betwixt each singular that was, is, or will be; an intimation of the All amidst the ecstasies of the mortal being. The magical notions of kinship, synergy, and *synastry* which lay behind a cosmic All become disrupted by a notion of "warring opposites," and their inherent possibility is displaced through the deconstruction of their mythopoetic dwelling via the incipient force of external mediation, of intervention, that is, cutting the knot.

The symbol of transmigration tells us of a transition from divine to the world; each singular issues forth with a divine vibrational state of being; mythically, souls are distributed through bodies. At death, this soul migrates across through death as a gateway, through and into which one exceeds toward a new birth; the soul transmits a vibrational pattern to the new body in consonance with its specific attunement in the prior embodiment, entering another being which longs for a soul, as this latter longs for a body.[14] This procession continues indefinitely, and although a single soul here and there may find its way through the labyrinth and return to the divine, many more still find themselves wandering about, throughout the *Kosmos*, postponing Ariadne's thread.[15]

What I think we can see is that a notion of a "harmony" as that which intervenes amidst a state of "warring opposites" is incompatible with the doctrine of an extended kinship, and thus, of the sympathetical, "magical" domain of transmigration. Philolaus writes of the joys of embodiment:

> The soul is introduced and associated with the body by Number, and by a harmony simultaneously immortal and incorporeal . . . the soul cherishes its body, because without it the soul cannot feel; but when death has separated the soul therefrom, the soul lives an incorporeal existence in the cosmos. (DK 22)[16]

Philolaus is not necessarily an advocate of an overt "mystical" renunciation of the body. It could even be suggested that the text of fragments attributed to him is problematic in that there lacks any ultimate consistency, lacking any "internal structure." Such a deficit is made quite clear if we consider another fragment of Philolaus, from *On the Soul*, preserved and reported by Stobeaus. Philolaus asserts that the world is eternal, as it is One, and thus, there is nothing to oppose it. And, moreover, there could not be any internal conflict which could destroy it. He describes the One as being divided into two spaces, of the soul to the moon and of the moon to the earth, one a place of compact repose, the other, one of change, respectively. However, the fragment clarifies the relation betwixt these distinguished spaces. Stobeaus reports:

> The composite of these two things, the divine eternally in motion, and of generation ever changing, is the world. That is why one is right in saying that the world is the eternal energy of God, and of becoming which obeys the laws of changing nature. The one remains eternally in the same state, self-identical; the remainder constitutes the domain of plurality, which is born and perishes. But nevertheless, the things that perish transmit their essence and form, thanks to generation, which reproduces the identical form of the father who has begotten and fashioned them.[17]

This fragment is nearly in accord with the magical interpretation of the Pythagorean teaching. It is in the "But nevertheless" in which the strict segregation of Limit and Unlimited, or, of any of the other "opposites" is rendered problematic by differing reports and evidence. The trace of the All which is here suggested amidst that which perishes, as the world is the energy of the divine, is a statement of the kinship of nature betwixt apparent oppositions. It is in this textual context that we can suggest with some surety that the fragments of Philolaus do not allow for an unproblematic interpretation, despite the historical judgment as to his position.

We can suggest that the doctrine of transmigration can make no sense in the context of a condition of "warring opposites." In the latter scenario, transmigration would make sense only as punishment. Indeed, in this view, there is no raison d'etre to enter into another body, whatever it may be. Once is surely enough, the lesson has been learned, one has been redeemed from the tomb, from the prison house of the body a la Hierocles. Yet, in this view, and on this topic, there will be no reason. As Plato narrates, there is a forced and extended purgation via many incarnations for those who are guilty. The warring opposites have set up an extreme opposition which has engendered a severe and bizarre hatred and contempt for the body. It is a punishment for the soul, a prison house, and torture chamber. It is enough only to have been embodied, to have fallen, once, in this view. Yet, although another dispensation would seem to be superfluous, according to the protocols of the politics of the soul, one is never enough. This illustration allows us to make the decision as to the notion of harmony which is consistent with the doctrine of transmigration: harmony as indigenous coordination versus an external mediation. The notion of harmony which is required for the doctrine of transmigration in its Pythagorean interpretation is not that of an external arbitration by means of an instrumentalized number, as if the existence of the All depended on the proper working out of an equation a la potion. The notion of harmony which displays a plausible concordance with the doctrine of transmigration is that which can account for an indigenous, extended kinship betwixt perspective-dependent "oppositions," such as Limit and Unlimited, soul and body. It is a symbolic interpretation.

The significance of the difference between an oral and a written dissemination of the doctrine cannot, due to a supreme lack of evidence, be thoroughly investigated. Much speculation may be set forth concentrating on the forms of these modes and what type of awareness may have been allowed to grow amidst any respective linguistic infrastructure—or, of the bodily prerequisites for any devotion to each. Yet, nothing can be decided on this basis for what is lacking is the appropriate samples of speech, writing, or indeed, music. As it was decided that the doctrine of transmigration requires a notion of harmony in the sense of an indigenous, vibrational coincidence of contraries, we could be lead to keep Philolaus at a distance from our interpretation of the doctrine. However, as we have seen, most of the fragments could be read as being in agreement with/implying (or at least not contradicting) the allegorical scenario of trans-migration. We must, instead of pushing Philolaus away, place heavy question marks over the interpretation of his fragments that perpetuates the notion of harmony as an external administration of warring opposites. If we can accept the alleged distinction between the sixth- and fifth-century teachings, we could portray the difference thus: the latter philosophy found expression amidst an empty physiology as a reactionary desire for transcendence, while the former spoke of a divine excession and an eventual recollection of exceeded souls. The fifth century desired liberation from conflict through mediation, while the sixth century practiced attunement amidst a divine opening, one which required an extended immersion in all aspects of the *Kosmos*, each and every possible body. The former turned inward, ennobling concentration and compactness, purification, detachment, the hope of a quick escape. The latter sought to cul-tivate a *bios* where there was enough space to allow each thing used and each possibility experienced to suggest a symbolic, that is, communicative dimension. We can perhaps fathom the uniqueness of Pythagorean harmony as, with the best word, friendship.

This investigation of Philolaus yields for us several provisional results. First, we take note of the vital significance of Philolaus as a source of the Pythagorean teaching for both Plato and Aristotle, and hence, for Western (via Arabic) phi-losophy per se. Second, we underline the fact of the written dissemination of the source material acquired through Philolaus, and the implications of such a transfiguration of mnemotechnic strategy with respect to philosophical practice. Third, we see the ambiguity of the fragments of Philolaus, but, allow for a critical appropriation of his fragments as evidence and source material. Fourth, by means of this ambiguity, we detect the possibility of distinct interpre-tations of the notion of "harmony," two of these possibilities we discussed above. What is at stake is the question of the status of the body amidst a world exceeded from the divine, and thus, of the coherence of the doctrine of transmigration.

Chapter 5

The Alleged Critique of Pythagoras by Parmenides

There is wide and longstanding agreement that the hexameter poem of Parmenides, a student of Xenophanes, contained a criticism of Pythagorean philosophy. We have already seen how Cornford has made use of his specific rendition of Parmenides in his interpretation and criticism of the alleged contradictions and confusions of Pythagorean thought. In this chapter, as a deepening of our engagement with Cornford, we will investigate not only his contention that Parmenides criticized Pythagoras, but also his use of this contention in his judgment that early Pythagorean philosophy was a contradictory construction and that the intellectualist, modernist wing of scientific Pythagoreanism was justified in their alleged demythologization of their founder's original teaching.

Cornford, in his 1922 essay, which was continued into 1923, 'Mysticism and Science in the Pythagorean Tradition', maintains that "two radically opposed systems of thought were elaborated within the Pythagorean school." They can be schematized as follows:

| Mystical | Sixth century BCE | Pythagoras—criticized by Parmenides |
| Scientific | Fifth century BCE | Number-atomism—criticized by Zeno |

The systems are distinguished by the "Eleatic criticism," around 500–490 BCE in which Parmenides is alleged to have attacked, much in the manner of the logical positivists, such as Rudolf Carnap, any philosophical system that sought to derive a manifold from an original unity. Cornford asserts that Parmenides detected and criticized a radical fault in sixth-century Pythagoreanism: "This fault is the attempt to combine a monistic inspiration with a dualistic system of nature."[1] This interpretation of Parmenides is deployed by Cornford to erect a reconstruction of the "mystical" system, "used as one might a mirror to see what was happening on the other side of a screen."[2] That which characterizes this system, Cornford explains, is its "religious" mingling of mysticism and science, or, expressed in a more rational way, its containment of the axioms of monism and dualism.

On this basis, Cornford then "infers"the existence of a fifth-century "scientific" system, which he claims to have found in Zeno, who is thought to be, along with Melissus, a follower of Parmenides. What must characterize this system, in the narrative set out by Cornford, is its attempt to come to terms with the alleged Eleatic criticism of the "mystical" system. Cornford writes concerning the split in the Pythagorean school:

> Tradition points to a split between the Acousmatics, who may, perhaps, be regarded as the "old believers" who clung to the religious doctrine, and the Mathematici, an intellectualist or modernist wing, who *I believe*, developed the number doctrine on rational, scientific lines, and dropped the mysticism.[3] (My italics)

It is quite possible that there was a differentiation in the Pythagorean movement, one that would have been the result of a pedagogical distinction arising from the problem of transmitting the doctrine between generations of participants. Yet, Cornford fails to consider whether it was truly possible to simply "drop the mysticism," if, indeed, it was mysticism at all. As Guthrie has suggested, in his interpretation of the early Pythagoreans as magical, there could be no simple "dropping," for, in the case of the Pythagoreans, the baby was the bathwater. Moreover, and what is consistently disturbing in Cornford's interpretation is his failure to consider the Pythagorean riots and the suppression of the *bios*. We have seen ample evidence that an interpretation which does not consider such a violent breach in a "tradition" will be radically misleading.

Cornford set forth two distinct though related characterizations of the critique by Parmenides: (1) the criticism of the generation of multiplicity from unity, and (2) the criticism of the presence in one system of the axioms of Monism and Dualism. The first characterization concerns the generation of the world from number, and the second refers to the positing of existential principles and aspects, such as light and darkness, alongside the contention that all is One. Both of these characterizations, however, rest upon limited interpretations of Parmenides doctrine of Being, disclosed to him by the Goddess who he visited at her instigation. Indeed, not only does the Goddess tell Parmenides of the way *It is* (to the exclusion of *It is not*), but she also counsels that he should learn the path of mortal knowing. This latter knowing, in this way, is not simply to be discarded, but as we will see in light of Schürmann's comments below, that the context of emergence for knowledge in mortal facticity allows for a radical reinterpretation of the significance of Parmenides' poetic philosophy.

In his own attempt to reconstruct the alleged sixth-century "mystical system," Cornford posits the "pivotal conceptions" of the teaching of the Pythagoreans. He writes:

These are: the ideal of "becoming like god" and the notion of *mimesis*; the correspondence of macrocosm and microcosm; the conception of *harmony*; the doctrine of numbers; the symbol known as the *tetractys.*[1]

This list of items contains, we must state before proceeding, philosophical and theoretical "content" which we usually regard as Pythagorean, and not merely that of the sixth century alone. Moreover, I have already suggested that one of the primary problems with Cornford's reconstruction of the early Pythagoreans is that he adopts in an uncritical fashion a pseudo-Orphic interpretation of the doctrine of transmigration. In this way, the proviso of "becoming like God" is interpreted in the "Orphic" sense of "purification," and, a general, and, indeed, mystical renunciation of the body and world; they want a "leap." In light of the "magical" interpretation of Guthrie, it is striking the extent to which Cornford allows his interpretation to be figured by the "mystical" perspective. For despite treatments of the notions of harmony, number, and kinship, he fails to detect the possibility that any "division" in the soul could be of the nature of an indigenous musical opposition, such as the musical 6th and the 12th, and not that of the warfare of a tonal flux. He writes concerning this opposition in the soul:

> This follows from the central religious experience of the divided self, the internal warfare between good and evil, the Orphic double nature of man, the sense of sin combined with the consciousness of inward good and light taking part against inward evil and darkness.[5]

This perspective is problematic in that there is no evidence, apart from the unquoted "Orphic" texts, that the Pythagoreans held there to be an "internal warfare" between light and darkness. What we have seen on the contrary is a mythopoetic articulation of contraries, opposites, of differences, such as limit and unlimited, light and dark, which when allowed to play (and not regarded as originary oppositions), are cast into relief as perspective and dimension. In light of this *reflective* play of the "many" and the "one," Cornford contradicts his own "Orphic" assumptions when he writes of a "tuneful adjustment," or, of a harmonization of the soul. We wallow in muddy waters.

We have seen that this notion of "attunement" stands opposed to that of purification since what is being adjusted, even if out of tune, is still of the same nature as that which is tuned. This kinship of nature, which Cornford does suggest, is what is not allowed in the 'Orphic' teaching. As Limit and the Unlimited issue forth from the divine, giving rise to the Limited, there can be no warfare between these opposites. We must keep in mind the problem of language in this context, and be clear with respect to the domains, some being regulative in Kant's sense, to which we are referring. In this context, I have interpreted the early Pythagoreans as a magical, as opposed to a mystical, philosophy which placed great emphasis on a contemplative way of life committed to a communal attunement with the divine. There is not a containment of the exclusive axioms of Monism and Dualism for there is no primal opposition between real principles. The "contradiction" only comes in with Cornford's 'Orphic' interpretation. Without this latter, the second criticism cannot stand. Indeed, the Pythagorean "system,"[6] from this perspective, would be a philosophical pantheism of an All that is indigenously self-differentiating, in a manner similar to the philosophies of Hölderlin, Schelling and Hegel, each of whom were influenced by Spinoza. Yet, the first criticism must still be addressed, not a repetition of the question of monism and dualism, but as a question of the facticity of existence.

The first criticism is still relevant as the Pythagoreans cannot account for the necessity of this singular opening as such. However, what is at issue is no longer *mysticism* and science, but a sixth-century magical and an alleged fifth-century logico-scientific system, separated via a great distance. The first criticism is relevant to the magical system in its use of number theory and cosmogony as *symbola* to intimate a kinship betwixt the divine and *this* world by means of a path of generation from number to sensible bodies. Cornford writes of Pythagoras:

> He could not yet distinguish clearly between a purely logical "process" such as the "generation" of a series, and an actual process in time such as the generation of the visible Heaven, which "is *harmony* and number." The cosmogonical process was thus confused with the generation of numbers from the One, and will appear to us as a transcription of this (*really logical*) process into physical terms.[7] (My italics)

What is being criticized is the "Byzantine" supposition that a One became Two through some process of pantheistic growth. The implication of this criticism is that the world of multiplicity, if we must affirm the reality of the One, must be "somehow unreal." In this way, Cornford asserts that a fifth-century scientific system arose to respond to the polemic by Parmenides—disregarding, of course, the clear continuity of Pythagorean doctrines in Empedocles and others.[8] The "system," which Cornford calls Number-atomism, sought to save the plurality of the world without infringing on the mandate that the One cannot come to be or pass away. Instead what is posited is a plurality of monads which assemble to construct the world of experience. Since these monads are eternal, there is no problem of the generation of the world from out of Nothing, or from out of a One, which in this scenario, would be forced to somehow change, to become not-One. Cornford details the implications of this "new system," anachronistically assuming that monadism meant materialism:[9]

> With this simple materialistic conception of a plurality of monads, the old mystical derivation of the world and its harmony from the divine Monad and

the "elements of number" disappears, and with it go all the religious notions of the harmony of warring opposites, good and evil, the correspondence of the macrocosm and the microcosm, and the ideal of the imitation of God. The real is reduced to discrete quantity with the single purpose of restoring plurality and motion.[10]

While such a set of purposes may reflect Cornford's own era, it is clear that in the magical interpretation of early Pythagorean philosophy, in which opposition is not "real" in the sense of a contradiction of exclusive principles, there would not be a problem of generation (of the world from the divine source) since the Divine All *is* the world. There need not be a conflict with Parmenides in that his notion of the One could be the same as the All in Pythagoreanism. As there is nothing outside it, the All is not one in the sense of being distinguished from an other. It is one in the sense that it exists as a unity that is the procession of its eternal life. Perhaps, it is this eternity, this oneness of the All, of which Parmenides speaks, as the Goddess counsels us that we must also familiarize ourselves with the knowledge of mortals which involves change. It is only of the Nothing that we should not inquire, as this is impossible. The One, in this light, could only be truly known by itself. Parmenides merely counsels us not to confuse our symbolizations in myth with the tragic truth of existence.

Another possibility presents itself in Dillon, who in his *Middle Platonists*, writes concerning Eudorus of Alexandria (active around 50–25 BCE), who wove his thought out of Pythagorean and Stoic threads:

From the *Philebus* (26E–30E) he could have gleaned the elements of this theory, since the monad and the dyad are inevitably also Limit and Limitlessness, and the Cause above them, though not called there the One, has a unifying purpose, and is identified with Mind and God (or at least with Zeus). The Old Pythagoreans on the other hand, do not seem to have postulated a single supreme principle, but rather a pair, Limit and the Unlimited, which for Eudorus is only secondary.[11]

From this perspective, the lack of a supreme principle (those not of the "unity" of the All) for the early Pythagoreans would be grounds to deny the alleged charge of contradiction by Parmenides. If there were two principles which were coalesced as, or, in our view, were aspects of a generative harmony, then the problem of a transition from the One to the Many is not extant, or becomes again, a question of semantics or poetics. In other words, it may be possible to conceive of the divine as a name for this coalescence of opposites, ones we remember through narrative as distinctions made in the temporal world. The All, the divine, like the earth, exhibits an indigenous harmony, that is not susceptible to "our manner of speaking" which seeks a beginning, middle, and end. Such a *dialectical* "system" may be described as a two-in-one, yet, we must not only remember that these are the classifying labels of post-Aristotelian logic, but are also not compatible with the terrestrial perspective of the *bios*; there is no vision, by the mortal, upon the One, only a participation amidst the All, one which will never be "outside." While the very existence of such a "scientific" system is merely inferred by Cornford from Zeno's criticism, it is not certain that these were Pythagoreans. He makes a reference to tradition and its mention of a split in the Pythagorean school between the "Acousmatica" and the "Mathematici", a distinction which I addressed earlier. In one account of Iamblichus, the *mathematikoi* were not even followers of Pythagoras, but of Hippasus. In another account of Iamblichus, as we have already seen, the *mathematikoi* were lower order students of the Pythagorean school dealing with the exoteric study of nature, but not yet initiated fully into the esoteric teaching.

If Cornford is correct in his division between the two systems, that which is implied is that the Pythagorean movement was "purified" of its overriding commitment to an esoteric program. And, contrary to Cornford, the early Pythagoreans would surely not have seen the alleged "logico-scientific" system as an advance, but as a *mutiny* by those who were not even yet initiates in the *bios*. It is in this context that we must deal with Parmenides' first criticism, one concerning the failure by the early Pythagoreans to make a distinction between number and being, and thus, of their alleged confusion between logic and physics.

I have described the doctrine of transmigration as a *complex symbola* with mnemotechnic purposes which sheltered the Pythagorean teaching within the oral tradition. Moreover, I will sketch out below two aspects of the doctrine of transmigration, in Chapter 7, the Path of the Event and the Path of Remembrance, or Return, which not only gave an account of the birth of the world, but also suggested a pathway by which the individual soul could participate in a collective *bios* which would allow for an attunement with, and thus, return to the divine.

Yet, as symbola, and as I have detailed at length, these myths have an exoteric and an esoteric dimension, which follow, one after the other, in a process of education. It is not necessary, like the doctrine of transmigration itself, to take these symbola literally, any more than to contend that they are false. Within a magical philosophy, the symbola, as with the monochord, indicate a depth of existence and indicate a pathway of disclosure, moving from the *manifest* to the *concealed*, that is, an *aletheiological* path.

In this context, the first criticism of Parmenides, a virtual "red herring," does not exactly apply to the Pythagorean teaching. Instead, what is important is that an initiate in the mortal realm engages in an education which makes use of allegories and analogies which are neither true nor false, but are necessary in that the wisdom that is pursued finds its point of departure amidst the phenomenal world. The mortal cannot glimpse the One, nor can there be any grasp of a many, except as the words we interject in order to "make a long story short." For the Pythagoreans, mortal beings do not have the ability to transcend their perspective bound awareness, except through the narrative of transmigration. For the perspective of *homo terra*, there are many things, and there is an intimation of the All. Yet, there is no One or Many; such insights would have to wait for Plato.

Cornford has given us the suspect gift of a Parmenides who writes of a world of radical oppositions, portrayed as the two paths, each at a crossroads, never to touch, even at the end. Yet, if we read the fragments of the poem of Parmenides, and do not take Cornford at his word, we instead fathom that the paths join at the root, interlace as the waves of an ocean. There exists a nexus of contraries amidst this web of mortal thought, which is not the contradiction of the One, but is held together by the One. What is in contradiction to the One is only that the One should somehow not exist. The presence of a world of contraries does not negate the One, but describes the situation of mortal thought, or knowing, with respect to the One. But, this is thought after all, and not life. Yet, we must gather such thoughts together for they are indicative of a much deeper remembrance of the All. Reiner Schürmann writes in his groundbreaking essay, "Tragic Differing: The Law of the One and the Law of Contraries in Parmenides":

> No reconciliation is possible between contradictories. They exclude each other as being excludes not-being. Not so between contraries. Their unity is not just thinkable, it is *given*. Otherwise, no contrariness would ever become unveiled. As he proceeds on the aletheiological path, the traveler learns to know that unity which held him from the very start. This is why the goddess does not instruct the neophyte in anything new. It is also why Parmenides never denounces the *doxai* as futile. He only exhibits their structure: contrariness. Mortals are "double-headed" (dikranoi, 6:5). They have spinning heads going back and forth between the opposites that they themselves posit ever anew.[12]

From this perspective, which it must be argued, remains more attentive to the basic teaching of the poem than does Cornford, Schürmann undermines any interpretation that Parmenides would regard *doxai* as futile, or in other words, that the doctrine of the one is merely a nullification of any mortal knowing in the world. He writes that mortals are "double-headed," which, in a manner similar to Kant, signifies a being which has access to both mortal knowing and the well-rounded truth bestowed by the Goddess. Indeed, much in the manner of Heidegger's sense of truth as *a-lethea*, that which is known to us as mortals, intimates that which is concealed either as that which is absent or as that which is a condition of that which is unconcealed or which shows itself. Schürmann writes:

> The traveler gains a knowledge that in a later vocabulary would be called both theoretical and practical: he learns how *esti* holds contrary *onta* together.

But he himself also learns how to hold contraries together. Whenever he
hears a present entity or force being named, he would have to hear in it and
with it the contrary name, the name of the absent.[13]

In this way, it could be argued that the use of Parmenides by Cornford against
the Pythagorean *doxai* is in essence an abuse of hexameter poem as it only—and
misleadingly—iterates the first way of truth—*It is*. In this sense, there is a far less
radical distinction between Parmenides and Pythagoras—indeed, it could even
be argued that there is a far greater divide between Xenophanes and the latter.
At the same time, it would be misleading to merely equivocate the teaching of
Parmenides and Pythagoras as it seems that there is a greater intimacy for the
latter of *praxis* in the world and the aspiration for a return to the divine. It must
be remembered that Parmenides was taken to the Goddess, and in a way which
did not—as far as we can discern—require any action on his part, excepting
perhaps, if we listen to Burkert, various possible shamanistic techniques. For
Parmenides, the One remains aloof, distant in its function of holding together
of contraries which disperse and gather in ever new configurations. This is why
Schürmann holds that *henology* (*logos* of the One) is ambiguous in terms of
mortal *nomos*, when he writes: "Henological power sustains one force as well as
the other." Schürmann designates such a seeming abandonment in the philosophy of Parmenides as "tragic knowledge," one which allows knowledge of a One
which, while it holds together contraries as such, was ultimately indifferent to
the ways and ramblings of mortal life. For the Pythagoreans, and in their version of tragic knowledge, each world is remembered even in its destruction, for
it is each of All. But, such remembrance still abides in the tragic myth as the
individuated self, much in the manner of the tragic hero, undergoes destruction after destruction, until it finally abides in the All. Parmenides, in this light,
represents a partial return to the Homeric separation of the mortal and the
immortal, except that a wanderer may be provided a glimpse beyond the mortal
realm, but only for an instant, and as the result of no *praxis* of its own. In this
way, the scenario suggested by Cornford that there was some kind of theoretical
advance over a confused, mystical system must be seen as untenable. For it is
clear that even Parmenides makes use of narrative and the allegory of the Goddess, which must be seen as "religious" in Cornford's perspective. And, indeed,
it is Parmenides who is much closer to the mystical renunciation of the world
than is Pythagoras. A better, though still unsubstantiated interpretation would
be that the magical comportment of the early Pythagoreans was regarded
by Parmenides as unnecessary, much in the manner of Luther's rejection of
works.

Schürmann describes mortal thought: "The law of contraries is nomadic in
that mortal 'posits' never settle for good on any canonic phantasm."[14] The way
around this radical contingency for the Pythagoreans was of course the assertion
that the latter was able to remember the contingency of his past incarnations

and therefore, on this basis, had access to divine wisdom, or in other words, to the philosophic *a priori*. Again, we must be clear about this use of myth to project a sense of our own being. The mortal perspective is again "double-headed", simultaneously entrapped in contraries, and compelled to look behind the veil so as to catch a glimpse of the underlying condition of the One. Schürmann writes,

> The goddess does not propose two directions to follow, one toward sunset, the other toward sunrise. The young traveler does not find himself at the parting of the ways. He is not faced with Hercules' choice. The one and sole course, which is unconcealing, runs though two phases, concealment and unconcealment. *Lethe* remains operational within *aletheia* like a persistent undertow. The one way of Parmenides integrates veiling in unveiling.[15]

It is Pythagoras, like Parmenides, who seeks to run through the two phases of concealment and unconcealment through his inducement to remembrance of the All amid the tragic dissemination of recurrence of mortal existence. The path toward sunset is a preparation for a death which is the gateway to the second path, that of the sunrise. At the door of the gateway, there is a threshold which will transport the soul to another incarnation or a return to the divine All. It is with this conviction of kinship with the divine that the soul can hope to *not* drink from the waters of Lethe, but like Apollo, disembark from the earth into the sky in full remembrance of its wanderings.

Chapter 6

Between the Earth and the Sky: On the Pythagorean Divine

It is widely agreed that the Pythagoreans are linked to the name of Apollo in some way. Of course, there is no irrefutable evidence that this is the case; yet, this affiliation has been documented to such an extent, that, as the original event of the early Pythagoreans will always be beyond our reach, we must give due notice to what is extant and explore the mythopoetic narrative of Apollo with the hope that such an encounter may cast light upon Pythagoras and upon the doctrine of transmigration. Once we are acquainted with this narrative, one which takes place amid the broader tapestry of a pantheistic polytheism, we begin to gather that Apollo, not only as the patron of stringed instruments, but also as the god of healing, may be a symbol harboring a much deeper insight into the Pythagorean teaching, one approaching a sense of the whole self achieved in the unity of the *bios*. In this way, the fragments of the mythopoetic narrative of Apollo may be treated as another artifact left by the Pythagoreans, that of, perhaps, of the healing of the rift in Being.

Such a narrative symbol, resembling that of the doctrine of transmigration, is not just a bunch of charming tales, but a sample of magical *symbola*, preserved as myth. We would be committing a grave injustice if we repeated the prejudice that these are only a random collection of surviving stories, and nothing else besides. This would be a repetition of the segregation enacted by Dacier, Cornford, and the positivist "tradition," a severance that attains its most hostile expression in the banishment of poets from the *polis*, which was only a mask for the bad faith of Plato. We must keep in mind that the early Pythagoreans participated in the oral tradition, in which, as Albright suggested, the role of verse, or *poiesis*, had an original symbolic and mnemotechnic significance. And, in this light, we must be exceedingly vigilant of the stratagems of a tradition that is founded upon the severance of poetry and philosophy. With such a severance, we risk remaining trapped in a distorted image of Presocratic philosophy deaf to its mythopoetic horizons and context of emergence. Indeed, these fragmentary tales can be read in a symbolic and phenomenological manner, as abiding many narrative dimensions: of terrestrial events, a type of "history," or, philosophy, or, to any other dimension related to Apollo, as a mythopoetic dwelling of remembrance. Such a poetical reading of the symbol of Apollo exhibits an attempt to read *mythos* as a symbolic "dwelling" of remembrances.

Apollo serves as a patron, a symbol, which distinguishes the Pythagoreans from other movements devoted to differing perspectives of the divine, such as the revelers of Apollo's brother, Dionysus. Yet, this mention of Dionysus reminds us that we cannot look at Apollo out of his mythopoetic context. It is this nexus of symbols which tells his story, allowing us to fathom his significance for Pythagorean philosophy. A tentative indication of this significance lies in its connection to the Pythagorean cultivation of the harmony of All. In this light, we must seek to understand Apollo, the principle of individuation, as symbolizing the intimacy amidst body and soul, in the *bios*, in that individuation is but one moment, together with communion, in the overriding movement of transmigration.

In the following, I will explore the mythopoetic dwelling of Apollo so as to fathom the significance and context of his flight from Delos; the ambiguity of his symbolic persona with respect to his relationship with the maternal and feminine vis-à-vis Artemis and Leto; and finally, his relationship with his brother Dionysus, explored in the context of the sublimation of Dionysian *ecstasis* in the Apollonian *bios*. Just as the Homeric world is the artwork of Olympian divinities, Apollo does not act alone. He is joined by his brother in a unity akin to the common nature of limit (Apollo) and unlimited (Dionysus). The divinity of the All, symbolized as the sublimation of Dionysus by Apollo, displaces the limitations of Homeric blood kinship, and dissolves the kingship of Zeus, via a notion of an extended kinship, that is, a non-patricidal *coup de grace*.[1]

The Mythopoetic Dwelling of Apollo

It would be dishonest to present Pythagoras as a monotheist, as a prophet who thrusts forth his god to the exclusion of other possible and/or actual gods or divine principles or notions. Such an inference seems to be suggested by K.S. Guthrie in his presentation of the post-platonic etymology of Apollo of Plutarch and later Plotinus as that which is "not many" (a = not; pollon = of many). This doubtful etymology, which may or may not posit an abstract One, may not be applicable to the early Pythagoreans, who, as Dillon suggests, held two basic principles, as the All cannot be reduced to a principle, or, arche.[2] At the very least, we might suggest that "not-many" may mean "some." In other words, Apollo is one divinity amongst other divinities, and has a narrative significance only amid this mythopoetic horizon. K.S. Guthrie also mentions a questionable etymology by Diogenes Laertius of Pythios, the name of Pythagoras, as being connected with the Delphic Oracle, and thus, meaning that Pythagoras told the truth to the same extent as Apollo. That which this tells us is only that Pythagoras is linked with Apollo. In other words, at their best, these etymologies merely indicate the necessity of a proper consideration of the myth of Apollo which states that he was born upon the island of Delos and eventually made his abode in the sky.

Cornford, in his narrative of division and strife, deploys many metaphors, taken from *mythos*, as with the "flight into the sky," or, a "cutting out at the root," and many others which suggest a specific interpretation of the myths. In his text, he suggests that there is a separation of the earth from the sky, that "transcendence" consists of purity, as a liberation of the soul from the confinement of matter, the body as a prison. There is much evidence which places a clear question mark over the emphasis upon a clean break by Cornford, suggesting that his interpretation is unfounded vis-à-vis the mythopoetic fragments. Once we have dispelled this interpretation, we can begin to fathom the manifold evidence which fills out this symbol, as a life-web of interaction, one which suggests, in retrospect, that Apollo has been torn by the likes of Cornford from his own most habitat amid a mythopoetic domain of many "things," creatures, and gods, and, made into an icon for detachment and the order of Science. Indeed, could the god of medicine (a branch of Magic) declare himself out of the loop, as independent from the domain in which medicine has any reason of being? What of the plethora of patients? Can a god of medicine segregate himself from disease? Can he be pure or even wish to be pure? And, do not these stories always involve other divinities, the horizons of a world, body, self? In this way, once again, Cornford uses a particular reading of a myth as a weapon against myth per se. In distinction from this self-refuting assertion of the absence of myth, as Bataille[3] would contend, the following will be oriented to a hermeneutics of myth as an intrinsic aspect of a renewed philosophical appraisal of the meaning of the symbol of Apollo.[4]

The Ambiguity of Apollo

Apollo is not a god of "purification" in the sense of a radical purgation, of cutting off, or cutting into two, in the sense of *ratio*, or, of elimination. He does not suppress the power and names of the other divinities, of Artemis, his twin sister, his half brother Dionysus, Hermes, the messenger of the gods, not to mention his father, Zeus. Apollo, moreover, offers his healing art, that of attunement, to mortals at his various temples. Even if he exceeds the successionist genealogy of the Hesiodic gods, he does so only as a healer of violence. As Nietzsche contends in his interpretation of Ancient Greek tragedy, Apollo, the god of the redemptive dream image, must maintain an intimacy with Dionysus, his half brother and the god of intoxication and the Dithyramb.

For, if Apollo not only sublimates the intensity of Dionysian *ecstasis*, but suffocates, strangles it, we will be left with the nihilistic results which Nietzsche, in his *Birth of Tragedy*, aptly describes in his diagnosis of the decline of Ancient Greek culture in the emergence of the "theoretical man" of Socrates-Euripides-Plato (Christianity). In this context, Dionysus and Apollo are transformed into the naturalistic figures of matter and form, of body and mind, a severance which is at the heart of our hermeneutical dilemma with respect to the "unity" of Pythagorean thought. For Nietzsche, on the contrary, these nihilistic apparitions of the "Last man" symptomatize an abandonment a biotic and exuberant harmony for a restricted economy of order of discipline and purgation through the models of the academy and monastery. It is in this way that *The Birth of Tragedy* is deeply akin to his *Thus Spoke Zarathustra*, which rearticulates the Presocratic doctrine of the eternal recurrence of the same as an overcoming of the nihilism of "theoretical man."

In the *scientistic* reading of Apollo, as we have seen in Cornford's emphasis upon the metaphors of flight and liberation, Apollo flees his mother, the 'barren' rock of Delos, to find liberation in the sky of his father. Yet, care must be taken in the interpretation of this story, and specifically in reference to the meaning of the flight, of its purpose, of its context and of its limits. Even from this meager fragment of Apollo's flight to the sky, we may recall another way to read this separation of the earth from the sky, in the example of Eurynome in the Pelasgian Creation Myth,[5] who rose naked from chaos, and finding nowhere to stand, separated the earth from the sky. In this case, separation allows for the emergence of world, as a terrestrial opening. Mythopoetically, it is the world which is a bridge between the earth and the sky, and in this context, Apollo, the god of individuation, could be seen to be, contrary to the divorcement central to Cornford's account, a symbol of an emergent world, one which arises harmoniously out of the inchoate communion of Dionysian ecstasy. This latter can also be read as rising from the Earth, which, as with Heidegger's "Origin of the Work of Art" (1936), inexorably circumscribes and ultimately subdues the Apollonian world (as is the case with the tragic hero in Greek tragedy). It is in this way that symbol of Apollo allows for the contemplation of a tragic perspective, as transmigration opens up a destination of remembrance and return to the divine All.

At the horizon, the earth and sky "touch" in a great panoramic circle, witnessed as we, with the Sufis, "turn ourselves around." This intimacy at the horizon itself suggests that the standard reading of this flight to the sky misses what is most essential in this mythological scenario: that the separation between the earth and the sky concerns only a distantiation of localities and perspectives. This is a distance only partially articulated, as a casting into relief of differing aspects amidst an extended kinship of the All. In this light, we can consider Apollo in his essential ambiguity as an individuated god *in-between* the earth and the sky, as a world abiding the double bind of tragic existence. The essential ambiguity of the Apollonian persona allows us to explore the specific orientation of the symbol of Apollo and of the horizons in which it acquires its meaning. We must remember that the principle of contradiction had never seen the light of day with the Pythagoreans, or, with any prior philosophical movement per se. Once again, we must remember the unique sense of "opposition" for the Pythagoreans as a symbol for the differing powers of the divine All. These powers, marked as symbols, mingle freely amongst each other in their interaction, juxtapositions, betwixt singulars, allowing us to assemble or decipher a story, a world, and ultimately, a meaning.

In this spirit, we can explore other mythological associations of Apollo which exert influence upon our portrayal of this god as a symbol, in this case, his relationship with his sister Artemis and his mother Leto. It is in this context that we can consider the relationship of opposites in terms of gender, and specifically the question of the gender of Apollo, and of the polytheistic sense of divinity as such. Harmony, as we have seen, consists of a coincidence of contraries as opposites analogous to the sense of musical opposition. This condition of interaction is not, in our view, an intervention into an *agon* of "warring opposites," but a synergy of differing powers of actuality, of the power of the All. In this context, a different metaphor for the divine All would be that of the alchemical marriage of the god and goddess. Ficino, in his *Book of Life*, seems unaware of what I have called the *scientistic* reading of the myth of Apollo. In this fascinating, though nearly forgotten work, he articulates the Apollonian and Phoebean character of his magico-medical philosophy. For him, Phoebe was the grandmother of Apollo and of his sister Artemis. While Apollo is of the sun and sky, Artemis is, like her grandmother, identified with the Moon. It is the Moon which is also a gateway betwixt the earth and the sky. In Ficino's account, Artemis, the eldest of the siblings, helped in the raising and nourishing of the infant Apollo, an account which comes initially from Apollodorus. Ficino writes:

> My dear sweet brothers in the love of the Muses, some among you have much more strength of mind than of body. Well, you should know, then, that as soon as she was born, Phoebe, the sister of Apollo, had to supply him with a little material for nourishment and with a lot of spirit at his own birth. Indeed, the humors and foods in the body are easily broken down into such spirit. Your entire spirit, therefore, is made of some such material.[6]

This provides us with a glimpse at the intimacy of the brother and sister, a similar intimacy as we will find between Apollo and his half brother Dionysus, or, of Isis and Osiris. This intimacy in the former case, together with no reference to the story of the maternal neglect of the mortal woman Leto, and thus, the feeding of Ambrosia to Apollo by Zeus, may indicate that there is another way to interpret Apollo and his mythopoetic context. This account would underline the continuity of Pythagoras with Homer, with their shared esteem and valorization of the body.

In the *Homeric Hymns*,[7] Apollo is said to have learned the art of divination from his sisters, the Letoides, in concealment from his father, Zeus. And, according to Harrison, not only does Apollo take the name of the goddess Phoebe as his own, but, would, so as to participate in the art of divination and prophesy, dress as a woman, as Phoebe, to escape the wrath of his father Zeus.[8] Since the genealogical line of Leto persisted in a condition of matriarchy (or, possibly, as matrilineal), together with the effective absence of his "procreative" father, Apollo abides amidst the maternal domain, incorporating the latter mentioned arts into his character, in defiance against the thunderous power of his father. It could be suggested that Apollo used these arts to migrate toward the sky, but as arts of the earth. In the spirit of Irigaray, we could suggest that Apollo has an ambiguous gender.[9]

As Apollo is the sky god, the god of light, he has detached himself from the earth in the sense of inhabiting the space between the earth and the sky, amid the terrestrial, the site of the temporality of unfolding. Apollo is not the sky itself, but is light which shows itself and points beyond itself, toward a source and situation. It is certain that Apollo desires and requires darkness, shadow, as well, in order to conjure forth the visions of dreams and the fluid figures of singulars, that is, individuation. This suggests once again his intimacy with Dionysus, or, at least with the contrary of light, shadow, this strange sharing of disease that does occur between a doctor and a patient, where often the doctor remains immune. Apollo and his brother Dionysus dress in their sister's garments in order to learn the mysteries. It is written that Zeus was not pleased with the essential ambiguity which was to be the character of his sons. The attempt to separate the pair, or to remove their ambiguous personae would displace the conditions for understanding the symbolism of divinity which is offered in this synergy of Apollo and Dionysus, as the two elements, limit and unlimited, of the early Pythagoreans in their articulation of an extended kinship of All. If we forget this feature of the Pythagorean teaching, we will not be able to grasp the significance of Apollo with respect to the doctrine of transmigration.

There has been a contention in a stream of scholarship, amongst feminist thinkers and others, who contend that there is a connection between Greek tragedy and the death of the matrilineal, that is, "primitive," principle of organization. The death is dramatized, as it were, through the display of a situation of ultimate, yet, conflicting loyalties.[10] In order to free oneself from this double bind, it was deemed necessary to sacrifice one of the loyalties. In this way, it is suggested that an explicit attempt to separate the doctor from the disease occurred with the explicit lack of a feminine *nomos* in fifth- and fourth-century Tragic Poetry, the *nomos* of the mother as such or as a possibility in the wake of the death of the father. The previous ambiguity and androgyny of Apollo is rent asunder and a "new" Apollo, in the guise of the masculine hero, has been set up who, regardless of the same nomenclature, has been divested from his link with the maternal. He is immortal for just that reason, according to this reading of the tragic perspective.

That the poets of the tragic age were documenting the ascendancy of the paternal principle, could be indicated, in this view, in *Oedipus Rex* of Sophocles, a text which shares with the *Orestia* of Aeschylus and the *Bacchae* of Euripides, a dispassionate narration of the death of the maternal principle, symbolized, for instance, in the anguished cry of Medea, "Nothing is possible anymore!" This text is fodder for commentators of the standard view of a "liberation" from the strangulation of the mother. Yet, these fifth- and fourth-century tragedies describe a breach or a catastrophe, paving the way for the mediators of Philolaus and Platonic philosophies. In *Oedipus Rex*, Jocasta asserts the "untruth" of divine prophesy, as she can only see amid the visible. It is no accident that the blind prophet, Tiresias, in order to see the "truth," need not have access to the light of the terrestrial. The manifestation of Apollo as a woman, as how things appear, and as a strangler, could also be read in the context of tragedy, as a strategic attack upon the maternal principle, and its earth bound vision.[11] In the tragic perspective, not only does the "female" Sphinx serve to undermine the seeming efficacy and strength of woman, but also, as it makes its appearance after the death of the father, and thus the law, it is implied that feminine assertion, like that of Antigone, can only be anarchic, bestowing an onslaught of disorder and despair for the children. Oedipus is a hero in that he seems to triumph over the woman, and in his victory, is given the reins of power and the possession of the mother.

Another example, to which I have already alluded, would be a correlation between the deception of Apollo, appearing in the form of a female monster, as the Sphinx, is an ironic attack against Hera, who, we will recall, attempted to prevent the birth of Apollo by sending the Python to kill him. This irony plays itself out not only with his killing of the python with an arrow, but also his confinement of the python within his temple. To appear as the Sphinx, as a woman who murders the children of Thebes, Apollo, in this view, at once demonizes the feminine, strategically executes his design to undermine the status of Jocasta, and escapes from his identification with this strangling female by killing from up close, that is, it is well known that Apollo kills only from afar.

I will attempt to respond to this contention. In a preliminary way, we could point out that the promised "liberation" which is alleged to arise from such a sacrifice of the maternal principle merely reasserts the insurmountability of the double bind which erupts with the destruction of the household. In other words, even if we are to accept this interpretation of the significance of Greek tragedy, it could be readily argued that the break from a maternal to a paternal principle is itself ambiguous, always haunted, as Schürmann contends in relation to Parmenides, by the undertow of reversal and difference. In this way, the tragedians could be read in a way that would not be in conflict with this variant of feminist interpretation, but would perhaps be more nuanced with respect to the ambiguous character of human existence. In this period, in the era from Pythagoras to Aeschylus, it is argued that matrilineal organizations of human *praxis* met their demise. Yet, it would seem from this criticism of tragedy, that there is the suggestion that the tragic poets were somehow agents of this demise, and not merely *poets of becoming*, documenting a transformation that had been well underway since the pre-Homeric ascendancy of Zeus. Moreover, this criticism of tragedy need not force us to abandon Nietzsche's reading of Apollo with respect to the notion of an Apollonized *bios*. As we have seen in our criticisms of the divisive reading of Cornford, and his pseudo-Orphic portrayal of the liberation of the soul from the body (as the liberation of Apollo from Delos), we need not read Greek tragedy in the manner of the liberation from the feminine or the subversion of the matrilineal genealogy. Indeed, that which is shown most clearly in the Apollonian figure of tragic individuality is the overwhelming superiority of the Earth, of the Dionysian communion, which forces the hero to succumb to his fate. The lesson is not a patriarchal one, but a tragic warning of any attempt to assert the primacy of one pole of an opposition. When this is attempted, the result is the destruction of *tragic myth*, or in the case of music, noise. With the Pythagoreans, the concern for continuity in the oral tradition and the significance of music, together with a symbolical manner of procedure, intimates a kinship with the "old ways." Such a consideration may help to cast perspective upon their enduring participation in the mythopoetic tradition and their continuity with so-called 'primitive' cultures. That which can be ascertained is the fundamental character of the Pythagoreans movement: the assertion of the kinship of the soul with the body of the *Kosmos*, as a return to the divine All via an Apollonian sublimation of Dionysian *ecstasis* at the site of the body.

Apollo is the Sun, sister Artemis is the Moon, and brother Dionysus is the vine. There is a necessary bond and an associative harmony betwixt these differing divinities, a bond and harmony which is the event, the extended kinship, of the All. This bond is instantiated amid the terrestrial *bios* in the acceptance and active participation of women, as such participation only became explicitly problematic with Aristotle, the father of logic. Each divinity, amid the symbolic terrain, plays its role, or, in other words, fulfills its "essence" in the unfolding of the fruitfulness and harmony of the *Kosmos*, the earth and all of its creatures. There is no cause for hatred of the Earth, as the father, Zeus, relied upon her to enfold human beings who desire to exceed their own proper limits.

What these offspring symbolize is at quite a distance from the significations of the Orthodox Pantheon of Homer. For while these divinities are technically, as progeny, included in the Pantheon, we can see a different order emerging, that of a displacement which occurs between Apollo and Zeus, as with the previous divisions of Uranus and Saturn, or Saturn and Zeus, but as suggested, one which sought to break the curse of the tyrant, of blood kinship, through the emergence of transmigration as a notion symbolizing the aspirations of an extended community. We may take this transfiguration of the context of reference as symbolic of the transformations of mythopoetic reference which occurred in the sixth century. This generation shift, which Pythagoras himself aided and abetted, was of Apollo and his consorts in their nonviolent succession of the Olympic Pantheon of Homer. These progeny displace the ancestors, place rosemary upon their graves, attempting to fathom and live a differing possibility. Apollo, the god of medicine, seeks to heal the wounds of the previous violent successions of the gods and to cultivate the indigenous harmony of the All.

It is in this way that Apollo acquires his significance and meaning amid the horizon of the other gods and goddesses who have an essential role to play in the effectuation of the harmony of the world. We can readily detect the ambiguity of Apollo (his own embeddedness in the mythopoetic horizons of existence) through a consideration of the interrelations of Apollo with respect to the other progeny of Zeus, Artemis, and Dionysus, and, moreover, their difference from other divinities who came from Zeus, such as Athena, who emerged from his head. While Athena, a female deity, is born without the mediation of a woman, from the head of Zeus, Apollo and Artemis, and again, Dionysus, (but with modifications) are born from the carnal union of Zeus with a mortal woman. For Artemis and Apollo, it was Leto, while, for Dionysus, it was Semele, who met an unfortunate death by being struck by lightening by Zeus, under the jealous enchantments of Hera. The embryonic Dionysus was instead carried to term in the leg of Zeus, and in this way, Dionysus, like Athena, symbolizes a partial or, as with the latter, a complete disruption of natural harmony.

That which is essential is the coalescence of human and divine upon this mythopoetic terrain. By having mortal mothers, Apollo, Artemis, and, amid disruption, Dionysus have mixed, ambiguous natures. This coalescence of the mortal and immortal sets forth the possibility of an eschatology of return of the mortal to the divine. In this way, as being both of the earth and the sky, Apollo serves an important symbol for the aspiration of return to the divine. The divinity is the All, but the All that manifests itself amidst a multifaceted excession of phenomenal domains, each being in the orbit of a singular divinity. It is through the play of these divinities, expressed in a mythopoetic narrative, that a "mingling" betwixt mortal and immortal dimensions exhibits the birth of the world. For Homer, of course, such an aspiration must have been *hubris*; yet, from this other perspective, a new possibility in the narrative of hope was opened up for mortals.

Apollo and Dionysus

From the Pythagorean perspective, Apollo, in his own gesture of Promethean sympathy, bestows to the mortal a path for the immortality of the soul. There is no direct access, no leap into nakedness before an illumined god, as if a god at his or her pleasure decided to make someone immortal or to place them in a constellation. There is instead a quest of becoming the All through being *each*. In the state of *human* be-ing, as opposed to being a bird or a bee, the path is a *bios* as a living *theoria* (magic) which will effectuate a return to the source of All. The *bios* is a sublimation of the Dionysian *ecstasis*. In this way, the Pythagoreans share an affinity with the Dionysian cult of the Orphic ritual *telete*. The similarity between the groups, as we have seen, lies in their respective commitments to a sacred *praxis*. Copleston writes:

> In Orphicism, we certainly find an organization in communities bound together by initiation and fidelity to a common way of life, as also the doc-trine of transmigration of souls—a doctrine conspicuous in Pythagorean teaching—and it is hard to think that Pythagoreans were uninfluenced by the Orphic beliefs and practices, even if it is with Delos that Pythagoras is to be connected, rather than with Thracian Dionysian religion.[12]

Copleston contends that the pursuits which characterize these cults is embed-ded in the doctrine of transmigration and naturally leads to the promotion of a "soul-culture." The essence of the Dionysian emphasis on worldly *praxis* (ecstasy) is maintained by the Pythagoreans, but, in our view, this ecstasy is sublimated through an analogical *bios* in correspondence with the symbolic implications of Apollo.

With their commitment to the god Apollo, the Pythagoreans, while display-ing many resemblances to these other wanderers and travelers, do express an explicit singularity of character. With Copleston's suggestion, it could be suggested that the Apollonian Pythagoreans stood mid-distance between the Dionysians and the Orphics.[13] That which the Pythagoreans shared with the bacchic Dionysians was a commitment to a communal bodily *praxis*, through a more intimate relationship to magical *physis*. They also shared the voice of spoken word (*logos* as breath) as a mnemotechnic medium and they shared music, but not necessarily the same music.[14] Orpheus, however, was a musician and poet, yet, differs from the others with his commitment to the written word and the image. The latter and his movement have also been described by Guthrie, as we have seen, as solitary practitioners.

It can be detected that the written word implies, as suggested above, serious implications as to its specific *praxis*, one which displaces and replaces the broader contours and the smallest features of a *bios* or an *ecstasis*. One could say, in a few words, that the reader or writer, or, for that matter, the ritualist of the imagist *telete*, assumes specific bodily postures and movements which differ than one who is concerned with gymnastics, walking, massage, herbal medicine or one who under the night sky contemplates the bodily dwelling of the soul—or, again, the ecstasies of a reveling Bacchante abandonment amid a communal hallucination. With reading and writing, the harmony of immediacy and spontaneous coalescence is eternally postponed through its captivation to the technique of the written word. But, beyond this predicament, we can congratulate the Pythagoreans' fortune to having been born at the right time.

To honor the self, the soul and body, as the *Golden Verses* advise, one must, as one would do with the monochord or especially the lyre, play amidst a biotic nexus which toti-potently intimates the divine excession of All, to become in tune with the All. Such a consideration brings back into focus the sublimation of Dionysian *ecstasis* via Apollonian *bios*, a sympathetic magic amidst an extended kinship. This philosophical and practical magic adheres to the contextualization of writing as an aid of natural memory. Writing for its own sake disseminated the labyrinth that ensnares the wanderer in forgetfulness. For, the magic of rhythm merely punctuates, if only fleetingly, the tonal flux to bring forth music, and in this way, Apollo is also a god of darkness, as the silence between the notes.

Marsilio Ficino writes in his *Book of Life*, 'Second Part: How To Prolong Your Life',

> Phoebus and Bacchus are always individual brothers, but they are very much the same. Phoebus is the soul of the sphere, the sphere is Bacchus. Phoebus is the whole circle of the sphere; Bacchus is that flaming ring within the circle. Phoebus is the nourishing light in this flaming globe; Bacchus represents the same healthful warmth from light. So they are always brothers and pals, always each other and the same.[15]

And, he also writes:

> They are certainly brothers and individuals, those pals, Phoebus and Bacchus. One of them gives you two of the most powerful things, light and the lyre. The other one gives you two more to refresh the spirit, wine and the odor of wine, with whose daily use the spirit itself becomes Phoeban and liberated.[16]

The kinship of these gods, the symbolical analogues of the "opposites" of Limit and Unlimited, or, of the aesthetic intimations of light and darkness, orchestrates a singular mythological complex of references, and serve, in much the same way as the doctrine of transmigration, as a symbolical reference matrix which points toward an esoteric wisdom of the generative divine, one shielded, once again, by exoteric artifices. As a further reminder of the types of reading that are possible, keeping in mind the vulgar "literalist" readings which have plagued the Pythagorean teaching since its inception, we can listen to an example of Ficino:

> The astrologers say that Venus and Saturn are enemies of each other. Nonetheless, in heaven, where all things are moved by love, where there is no fault, there can be no hatred. When they say enemies, therefore, we must interpret this as meaning that they differ in their effect.[17]

Once again, we must remember that it is the All which is the destination of any aspiration of return to the divine. And, this implies that one looks to oneself and to the gods, to the earth and the sky, and must amid the world in-between, orchestrate a *bios* which confirms and strengthens the kinship and harmony of All. There is a synchronicity between self, world, and the divine, the former two being living analogues of the divine. Along the pathway from the self to the divine, each wanders through the world, and it is here that we can get sidetracked into a superficial forgetfulness characterized by a one-sided latching-on to a merely foreground signification. While this sign may contain the answer to the riddle, or at least point the wanderer toward an answer, forgetfulness reigns when this sign is taken for an end in itself. To put this point more directly, the wanderer has been shown to the gateway, but instead of going through this gateway to find what lies beyond, he bows down and worships the gateway itself. He proceeds no further as he is lost in the forgetfulness of conviction.

Apollo, the divinity of harmonic order and individuality, has an intimate relation with his brother Dionysus, a divinity of exuberant life and communion. This intimacy between brothers points the wanderer toward a sense of divinity that does not take sides between antitheticals which display their relevance only amidst the terrestrial opening, between the earth and the sky. Indeed, there are differences amidst world, yet, this points to the *logos*, not a *polemos*, sent forth from a living divine, one that is dancing, like Shiva, amid its alleged contradictions.

We will recall, in our previous discussion of harmony, that *logos*, as the two, desires the three, harmony, which is necessary for the cohesion of the divine out-flashing into world and self. Yet, if we are not confused by the numerical order of 1, 2, 3, 4, we can suggest that the harmony, a coherent chaos, is and must always be there already. Or, the *logos* is the circulation of an harmonic order of extended kinship. It is crucial not to forget the living harmony of the All, and get lost in supposed opposites such as light and darkness, or, male and female. Of course, each is an aspect with its own specific character. Yet, to think that there must be an external mediation via the philosopher to secure the very fabric of reality is ludicrous. We must remember that while there is manifold difference, all and each of this must be of the Same in the character of the All, as the All.

We can suggest that Apollo and Dionysus, as well as Artemis and the myriad other divinities are symbols of a polytheistic pantheism which, from a modernist perspective, would be contradiction itself. And, while the Pythagoreans did not replicate the religion of the goddess, they did not reject it either. In his ascent into the sky, Apollo was merely seeking a place for himself amidst the world. This is promised by the path of return, a path which does not require sacrifice, but only remembrance, memory as a perception of the manifest harmony of All (Apollonian prophesy is a remembrance of the future). In this way, none of the gods and goddesses as ultimate referents in themselves, but each intimates the divine *as such*.[18]

Apollo leaves his mother without malice or regret, with joyful memory played out as symbols of his life. He takes the place of his father, in alliance with his brother, but without patricide. The awakening of extended kinship throws away the separation of mortal and immortal a la Homer and cuts the knot of successive overthrows of father by son (Uranus-Saturn-Zeus), and originally of the mother by father (Gaia, Uranus). In this light, Pythagoras is seeking to suspend the succession of overthrow, a suspension that is enacted as a *bios*, a modality of the self amid the kinship of All, as emergence of a world, which, conceived as an association of friendship, heals the wound of being.

Chapter 7

The Pythagorean *Bios* and the Doctrine of Transmigration

The fellowship which characterized the Pythagorean *bios* was a "self-chosen association of individuals."[1] The association was, in this way, one that was based upon freedom, grounded as it was upon the resolution of the individual members. The *bios* was a practical topology and affiliation of philosophers, dissidents amid the established *polis*, in dissension with regard to not only *theoria* bound up with the notions of soul, cosmogony, and theology, but also, a divergence with respect to the concrete way of life bound up with these conceptions. This association effectuated its dissent through an orchestration of a communal lifeworld, a *praxis* disseminated through the mnemotechnic *symbola* of the doctrine of transmigration.

Michel Foucault, in his *History of Sexuality, volume I*, may be of some aid to our attempt to close in on the early Pythagoreans with his description of the terrain of various philosophic, poetic, ecstatic, and mystical tendencies and styles. He writes:

> In classical thought, . . . the demands of austerity were not organized into a unified, coherent, authoritarian moral system that was imposed on everyone in the same manner; they were more in the nature of a supplement, a "luxury" in relation to the commonly accepted morality. Further, they appeared in "scattered centers" whose origins were in different philosophical and religious movements. They developed in the midst of many separate groups. They proposed—more than they imposed—different styles of moderation or strictness, each having its specific character or "shape." Pythagorean austerity was not the same as that of the Stoics, which was very different in turn from that recommended by Epicurus.[2]

The initiation into a way of life which existed as one movement of many in some degree of conflict with the established order had the significance of a radical singularization of the self in the moment of initiation, or beginning. Such a decision concerns, in the context of the narrative of transmigration, one's own attunement amid the All, of that rhythm with which one merges in the cosmic dance. The mortal self must have the freedom to decide, for, as implied in the doctrine of transmigration, each must, in this cultivation of remembrance, look into himself or herself so as to fathom what must be done in order to cultivate a growing intimacy amid the All. Each self must decide his or her own most pathway, as only the self has access to its own secret. Burkert describes the punctuating character of the event of initiation:

> Every initiation means a change in status that is irreversible; whoever has himself initiated on the basis of his independent decision separates himself from others and integrates himself into a new group. In his own eyes the *mystes* is distinguished by a special relation to the divine, by a form of piety. Every festival stands in contrast to everyday life.[3]

For there to be the fulfillment of its purpose, the Pythagorean philosophy required distantiation from the Olympian *polis*. This distinction required the cultivation of a separate philosophical space, for the fulfillment of a different conception of extended kinship expressed in the rather *subversive* doctrine of friendship. Friendship as a kinship of self-chosen individuals subverts the blood kinship portrayed by Homer and the hereditary aristocracy of the Olympian *polis*. It is not necessarily tied any longer to any sacred soil, or, to any sacred grove, except of course, for the earth and the sky.

The Pythagorean subversion of blood kinship is accomplished via the synchronous happening of "scattered centers" of thought and practice, each nucleus, perhaps a network of groupings with a shared *ethos*, operating amidst the hegemonic cultural terrain of its day. In this great mosaic of styles, that which distinguishes the *bios* is its radical displacement of ritual practices, underscoring not only the necessity of a singular way of terrestrial (perspective) life to accomplish this divine occurrence, but also its emphasis upon the integral self, one not reducible to the "metaphoricity of sight," of the visible and the invisible of mere theory. The Pythagorean *bios* effectuated this complete self via the plethora of phenomenal dimensions of affectivity, of bodily motion, touch, sound, smell, and taste. These points of contact amid the All, of synchronicity, with that which lies beyond the surface of the body become the conduits for a remembrance that shelters an esoteric wisdom, and for its manifestation as a terrestrial symbol. Burkert describes of the many rules of life, symbola, observed amidst this *bios*, which like the monochord, provide guidance in the tuneful adjustment of the soul amidst body.

> It is hardly possible to find a single basic idea in the conglomerate of prescriptions that make up the Pythagorean life. They are called *akousmata*, things heard, derived from the oral teaching of the master, or symbola, tokens of identity. These are not part of ritual: there is no Pythagorean *telete*, the *bios* had discarded cult. Certain parallels to mystery rites remain: the prohibition of beans, the preference for white garments.[1]

There may be no single idea for these prescriptions, but we can suggest that there is a poetic *topos*, that of the narrative of transmigration, which serves as a background for the meaning of *symbola* as stated in everyday life. Specific symbola are suggestions amid the everyday, the significance of the *bios* resides in synchronous relationship with the doctrine to which it is analogous. This doctrine discloses a complicated portrayal of the predicament of the initiate. Certain prohibitions against eating flesh, past-life regression, even the narrative of transmigration itself, may seem to be rhapsodic anecdotes with no single idea to be found in them, but these in fact stand as signposts and marks of remembrance of the essential kinship of the soul with the world and the divine, and as the divine. Amid the terrestrial perspective of the body, of bodies, of collocations of selves, there will not exist an absolute idea, an *eidos* seen by a divine Cyclops; there will only be stories, persisting each amidst a tenuous persistence of memory, threatened by displacement, erasure, and oblivion.

As we saw earlier in Guthrie's reference to Socrates, leaving the body is not something that is so eagerly demanded, but one hopes to have good courage in death. The courage arises when one realizes that death is only a gateway, a transition, an event. It is philosophy that may prepare one for this event and give good courage to one who has lived a life analogous to the divine. The kinship of the soul with the divine, therefore, is remembered even if it is expressed in a "superstitious" maxim. For, in the depths of a superstition, beyond an exoteric *eidos*, its presentation, lies the depth of an esoteric meaning, one which is the music of the life that exists beyond the geometric containment of surfaces. Guthrie writes concerning the uniqueness of the Pythagorean *bios*, although repeating the tired line of mystical asceticism, with its misleading connotations:

> Each of us is shut up in his separate body and marked with the impurity of the lower forms of matter. How are we to shake this off and bring the moment nearer when our own small part will reunite with the whole and we shall be god ourselves? What is the way of salvation? Eleusis offered it by way of revelation, granted to the initiate after suitable preparatory purification. The Orphic sought it through some form of sacramental *orgia* or *teletai* and the observation of taboos. Pythagoras retained much of this, but because he was a philosopher he added a method of his own.[5]

What is being attempted is a thought-provoking *bios*, which through its practical effectuation there is constructed a "magical" bridge between the everyday and the divine. This bridging is an attunement of harmony bringing together the soul and the divine in the fulfillment of nature as kinship. It is the *bios* which is a *praxis* of turning toward the All, as imitating the divine as *Kosmos*, as opposed to any ritual image of the divine, for the *bios* is an *activity* which seeks to cultivate a state of harmony from out of this incarnation. As written earlier, the doctrine of transmigration contains both an account of the opening from the divine to the world and suggests a path of return of the soul to the divine.

One way to briefly grasp how these paths are encompassed in the doctrine of transmigration comes from a brief consideration of the notions of kinship and sympathetic magic. James Frazer, another of the contemporaries of Cornford, who, while not in any way friendly to a notion of magic (as Wittgenstein laments in his own *Remarks on Frazer's Golden Bough*), portrays the notions of kinship and sympathetic magic in the following logical schema:

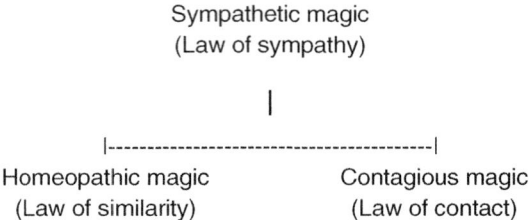

If we consider philosophy as a way of life and *theoria* which is an Apollonized version of sympathetic magic, and if we consider the doctrine of transmigration as a "totemic chant" of this teaching, then we can hear in this chant the specific laws of philosophy as those of similarity and contact. Each of these laws plays a role in the paths of event and remembrance or return contained within the doctrine of transmigration. The opening displays the law of similarity, or homeopathic magic, in that it shows an elaboration of an identical harmonic matrices which contain reinforcing opposites, as for instance the harmony of the body resembles the harmony of the Kosmos. It displays, moreover, the law of contact, or contagious magic, in that the "effect," or the soul, is similar to the "cause," and thus, these persist together amid their distance. The path of remembrance or return contains the law of similarity, for the basic requirement of return is an imitation of the divine by means of an attunement of its double, the soul. It contains the law of contact in that the presence of the divine spark amid the body incites the one to trace and seek its source.

The doctrine of transmigration, like the monochord, organizes these laws of kinship and magic within a narrative which does not position the motions of opening and return within a fatalistic providence, but instead, within a scenario which requires for its effectuation the decision of the initiate. It is a self-chosen pursuit which has as its goal the individual and collective transmigration through the life of the All, and it places its resources into achieving this return to the divine. Yet, it is not necessary from the everyday perspective for one to choose this path; it is only necessary if one decides to affirm this task. The overt "magical" element of free decision at the heart of the doctrine of transmigration consists not only as a description of the nature of self and world, but also of action and belief, of either the recognition and affirmation of this "account of truth," disclosed as sympathetic kinship of All, or, of a rejection of this scenario.

It is certain that many chose the latter option. Those who did take this decision attempted to become participants within the Pythagorean *bios*, those who, perhaps, already swayed amidst a similar rhythm. Nietzsche writing in an early fragment, *On Rhythm*, sets forth an explicit tie between magic and the harmonic association of rhythm (Apollo) to the tonal flux (Dionysus):

> The magic in rhythm consists in a quite elementary symbolism by which the regular and the orderly imposes itself on our understanding as a higher realm, a life above and beyond this irregular life; that part of us which has the power to move with the same rhythm follows the urging of that symbolic feeling and moves in unison with it or at least feels a strong urge to do so.[6]

For although the teaching implies that all and each will eventually choose this path, as required by the supposition of a divine All, it is not intimated that there is any urgency or compulsion to choose an explicit return to the divine. As we see in the *Phaedrus*, many, including Orpheus, who himself chose to become a bird, were criticized by Socrates, as life was simply a sickness healed by death. The Pythagorean doctrine specifies for the initiate a path of return to the divine through the *bios* and *theoria* of philosophy. But, is this just another empty promise, a fiction to seduce the self into a way of life, amidst a "truth regime?" A little lie to aid the breeding of exemplary specimens a la Plato? And, what of the time scale? Why must I sacrifice my discretion to a *bios* and *theoria* (magic) if that is not what I wish? These questions are significant, but merely intimate the murky region of belief. There is no way for us to gain access to the *alterity* of a personal event of decision in the other. What we can do, however, is to fathom the horizons which are operative in the incitement of the necessity for any initiatory decision as such. We have indicated the broad historical horizons of the Pythagorean movement, and we have hinted at the moment of belonging, or decision, via Nietzsche's thought of a "magic" of rhythm. But, we do not know why, beyond perhaps political or philosophical speculation, the Pythagoreans set forth a notion of an immortal soul with a destination that radically differed from the traditional Homeric narrative. The Pythagorean teaching tells us that the self relates to the All as a microcosm to a greater macrocosm. But, we must focus on the very fact of distinction as such, and thus, upon the meaning of the naming act which produces indicators to "identify" entities. A distinction per se is provoked via the limitedness of perspective and of mortal life. The impending event of death is intimated in the deaths of similars, and casts into relief the primary horizons for the possibility of the finite self. Our perspective is limited; yet, amidst this bodily opening, we sense the continuity of our own life with the life of All. With our imagination, we seek to fathom, to infer, the possibility of an All of which each of our lives is a singular expression. It is this intimacy betwixt the self and the All which unleashes a response to the decrees of Dike, the Goddess of terrestrial justice who demands the demise of each life which had so audaciously sought to live. This is a reference to the fragment of Anaximander, purported to be a teacher of Pythagoras. Nietzsche's translation of this first fragment of Western philosophy, reads:

> Whence things have their origin, there they must also pass away according to necessity; for they must pay penalty and be judged for their injustice, according to the ordinance of time.[7]

This is an allegory of the situation of the mortal, one who must meet her demise "according to the ordinance of time." References, however, to "penalty" and "injustice" must not be equivocated with their Hinduist, Christian, or Platonic relatives. The mortal does not want to die; the penalty is the denial of its bodily self and its life amid the dimension of its being. Life is colored with the metaphor of injustice, as justice resides in humility.

Amidst these horizons, we can suggest that Pythagoras seeks to bring a determinant notion of return within the horizons of Anaximander, one that would accord with the Orphic background of the latter in his focus upon time and necessity. The latter offers us a source which is unlimited, drawn into limit and thus giving rise to tragic individuals, condemned to die for their own injustice. This strategy of Pythagoras consists in proposing a binding link or conduit between the limited and unlimited in a manner which resembles what was suggested earlier in our considerations of the relation of Homer and Pythagoras. The body, this one here, will meet its demise; yet, the soul which had animated that body, and others before it, will inhabit another body as a constituent of the All. An extended kinship is suggested in this way for the *Kosmos*, yet, there remains the self, this coalescence of the body and soul. The finite self as be-ing, a phenomenon, must also be counted amongst the kinship of the All. With this realization, we can ascertain that the soul is not that of a shadow of nostalgia as with Homer; nor does the soul die even before the body meets its demise. The soul migrates on through the life of the All, abiding the memory of each singular self along on its pathways toward the All, and in this way, abides a greater self. One pursues these intimations of the divine through remembrance, in which one becomes open to the migration of the "soul" across the Unlimited into another manifestation of self. There is of course the question of the *telos*, the end, the attainment of the goal, of a return to the divine All. In other words, the question is that of the possibility for an ultimate "transcendence of the wheel of incarnations," an event via which a self of remembered selves, becomes the All. It would seem from our previous discussions, that such a transcendence of the wheel maintains the connotations of transmigration as 'justice' and punishment with its inherent denial of the body. As we will see in more detail, the specific magical character of the Pythagorean philosophy precludes the notion of a mystical end or transcendence. In its stead, there is a magical *praxis* of remembrance and attunement in the cultivation of a way of life that was attuned to, and was sheltered by, the divine All. In other words, there is no need to go anywhere, despite the confusions engendered by our language.

The doctrine of transmigration contains, if we contemplate the implications of the narrative (and what we must already know in order to understand the story even at a simple level) an account of the poetic opening of the divine to the soul amidst body, an account encompassed to a great extent through the exoteric study of the physical, mathematical, and musical nature of the universe. It also contains an account and practice of attunement effectuated by a recollection of this opening, but a remembrance which begins, not from the position of the divine, but from the phenomenal regions of the soul and body, of the finite self. In the following pages, I will therefore examine these pathways which are implied within and required by the doctrine of transmigration. I will first present the "Path of the Event" (or opening, to speak as we do) which concerns itself with a speculative elaboration of the event of the world. This will concern itself with cosmogony, number theory, harmony, and body. I will next examine the "Path of Remembrance, or Return," through an examination of the rudiments of a path of resemblance and remembrance which will be the cultivation of attunement in the esoteric initiate. This will emphasize the situation of the initiate as being amidst body, and thus, will highlight the practices relating to the *symbola*, or rules of piety, concerning such issues as herbalism, dietetics, medicine, music, and dreams.

The Path of the Event[8]

It has been suggested that the doctrine of transmigration, as a mythopoetic symbol, implies a doctrine of the opening of the One to the Many. This doctrine is an assemblage of cosmogonical and cosmological principles which through an indefinite divine event, there is the "generation" of number, harmony, sensible objects, and life, an event which gives forth the present world-order. Initially, under the aspect of this "grammar of the event," what we have to examine is the coming into being of a world in which there is delineated a continuum from its source in the divine to the everyday sensible bodies which surround us. The path of event not only gives an explicit account of the existence and horizons of the self, but also displays a resemblance betwixt the self and the All, or the microcosm and macrocosm, thus implying a path of return to the All by the self.

One way to embark upon this discussion is with a consideration of the *tetractys*, or tetrad, also known as the Divine Quaternary. Theon of Smyrna, in a work, entitled, "How many Tetractys Are There?," describes eleven quaternaries which are constitutive of a perfect world, a *Kosmos* which is "geometrically, harmonically and arithmetically arranged, containing in power the entire nature of number, every magnitude and every body, whether simple or composite."[9] Such a world is perfect since "everything is part of it, and it is itself apart of nothing else."[10] In this way, the *tetractys* is a "universal pattern" that underlies all reality, from the primary entities of number to the life of the self, united in an extended field of kinship. Theon of Smyrna summarizes:

> Thus the first quaternary is 1, 2, 3, 4. The second is unity, the side, the square, the cube. The third is the point, line, the surface, the solid. The fourth is fire, air, water, earth. The fifth is the pyramid, the octahedron, the icosahedron, the cube. The sixth is the seed, the length, the width, the height. The seventh is man, the family, the village, the city. The eighth is thought, science, opinion, sense. The ninth is the rational, the emotional and the willful parts of the soul, and the body. The tenth is spring, summer, autumn, and winter. The eleventh is childhood, adolescence, maturity, and old age.[11]

The symbolism of the tetractys, the "fount of everflowing nature," itself an excession of the divine, intimates the entirety of experience and being, amidst an opening of an extended kinship, and can be easily encompassed by the doctrine of transmigration. Cornford, in his "Mysticism and Science," lists the notions which are contained in the *tetractys*, displaying how a symbol can imply or contain a depth of wisdom and knowledge:

1. a system of numbers;
2. it symbolizes the elements of number which are the elements of things;
3. it contains the concordant ratios of musical harmony;
4. it contains the root and fountain of everything in nature.

We see that the tetractys, symbolizing the world order, contains within itself the traces of its emergence, and thus guides us in an elaboration of the event. Cornford writes:

> We have seen how, in the primitive symbolism of the tetractys, the Monad was the divine, all-inclusive unity, containing both the opposites, male and female, Limited and Unlimited according to the old cosmogonical scheme, from the undifferentiated unity emerge two opposite principles, and these are recombined to generate determinate (limited/things—the series of numbers and the things which represent or embody (μιμεισθαι) numbers, thus any determinate thing will, like the Orphic soul, contain both principles, good and evil, light and darkness.[12]

Cornford indicates here the radical continuum which we seek to elaborate the path of the tetractys. Such a path, we will remark, moves from the invisible (number) to the visible (being), a specification, once again, which may be lost if one fails to adequately distinguish the Pythagorean from Orphic teaching with regards to an attunement in the *bios* and a ritual purification in the *teletai*, respectively. If number is the symbolic principle, the source, and the roots of all things, it is the All which is the source and "principle" of number, of a "unity" which is not number, but the marriage of the limited and unlimited. Theon of Smyrna writes:

> Unity is the principle of all things and the most dominant of all that is: all things emanate from it and it emanates from nothing. It is immutable and never departs from its own nature through multiplication (1×1=1). Everything that is intelligible and not yet created exists in it: the nature of ideas, God himself, the soul, the beautiful and the good and every intelligible essence such as beauty itself, justice itself, equality itself for we conceive of each of these things as being one and as existing in itself.[13]

But, yet, in some way, in our narrative, the One becomes something else, or there is the emergence of Two. The transition from One to Two, of a unity to a multiplicity has been cast to a great extent within the horizons of cosmology.

The principle of number is the Monad, which is itself not a number; the elements of number are the Limit (*peras*) and Unlimited (*apeiron*). One can recall the significance of these elements in the conception of a universal sympathetic being which breathes in the Void, or is engendered via the drawing into itself of the Unlimited by the Limited, that is, the projection of boundaries. These elements, and this predicament, are either generated by or issued forth from the Monad, which, as Cornford suggests, are contained by this "Unity." It is through this "opposition," between *peras* and *apeiron*, that One becomes explicitly other than itself. This transition is necessarily involved in this scenario of opposites. For, instead of characterizing the generation of the sensible world as an artifact of conflict, one could contend that Limit sublimates the Unlimited, thus, generating the All and each. Theon of Smyrna writes about this transition:

> The first increase, the first change from unity is made by the doubling of unity which becomes 2, in which are seen matter and all that is perceptible, the generation of motion, multiplicity and addition, composition and the relationship of one thing to another.[14]

This symbolic "doubling" of the Monad opens up the possibility of the physical state of being, and thus of a relationship betwixt the dimensions of *physis* and *deos*. This relationship, the first possibility of *logos*, as the Dyad, is completed in the Three, the triad, which bridges duality, and as will be detailed below, first introduces *harmonia*, mythically described as a "joining together." This is distinct from a scenario of external mediation, as what is cast into relief is the symbolic emergence of a world order, exemplified in the Four, or the *tetractys*, an order that is primordial. In this way, the tetractys is the "numerical paradigm of whole systems."[15] It contains within itself the full definition of the continuity between the divine and the world, conceived in this allegorical scenario, as the radical continuum of the invisible to the visible. It "represents the vertical hierarchy between one and many."[16]

Implicit in the symbol of the tetractys, therefore, is not only an elaboration of the relationship between the divine and the world, but also the relationship between the divine and, on the one hand, the sensible object itself, and on the other hand, the soul. An examination of these relationships allows us to fathom the symbolic generation of the body and soul from the "original" excession of the divine. This generation moves from points to plane and to regular solids, which when they approach the fractal, are imbued with the interior and exterior life of music, as the song that is sung from this "meeting place" of Limit and Unlimited amidst the body, the living singular. K.S. Guthrie writes:

> Hence in the realm of space, the tetractys represents the continuity linking the dimensionless point with the manifestation of the first body.[17]

This is a pathway from the invisibility of number to the visibility of things, these being differing states within a single harmonious being. We thus must consider how the invisible becomes visible. A first indication of this comes from an analogy provided by a graphic representation of the tetractys:

The sequence of numbers becomes represented in the form of a triangle. Or, perhaps, it displays an excession of the One to the Many? Yet, staying within the parameters of cosmology, each of these numbers is analogous to differing yet static geometrical formations. One is the point, while although we know these do not really exist, can be plotted with a simple dot. Likewise, the Two becomes a line, Three, a surface, and Four, a solid. The geometrical formation is thus analogous to the monochord and the body, for it points to, or lets you hear, the invisible from the standpoint of the visible, the silent. The geometrical formation provides a resemblance to that which is there, but cannot show itself except through analogy. But, as these analogies are threaded into the narrative of the doctrine of transmigration, they are only of temporary service, for there is not an analogy for the divine, but as we will see in the next section, only a way of life which emphasizes the "invisible" motions of the body, and not of the ritual image.

We can thus see that the tetractys intimates the possibility of a transition from number to being, but also accounts for the manifestation of the world order. How the tetractys, as a system of numbers, accounts for the generation of sensible objects is indicated by its containment of the elements of numbers which are the elements of things. The elements of number, *peras* and *apeiron* coalesce in the generation of number, which is itself therefore an artifact of the original unity of the divine. It is number which harbors these elements within the world order. For instance, the tetractys is a triangular number composed of consecutive integers, incorporating odd and even numbers. The distinction between odd and even numbers and its relationship to *peras* and *apeiron*, as the elements of number, can be shown graphically:

Odd number   Even number

An odd integer is a square number composed of consecutive odd integers of 1, 3, 5, and 7, which displays an analogy of Limit in the form of a square. An even integer is an oblong number composed of consecutive even integers 2, 4, 6, and 8, displaying an analogy of the Unlimited in the form of a rectangle. This intimation of the relationship of number and being indicates an emphasis upon symmetry, and thus, of a distance between divine and nature, thus illuminating the path of opening from the divine. Moreover, this geometrical example suggests the participation of the elements of number in the elements of things, thereby casting light on the claim that the tetractys is a fountain of everflowing nature. Cornford comments on the analogy between number and being:

> The geometrical character of Pythagorean arithmetic must not be forgotten. Indeed, we are told that Pythagoras identified geometry with science (ιστορια) in general. In the unlimited darkness of night all objects lose to the eye their colors and shapes; in the daily renewed creation of the dawn of light they resume their distinct forms, their surfaces and colors (χροια in Pythagorean language means both). Thus, in the physical world, light, the vehicle of knowledge, acts as a limiting principle, which informs the blank darkness with bodies bounded by measurable planes and distinguished by all varieties of color. The body is thus a visible thing in which two opposite principles meet—the Unlimited (darkness, "air," void space) and Limit, identified with the colored space (ειδος, ιδεα, μορφή, σχεμα). True to its mathematical

character, Pythagoreanism tends to conceive a visible body as essentially a geometrical solid, whose surfaces are ultimately reducible to number and their relations.[18]

If, as Cornford suggests, Pythagoras "identified geometry with science," we can clearly discern the problematic surrounding his strict separation of mysticism and science. As we have seen, he has chosen to interpret the presence of "opposites," of *peras* and *apeiron*, in the body as contradictory elements. Yet, what he fails to see is that these elements are previously unified in the divine, which through the interaction of these elements accomplishes the generation of a single, harmonious being.

In this way, if geometry is designated as "science," then it could be suggested that geometry is a unique *symbola* of a "magic" which seeks the transcendence of the visible into the invisible. The exoteric, geometrical elaboration of the path of event presents a delineation of visible forms which resemble not only the world as such, but a world which is the visible testimony of an originative act of the divine, an act which is approached through the esoteric practice of the cultivation of attunement with the All.

The elements of number meet to generate bodies of ever variable and complex geometrical compositions. And, keeping in mind Dillon's suggestion that the Pythagoreans employed *symbola* in their method of education, each number is analogous to various physical elements contained within the world order. From Plato's *Timaeus*, we have the report of number as generating the regular solids, these which symbolize the constituent elements of the world: the dodecahedron, a solid of 12 sides, symbolizes Aither; the icosahedron, a solid of 20 sides, symbolizes water; the cube, 6 sides, earth; the tetrahedron, 4 sides, fire; and the octahedron, 8 sides, air. If we consider number and being as "positions" along a continuum of inauguration, there would be no difficulty in conceiving of the link between the two, even in terms of contemporary science. In many ways, this consideration of number has provided many of the tools we will need to comprehend the excession, in the poetic narrative, of a divinely generated physical *Kosmos*. Number intimates the symbolical bridge betwixt the everyday and the divine.

Yet, it seems that we remain, in this region of geometry, only upon the surface of things, and with these sources, contained within the narrow horizons of the metaphoricity of light. However, as we will see, the tetractys as a symbol of the world order also brings us beyond the surface. For if we only attempt an understanding of the world based solely on an application of the elements of number, and upon the table of opposites which is essentially derivative of these elements, we cannot conceive of life, or, of soul amidst this geometrical matrix. Or, in other words, there must be the analogy of the divine Monad, or unity, for each region of being, and in the dimension of the physical *Kosmos*, the analogy is that of the soul.

It is mathematical harmony (Music) which allows the inquiry to pass beyond the surface into the fluctuations and movements of cosmic life. An understanding of this will allow us to grasp my earlier comment that the "joining together" of *harmonia* is not an act of mere mediation of extremes, but shows these contraries, the elements of number, *peras* and *apeiron* as generated from the original "unity" of the All. If it was said that two brought about the possibility of *logos*, three establishes this *logos* as harmony. This harmonia is the *mythical* "coalescence" of numerical *peras* and the "otherwise indefinite realm of manifestation."[19] Harmony arises through a joining of the latter and the "limiting power of number." If we take musical harmony as our example, this limiting power would translate into the following: "Number bridges tonal flux by mediation or harmonia."[20] This can be displayed through a consideration of the monochord: [21]

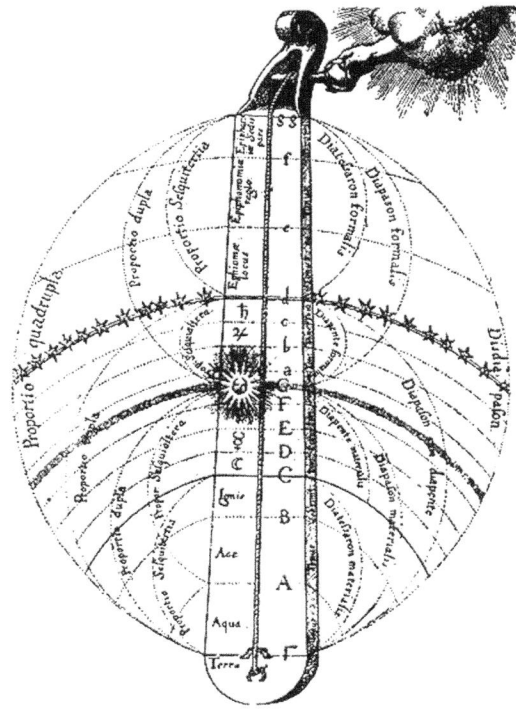

The Divine Monochord[22]

The monochord reveals that "the primary principles of *peras* and *apeiron* underlie the realm of acoustic phenomena."[23] In that numerical proportions underlie musical harmony, the indefinite continuum of tonal flux, succumbs to the limiting power of number. Kenneth Guthrie writes:

> Through the power of limit, the most formal manifestation of which is Number, harmonic nodal points naturally and innately exist on the string, dividing its length in halves, thirds, fourths and so on.[24]

This displays the possibility of a harmonic tonal and overtone series, the latter being the foundation of the musical scale. This can be demonstrated by lightly placing a finger on the string of a lyre (or guitar) over the harmonic divisions. This will reveal the overtones, which will not sound anywhere except at these specific divisions. K.S. Guthrie writes with respect to this overtone series:

> The overtone series provides, as it were, the architectural foundation of the musical scale, the basic "field" of which is the octave, 1:2, or the doubling of the vibrational frequency, which inversely correlates with a halving of the string.[25]

In this way, we can see the first mediation of the extremes which exist on the monochord, which is, if its string is plucked alone, the analogy for the tonal flux. The tonal flux is bridged by number in the sense of a *harmonia* that is engendered "through the medium of numerical proportion or *logos*."[26] From this insight that this propaedeutic mediation of extremes takes place as such through numerical *logos*, there remain but two steps which lead to the construction of the musical scale. These steps are two different kinds of numerical mediation, arithmetic and harmonic (the octave of 6:12 is his frame of reference). The first is represented as follows:

$$\frac{A + B}{2} \qquad \frac{6 + 12}{2}$$

The arithmetic medium is thus a vibration of 9, which, if placed into relation with 6, yields the ratio of 2:3, which is the perfect fifth. The harmonic mean is represented as follows:

$$\frac{2AB}{A + B} \qquad \frac{2(6)(12)}{6 + 12}$$

The harmonic mean in the octave 6:12 is 8, and in relation to 6, there is generated 6:8, or 3:4, the perfect fourth, which is the inverse of the perfect fifth. We can thus see that *given a tonal flux*, we can generate the foundations of the musical scale through a process of numerical—arithmetic and harmonic—mediation.

Yet, what we can also see is that *this music scale as such is already contained in the flux*, or in the string of the monochord, and it was us, who through the intervention of our constructions and measurements, revealed this to be the case. Once again, it is a case of "our way of speaking" and the misleading grammar of our mythical rearticulation.

In an appendix to Guthrie's *Pythagorean Sourcebook*, entitled, "The Formation and Ratios of the Pythagorean Scale," David Fideler elaborates on the previous by providing a chart of the ratios of the Pythagorean scale and the corresponding string lengths for these ratios on the monochord. He writes with respect to the Pythagorean scale:

> In the case of the scale, the "opposite" of the high (2) and the low (1)—the two extremes of the octave—are united in one continuum of tonal relationships through the use of a variety of forms of proportion which actively mediate between two extremes.[27]

For the rest of the article, he invites us to witness the formation of the musical scale through the construction of a monochord. In light of its analogous status to the body, this suggestion is very important for grasping the intimate connection the Pythagoreans had considered the *bios* and *theoria*, or in other, ultimately misleading words, the theoretical and the practical. I will therefore present this exercise in the following.

Fideler begins:

> The best way to understand the mathematical principles of harmonic mediation involves actually charting out and playing out the ratios of the scale on the monochord.[28]

After detailing the construction of the monochord, he describes the playing of the overtone series, the tones of which are located at the half, quarter, and third lengths of the string, played by lightly touching the nodal point on the string with the finger, and plucking with a finger on the other hand. He also details the playing of what he calls the "harmonic 'Tetractys,' or the perfect consonances: 1:2 (octave), 2:3 (perfect fifth), and 3:4 (perfect fourth)." He writes, as a guide for the playing:

> Listen carefully to these ratios and reflect on the fact that you are actually hearing the relationships between these primary whole numbers.[29]

Fideler continues to generate the Pythagorean scale, exhibited in deference to the god of grammar as a bridging of extremes by the *logos* of musical harmony. The alleged means of the bridging of the extremes, however, as we see in his further demonstration, are already there, resonating not only as the numerical ratios, but in the "living" body of the monochord itself. The basic ratios are there in any string with tension. The completed scale of notes can only be elaborated after the monochord has been tensed. We see here an intimate interaction between musical harmony and the instrument, or as we have characterized the monochord, as a symbol.

Fideler details the steps to the final scale:

1. the octave (1:2);
2. the arithmetic mean, or the perfect fifth (C-G-c);
3. the harmonic mean, or the perfect fourth (C-F-c);
4. the musical proportion, the basis of the scale (C-F-G-c);
5. the remaining whole tone intervals (C-D, D-E, G-A, A-B);
6. the leimma or semitone (E-F and B-c), the relationship between the perfect fourth and three whole tones;
7. the entire scale (C-D-E-F-G-A-B-C).

He concludes this instruction with this statement:

> Through the use of arithmetic, harmonic and geometric proportion the two extremes have be successfully united.[30]

This provides us with an interesting glimpse of what may have some resemblance to a genuine method of Pythagorean instruction. What is important is that this "unification" is not a "mediation" of existent "extremes," but an exoteric procedure of disclosing to the initiate an esoteric harmony which is always already there.

As suggested earlier, the doctrine of transmigration is yet another of these mnemotechnic devices, but one that is ultimately less tangible in that it can only be recounted in spoken, worldly narrative. And this is where we must recall the essay of Theon of Smyrna concerning the tetractys, an abbreviation of transmigration which sets forth the world and its source. It is in the last five levels which describe the factical world of life, of the world of the present, a dimension which as finite existence is the natural home and perspective for the doctrine of transmigration as a mnemotechnic symbol of an oral dissemination of terrestrial life. Theon writes:

> The seventh is man, the family, the village, the city. The eighth is thought, science, opinion, sense. The ninth is the rational, the emotional and the willful parts of the soul, and the body. The tenth is spring, summer, autumn, and winter. The eleventh is childhood, adolescence, maturity, and old age.[31]

Amidst the myth of transmigration, a plethora of souls abides successive bodies throughout differing temporal and political worlds. In addition, it is just not human bodies, but all living bodies. A vast reproduction (birth, life, death) of bodies is therefore implied in the doctrine of transmigration. In a living symbolism of divine love, a male and a female, bring forth a novel body and self. As each body eventually dies, its soul is released, perhaps, as a vibration, a song, one that may continue to wander upon the earth, waiting for another body. The soul of this new self is that of the wanderer who awaited this birth. Yet, to speak in the jargon of Cornford, the parents give the child its animal spirit, its life and its biological heredity, but, they do not give the child its soul. The wandering souls that enter the new bodies to become new selves are nomadic, drawn, like to like, toward this new body, at a similar rhythm these dance. In this way, the soul transcends the lineage of blood kinship, and perhaps, of political allegiance, in that the soul is older than its body and blood. The soul migrates throughout the extended kinship of the bodies of the All. One does not suffer the "sins of the father" for the soul comes from another source, from another deceased self.

It could be suggested that amid this domain of the terrestrial, it is the body which is Limited, and it is the soul, and that which it points to, as its sets over actuality a myriad constellation of infinite possibility, is Unlimited. Amid such a domain and field of horizons, of a terrestrial perspective, it is the body which innately coordinates the field of priorities. Amidst this domain, together with our fellow wanderers, we seek remembrance, memory, or at least clues to this memory, which indicates itself everywhere, in the diurnal cycle, in the orbits of the stars, sun, moon, and planets.

Yet, one may not be able to see what is right in front of his or her eyes due to the noise and confusion of the din, of that realm where *bios* and *theoria* persist in dissonant rupture, in the realm of human forgetfulness. It is in the context of this state of forgetfulness, of inexorable distraction, that a symbol with depth can provide a focus for the continuation of memory into the future. The doctrine of transmigration contains, in analogy to the monochord and the generation of *physis* from number, an account of the coming into being of the world and soul in what I have called the path of opening. This path is required by the doctrine as it posits a soul which has come to be in a world from its source in the All. The path of the event provides the account that is required by the doctrine. This path shows the intimacy between notions of a "mathematical conception of nature" and the conception of the "embodied" soul which finds itself amidst this "natural" world.

The Path of Remembrance, or Return[32]

Dillon in his work, *The Golden Chain*, writes that the notion of an extended sympathy is the horizon necessary for the practice of sympathetic magic. In this way, a phenomenal, symbolic act or being, may be plied to effectuate some intention within a continuity of resemblance. Dillon portrays this notion of sympathy:

> Here we find Origen drawing on the notion of *sympatheia* to explain what physical effect powerful names can have on us, or on others when we make use of them. The resonances they give forth set up favorable vibrations within us, rather as the Pythagoreans felt was done by the right sort of music. Such resonances are independent of the purpose or state of the utterer: they have a natural power independent of meaning.[33]

This "natural power independent of meaning," gives life to the "powerful name" as it is spoken. It is the "right sort of music" which sets forth "favorable vibrations within us." This "natural power," the divine spark amidst the phenomenal opening of sympathy, can be sublimated and directed in order to affect specific intentions. It is important how one conceives of this "natural power" in order to specify the precise pathway to be chosen. For the power is clearly there, only the intention and method remain to be decided and initiated. Confronted by the question, "What is a Philosopher?" it is reported that Pythagoras, who allegedly first spoke "philosophy," responded with the following parable:

> Pythagoras replied that life seemed to him like the gathering when the great games were held, which were attended by the whole of Greece. For there some men sought to win fame and the glory of the crown by exciting their bodies, others were attracted by the gain and profit of buying and selling, but there was one kind of man, the noblest of all, who sought neither applause nor profit, but came in order to watch and wanted to see what was happening and how. So too among us, who have migrated into this life from a different life and mode of being, as if from some city to a crowded festival, some are slaves to fame, others to money, but there are some rare spirits who, holding all else as nothing, eagerly contemplate the universe, these he calls lovers of wisdom (philosopher); and as the festival it most becomes a gentleman to be a spectator without thought of personal gain so in life the contemplation and understanding of the universe is fall superior to other pursuits.[34]

According to the mythical narrative, this life is "one" in a succession of lives, persisting in a cycle of incarnations which derives its "providence" from the divine source from which it originally emanated. This insight allows the philosopher to gain a sense of detachment from the tenuousness of fame and fortune, though his contemplation can never be detached from a specific *praxis*. To detach oneself is to pursue a path to the divine that requires the cultivation of a space which "nurtures" a specific *bios* and *theoria*, one apart from the pretentious and banal wastelands of fame and fortune.

The description of the philosopher in the previous citation could well be construed, with its emphasis on the notion of the "spectator," to resemble the "objective" scientist. Yet, what is crucial is the meaning of "what is happening and how." For the "object" of contemplation for the Pythagoreans is the world in its effusion from and as the visible and musical analogue of the divine. In this way, "what is happening and how," described in the doctrine of transmigration, renders the "spectator" a necessary participant within the divine process. We saw the "numerological bridge" which extends from the divine to the world, and have seen how this bridge situates the "presence" of the divine in the world. It is in this context that we must gain an understanding of the personal decision to participate in a Pythagorean "magic" that is construed as a philosophical *bios*.

It is this "magic," conceived as the sublimation of a "natural power independent of meaning," which provides for the possibility of a path of return. This element of "magic," as the sublimation of a "natural power" corresponds in the Pythagorean philosophy to the *bios*. It is a way of life, moreover, which is Apollonized through a coherent *theoria*, of the path of opening and the symbola of practical life. This serves to distinguish the Pythagoreans from other ways of life. Guthrie specifies the basis of this distinction:

> Assimilation to God was for him, as we have seen, the goal of life. At the same time, unlike the Orphics and their kind, he and his followers united with these aspirations a philosophy rooted in the twin ideas of limit and order, *peras* and *Kosmos*.[35]

The practice of sympathetic magic, or the *bios*, is Apollonized by a *theoria* which is organized around the ideas of limit and self-knowledge. The site of the soul is the body, and it is from this point of departure, of limit, which the initiate must set off on the journey of this self through the ways and byways of the All. For while it could be argued that each of these are elements of a *theoria*, it is significant that the transition from the exoteric to the esoteric dimensions of the teaching was associated with the "cultivation" of a way of life of attunement, one guided by the spoken words of *akousmatikoi*, words about the body, self, and life. The living body is not to be forgotten, for it, like the *Kosmos*, opens from a divine source. In this way, we can compare a mere mathematical education with the ritual of Cornford's pseudo-Orphics. For both of these are ultimately enmeshed in the visible only, their images are static, narrow, dead and are thus disconnected from a philosophical life which participates in and may become attuned with the All. It is the way of life which allows the images of mathematics to come to life in a *bios* which consists in a "tuning of the soul in consonance with the celestial *harmony*."[36] This tuning cannot and must not discard the body, which bestows an intimation of the wisdom of the integral self.

Dillon provides us with an indication of the meaning of this tuning of the soul referring to "Pythagoras' discovery of musical harmony, and the regulation of the disorder of sense of hearing by the application of *logos*."[37] An application of a *logos* does not consist in an external regimentation of sense, but of an awakening of the All in the remembrance of each. As we have seen, the original diremption of the One to the Two set forth the first possibility for *logos*, while the Three, or harmony, made this *logos* actual in the Four, or world order. The application of a *logos*, one which sends from the divine out flashing, is thus the explicit recognition of the divine amidst and as the world.

This calls to mind the suggestion by Guthrie that the doctrine of transmigration provides for the possibility of the *a priori*, and the discovery of this *a priori* through a process of recollection. A contemplation of the world, as we saw in the last section with the monochord, draws us on beyond this perspective toward a broader dimension of experience. In this way, the path of return is a process of recollecting the prior opening, but from the standpoint of the soul amidst body. And thus, the path of return requires a specific *bios* in order to accomplish its aspiration.

This is not to suggest however that nothing is known of this path, that each must begin this process *ex nihilo*. We have many sources which describes the activities of the Pythagoreans, the testimonial "evidence" given by and about Pythagoras with regard to his past lives and his various, seemingly impossible abilities and actions. These references, although taken with a prudent caution, harbor a promise and are meant to convey authority for the doctrine of transmigration as a founding myth. However, these references also contain, if we look more deeply, the elements which constitute the path of remembrance or return, but one which blossoms as yet another allegory.

The Pythagorean Bios: A Tentative Indication

The various *Lives of Pythagoras* which I briefly outlined above will provide us with a meager glimpse of the various elements of the *bios*. But, what we must remember is the forgetfulness of an historical culture which has few mnemotechnic resources. And, coupled with the early Pythagorean resistance to writing, and preference for the spoken word, we have little else to go on. We have a motley throng of testimonies, which can aid our interpretation, if, we remember the symbolic character of this discussion, and of the overriding influence of the doctrine of transmigration. Indeed, there are many *magics*, and there are many interpretations of the doctrine of transmigration. Burkert lists haphazardly our many possible fates: we either run forever in a circle through all spheres of the cosmos; sheer chance decides on the reincarnation, or else a judgment of the dead; it is a morally blameless conduct that guarantees the better lot or else the bare fact of ritual initiation that frees from guilt. Yet, before we decide amongst these possible fates, we must be guided by the notion of an extended kinship and the necessity of many bodies for one soul. In this light, we can ascertain that the location of the self lies before, beyond, and after any singular individuality, pointing the self toward its *greater self*, and to its condition in the All. A grand mixture of souls and bodies, strangers and friends, dwell together, experience together, hoping to remember more of themselves. Yet, it is one thing to *say* or *write* remembrance, and another to *do* remembrance. For instance, Photius relates that the path of return is a discipline, a training of ascent which aspires to higher levels of being.[38] Diogenes Laertius informs us that the path of return is intimately associated with memory, as we can see in the parable in which Pythagoras chose memory when he was denied immortality. Although this choice implied that he would have to be mortal, it is memory which is the key to immortality, the thread out of the labyrinth. Moreover, memory is emphasized by Iamblichus and Porphyry as a process of recollection, the former in the sense of a pedagogical practice of regression, the latter in the context of a cultivation of remembrance of the divine through the detection of resemblances in the world. And, this remembrance, for the latter, is associated with practical, ethical imperatives such as respect for each of the All, practiced through vegetarianism.

The Pythagorean *bios* therefore can be seen as a cultivation of attunement, or a training of attunement, awakening memory, not only to establish the *a priori* connection of the divine and the world, a service provided by Pythagoras, but also as a guide along a path a deeper remembrance via an exploration of the gifts of the divine, the exuberant world of the play betwixt the gods. In this way, we can appreciate the significance of the *symbola* disseminated by the Pythagoreans in their teaching. Yet, we must take these symbola in their broadest sense, as an exoteric trace of an esoteric wisdom. Diogenes Laertius explains:

> These disciplines he used as degrees of preparation to the contemplation of the really existent things, by an artistic principle diverting the eyes of the mind from corporal things, whose manner and state never remain in the same condition, to a desire for true spiritual food.[39]

Symbola, as considered in this context, may therefore include the mathematical studies, the rules of piety in the *Golden Verses* and the Pythagorean sentences of Sextus Empiricus, which guided one in the realm of the everyday, the strictures upon the treatment of the body and the world, and finally, various practices such as musical healing, meditation, and the burning of incense, aromas, massage, and suggestions for a diet. The broadening of the usual notion of a "text" to include these symbols allows us to at least intimate an integral self amidst its world, body, life. This "text" is a tangible "thing" which may allow a reminiscence of the divine source of All.

It is in this context which we must interpret the notion of a "natural power independent of meaning," which provides for the possibility of a philosophical magic, as a matrix of practices which explore the "hidden virtues," or qualities of phenomenal manifestations, such as music, color, aroma, herbs, talismans, and shamanistic techniques. In this sense, the symbola are the "totems" which will be deployed as mediums pointing toward a dimension beyond the prevailing lifeworld, and through this enactment of a pathway, as a building of futurity, we apprehend the intimate interplay of singulars amidst these dimensions along the road of an exploration of the All. These "totems," as the proper techniques,[40] or the *symbola* thereof, are arranged in the *bios* which is chosen and lived, and are the necessary analogues to a transmigration throughout the myriad circuits of the All.

We have seen how Cornford describes this analogy between *theoria* and *bios* with his statement that the "beliefs of a religious community in its earliest stages are externalized in its rule of life . . . "[41] It is this process of symbolic externalization, if we can indeed isolate it so neatly, that responds to the "natural power independent of meaning." This sheds light upon Cornford's reference to the "construction of the seen-order providing for the needs of the unseen." And, this seen-order is the symbolic *bios* and *theoria* of a philosophic, that is, sublimated, magical *praxis*.

In the following, I will outline certain aspects of this process of "externalization," of a "harmonious grouping" which combines "all the means and objects of knowledge," by which a "natural power," such as music, is to be "harnessed" to allow a *theoria* of measure, limit and order to be analogous, or attuned, with a *bios* seeking a return to the divine through the training, or less athletically, less gravely, as an ironic path of *closing-in-on*.

Iamblichus writes of a daily program of the Pythagoreans. It begins with solitary morning walks in quiet places "until they had gained inner serenity." This follows a gathering of friends for the "discussion of disciplines and doctrines, and in the correction of manners." After this gathering, they "turned their attention to the health of the body," engaging in massage, exercise, oratory, and sometimes wrestling. They "lunched on bread and honey, or on the honeycomb, avoiding wine," meeting with guests and strangers. They "once more betook themselves to walking, yet not alone, as in the morning walk, but in parties of two or three." They returned for bathing and gathered in a common dining room. "Then were performed libations and sacrifices, with fumigations and incense," after which followed a supper of "herbs, raw and boiled, maize, wine, and every food that is eaten with bread."[42] The supper was followed by libations and readings[43] by younger members of what the "eldest advised." The gathering was closed with the speaking of precepts by the eldest, after which "all separated to go home." Porphyry also writes about the daily routine of living:

> He himself held morning conferences at his residence, composing his soul with the music of the lyre, and singing certain ancient paeans of Thales. He also sang verses of Homer and Hesiod, which seemed to soothe the mind. He danced certain dances which he thought conferred on the body agility and health. Walks he took not too promiscuously, but only in company of

one or two companions, in temples of sacred graves, selecting the most quiet and beautiful places.[44]

Porphyry emphasizes the elements of friendship and community in this depiction, pointing out the role of Pythagoras as a healer:

> While they were in good health he always conversed with them; if they were sick, he nursed them; if they were afflicted in mind, he solaced them, some by incantations and magic charms, others by music. He had prepared songs for the diseases of the body, by singing which he cured the sick. He had also some that caused forgetfulness of sorrow, mitigation of anger, and destruction of lust.[45]

Porphyry describes a vegetarian diet of honey for breakfast; millet, barley, and herbs for dinner; poppy seed, sesame, skin of the sea-onion, the flowers of daffodils, the leaves of mallows, and chick peas to "quiet his hunger;" and to "quench his thirst," cucumber seeds, raisins, coriander flowers, mallow seeds, purslane, scraped cheese, wheat meal and cream, "all of which is mixed up with wild honey."[46]

There is a strong symbolic significance in this selection of diet, one that is closely related to the Pythagorean notion of biotic health. For instance, with regard to the herbs, poppy seed procures rest and sleep, and it contributes to the health of the lungs. Purslane also aids the respiratory system and wards off "venereous dreams." Cucumber works in a similar way to the latter and like the poppy and purslane, is associated with the moon and with cold, the agents of bad sleep.[47] Mallow seeds also aid the respiratory system and can be used to cure bronchitis.[48] It is interesting that these herbs have beneficial effects on the respiratory system in that the Pythagorean teaching described the soul as breath. Yet, it is not just the air, but each of the elements. For instance, there are also symbols which intimate the prohibition of certain foods. Clarkson writes in *Magic Gardens*:

> The Greek Pythagoras, sixth century B.C., advised against eating beans because the black spot was indicative of death, this superstition thus identifying the type of beans common at that time.[49]

Here she gives an alternative interpretation to the banality that everyone already always knows about flatulence; but, with a little more seriousness and thought, Clarkson provides further examples of plants which intimate the symbolic nature of food in general: "The Greeks valued vegetables so highly that representations of them were offered to the god Apollo, the radish in gold, the beet in silver, and the turnip in lead."[50] Once again, the radish is a cure for chronic bronchitis, and interestingly, it is also an aid for insomnia, which underscores the patronage of the *bios* by Apollo, the god of dreams. Another example which suggests the shamanistic dimensions of the practical *bios*, is indicated by Schultes and Hofmann, in their work, *Plants of the Gods*, where they discuss, along with the practices of many indigenous tribes, the mandrake root:

> Theophrastus in the third century B.C. wrote that collectors of medicinal plants drew circles around Mandrake, and they cut off the top part of the root while facing west; the remainder of the root was gathered after the collectors had performed certain dances and recited specific formulas. Two centuries earlier, the Greek Pythagoras had described mandrake root as an anthropo-morph or tiny human being. In Roman times that magic began extensively to be associated with the psychoactive properties of the plant.[51]

What we can ascertain from this reference to Pythagoras is the significance of the *doctrine of signatures*[52], or resemblance, of like of like, of sympathetic magic, which in this example is that of the root and the human being, one suggesting a relationship of kinship between similars. While we cannot decide whether or not Pythagoras actually advocated the use of mandrake, we can, as with the monochord, see the symbolic and practical importance of tangible entities in the life-web of the *bios*. And, similar to our description of the formation of the Pythagorean musical scale through the playing of the monochord, we can see that the body harbors within itself a wisdom which can be set free through the appropriate practices. The importance of the daily routine is the happening of a life of attuning, one that seeks to dance amidst the rhythms of the All, by a way of life which remained consistent with its return to the All, or, as a closing in on the divine.

This is a way of life of active participation amidst the world. It is, in this way that the initiate may become explicitly attuned to the cyclical precision of the *Kosmos*, and to the divine source that this latter intimates. It is in the same way that musical composition and healing, together with dance, allowed the Pythagoreans to "remember" the wisdom that is intimated in the living body. Iamblichus describes the practice of musical healing:

> Here is also, by Zeus, something which deserves to be mentioned above all: namely, that for his disciples he arranged and adjusted what might be called "preparations" and "touchings," divinely contriving mingling of certain dia-tonic, chromatic and enharmonic melodies, through which he easily switched and circulated the passions of the soul in a contrary direction, whenever they had accumulated recently, irrationally, or clandestinely—such as sorrow, rage, pity, over-emulation, fear, manifold desires, angers, appetites, pride, col-lapse or spasms. Each of these he corrected by the rule of virtue, attempting them through appropriate melodies, as through some salutary medicine.[53]

A specific criteria arises through the experience of contraries by which disease and emotional discordances may be transformed through music and other practices into a state of health. To find this health and to bring about a "natural" harmony of a living being requires an interaction amid the body which will bring forth an "innate" harmony, similar to Chinese medicine. To this extent, although discordance seems to stand opposed to concordance, the former exists as do the shadows which allow for a relief and dimension, not possible by light alone. The priority, however, of light over darkness, and health over illness, and thus divinity over *this* world, arises with the apprehension of a tragic cycle of life which perdures despite illness and death. In other words, notes may seem much more pleasing than the silent spaces between these notes, but that does not make the silence less "there"—or any less important.

It is also significant that each of these practices harbor within themselves the implication of a *theoria* which bestows through the *bios* a commitment to the remembrance of the divine. This is shown in the burning of incense in sacrifices. Maple writes:

> Ancient man seems to have taken for granted the existence of an animus or indwelling soul in every object, and he believed the same of the food he offered his gods. The gods, being non-physical, could not be expected to consume solid food, so it was processed into smoke by burning. They could then assimilate the spirit or essence of the food represented by the smoke that arose from the altar. It goes without saying that the aroma of burnt flesh is far from pleasing and as man became gradually more aesthetically aware, he sees to have assumed, with some justice, that a pungent stench might be offensive to the gods.[54]

Although this may be seen as speculative, we can see that such an *æsthetic* awareness, one which was centered in a specific *theoria* and *bios*, seems to have been present among the Pythagoreans. What is striking is the consistency of the analogies between the varying aspects of the constructed seen-order. The needs of the invisible acquire artistic preeminence in a way of life dedicated to a thoughtful, bodily *praxis*.

It must be admitted that it is not possible for us to understand further the precise exercises that may have surrounded a practice of past-life regression for the Pythagoreans, or of the use that were made of dreams described by Iamblichus and Porphyry. Yet, it seems clear that such practices can be imagined as analogous to those of musical healing, dietary regulation, or meditation. The realm of dreams or of regression would simply be additional fields, which like the monochord, provide access to remembrance. It is in the context of these practices that the "identification" of the microcosm and the macrocosm acquires a tangible expression. This cultivation of remembrance, as a cultivation of the soul, demonstrates that the "oppositions," posited by a separation of terms, as in the case of the "opposition" of musical harmony, are more appropriately conceived as residing in the quality of friendship. Iamblichus writes:

> Friendship of all things towards all was most clearly unfolded by Pythagoras. Indeed, the friendship of Gods towards men he explained through piety and scientific cultivation; but that of teachings towards each other, and generally of the soul to the body, of the rational towards the irrational part he unfolded, through philosophy and its teachings.[55]

We can see that while these "opposites" are expressed as distinct, and that a hierarchy is posited between these terms, there is not an irreconcilable conflict or natural antipathy between these, but a condition of communication. This notion, applied to the quality of friendship, demarcates the Pythagorean concepts of "equality" and "justice." From this notion, we can ascertain the rudiments of a Pythagorean terrestrial *ethos* (that ancient musical term), one which did eventually find historical expression, especially in southern Italy, at Croton. In light of the "identity" of the microcosm and the macrocosm, it is not difficult to recognize the "identity" of the self and the polity conceived as harmonies which operate on different scales, but as essentially the same nature. The notions of friendship and mutual aid allow us to fathom an *ethos* of harmony among each self amid its path of remembrance or return.

This happening of reciprocity calls to mind the discussion of the tetractys by Theon of Smyrna, that this is a continuity of harmonies, harmonics as the "magical bridge" whose grades of texture and color span the ineffable excession of possibilities, making possible talk about different dimensions. There is an "unfathomable intentionality"[56] and this "unknown" incites our quest for meaning amidst the encroaching horizons of nothingness. It will be through friendship and social intercourse amidst the lifeworld that we will acquire the perspective to fathom our questions. Iamblichus illustrates this conception of friendship, and provides us with a glimpse of the significance of the holding of property in common:

> But much more admirable than the above examples were the Pythagoreans' teachings respecting the communion of divine goods, the agreement of intellect, and their doctrines about the divine soul. They were ever exhorting each other not to tear apart the divine soul within them. The significance of their friendship both in words and in deeds was an effort to achieve a certain divine union, or communion of intellect with the divine soul. Anything better than this, either in what is uttered in words, or performed in deeds, is not possible to find.[57]

The way of life, as a communal and individual practice of remembrance which is a working toward a goal, is an emulation of, and participation in, the extended sympathy of the visible world, one which aspires to become divine. It is in this notion of friendship that the authentic character of philosophy is intimated, one that is made manifest in a true community.

Chapter 8

The Platonic Rupture: Writing and Difference

It seems that in order to inscribe themselves in the hearts of humanity with eternal demands, all great things have first to wander the earth as monstrous and fear-inspiring grotesques; dogmatic philosophy, the doctrine of the Vedanta in Asia and Platonism in Europe for example, was a grotesque of this kind. Let us not be ungrateful to it, even though it certainly has to be admitted that the worst, most wearisomely protracted and most dangerous of all errors hitherto has been a dogmatist's error, namely Plato's invention of pure spirit and the good in itself. [1]

In order to more clearly bring out the specificity of Pythagorean philosophy, and of the singularity of its interpretation of the doctrine of transmigration, I will turn to the doctrine of *metempsychosis* in the dialogues of Plato. It will be in a contrast between these philosophies, and especially in light of the transition that had occurred with Philolaus, that we will be able to glimpse a negative reflection of the Pythagorean *bios*—in the political mirror, as it were, of the *polis* of the *Republic*. In his younger days, Plato wished to be a writer of tragic dramas, yet, after he met Socrates, he burned his copies of Orphic poetry and decided to write his philosophical "dialogues" instead. Beyond the casual reference to his early life in various biographical sketches, not much *philosophical* significance has been given to this early "poetic" aspiration, Nietzsche being nearly a lone wanderer in this field. It was when Plato burned his early poetry and trage-dies that he left the tragic age of the Greeks and entered into the Alexandrian age of the "theoretical" man. For Nietzsche, such an event is indicative of the flight from the tragic double bind of existence toward the dialectical escapism of Socratic optimism.

It might seem perverse to expect Nietzsche to guide us in a specification of the Pythagorean doctrine, given his beliefs on the alleged Orphic and Platonic character of Pythagoreanism. Even if we disagree with Nietzsche, his diagnosis of the theoretical triumvirate of Euripides-Socrates-Plato as a symptom of a deep cultural decline in Ancient Greece does suggest parallels with the destruc-tion of the Pythagorean *bios* of the oral tradition. It will be the radical Platonic turn toward the ascetic ideal which will concern us in this interpretive context, as a turn which displaced a teaching with a unique emphasis upon a philosophical *bios* amid the horizons of which *theoria* would be situated and enacted. As we will see, the Pythagorean teaching, in contrast to Plato's *otherworldly hope*, consisted in an affirmation of the harmony of the world, as the *Kosmos* was regarded as the body of the All.[2] It is in this sense that Pythagoras has a distinctly *this-worldly* orientation, one focused upon the healthy body and the affirmation of the sufficiency of the All.

In the *Birth of Tragedy*, Nietzsche declared that the New Attic Comedy of Euripides was a symptom of the victory of a decadent "Socratism," of the "theoretical man" over the dithyramb of the tragic chorus. The novel "comedies" of Euripides, who late in his life would recant his destruction of tragedy, were characterized, for Nietzsche, by an excessive, fratricidal Apollonism which sought to stamp out music, his half brother Dionysus, from the drama of life. The younger Euripides sought to rid tragic life of the ecstasy of the chorus, inserting in its stead the unsuspenseful and rational elucidation of a morality play, not a sublimation, but a purification, often ending in a *deus ex machina* in which the "truth" is explained and summarized, that is, interpretation as command.[3] In such a scenario, the tragedies of Aeschylus and Sophocles, which revel in ambiguity and ultimate double binds, are cast aside for an inartistic project with an overriding significance of moral, political education. Indeed, the plays of Euripides begin with a thorough elucidation of that which was to come, thereby removing suspense and poetic tension from a genre which must henceforward be regarded as works of propaganda. In the earlier tragedies, the chorus relishes in the destruction of the tragic hero as an affirmation of the community and of the paradoxical mortality/immortality of life. It is the tragic destruction of the hero which intimates the *terrible truth* of mortality, but a truth that abides a deeper affirmation of life in the inexorable rebirth of Nature, of the All. Nothing can be known beyond the *terrible truth*, and for Nietzsche, any will to truth, that is merely a will to bridge over the paradoxical with an aesthetic posture is not in accord with the tragic, and is thus *hubris* against life, against the All. For, in the context of Nietzsche's perspective, such a will to truth, of one that pretends to seek an escape from life, is, at the end of the day, merely a symptom of an all-too-human will to power, which is to be simply unmasked.

For Nietzsche, the desire to construct a solution to the paradox is a symptom of weakness, and one ultimately, of nihilism. The construction of the resolution as the law of the *polis* is a *simulacrum*, but if it is regarded as a "reality" to the detriment of a joyous and powerful life, it is *ressentiment* and a negation of life. This is the *ressentiment* of Socrates who denied the "world" in favor of that void of an "other world" of reason, truth, good, pure, detached, in its own peculiar movement apart from the truth of being – as if the *terrible truth* of the mortality of the self and world is the *only* illusion, *maya*. In this way, as we will see, Socrates conjures out of the void the ideal of an escape from this world—to break oneself off cleanly, as pure spirit—such is the truth, a truth we can only share once we have forsaken this world, once we have died, when the music is over.

As Nietzsche writes in *The Will to Power*, "We have art lest we perish of the truth."[4] In this way, Socrates *is* the artist of death.

In this context, we can see the dialogues of Plato as the *aestheticized* distillations of the form of life which was Socratic optimism, with its deconstructive and reconstructive pattern of dialectical reason. That which is deconstructed is our instinctive self-awareness of the terrible truth of existence, together with the customs of valuation and practice with regard to the body and a way of life. Yet, before, during and after this dismantling, there "bubbles up" the projection of a reconstructive agenda in which the scale of values have been disrupted, inverted, displaced by a novel paradigm and regime of learning, one which is captivated by the intelligible only, detached in its repose of eternity and a divine that is *other*. The *otherness* of the divine and thus of the seat of value underscores the ascetic relation of the self to the body as the denial of the latter is regarded as the *modus operandi* of an ascent to the intelligible. In the wake of the severance of *topoi*, with their associated power and evaluations, the god and truth of eternity are set against the sensible world of flux, which, having been constructed in the severance, becomes only a disposable model, a chaos that begs for a principle of order, of that which is moved, finite. With the destruction of the old law tablets of reference and truth, it is asserted that the flux of the living world is antithetical to the nature and truth of the divine, and thus, can have no part in it, as like is of like. The only truth, for Plato, is that there is no truth *here*. If we desire to discover the truth, we must transcend the ways and byways of this world of flux (Heraclitus), become strangers to this world, and, welcoming death as the release from the *samsara* of suffering and death, rise up out of this sea of ambiguity into the purity of the light. This deity of the eternal, and its mirror in the soul, while it may have its own "self-movement," is not the movement, however, of the body, music and *praxis* which is the state of the Pythagorean notion of the soul. Socrates may have seduced Plato after all to believe in the severance of the *nous* from the *Kosmos* in a radical devaluation of the world, a truth which saw life as a long sickness only to be healed in death.

It is against this cautionary backdrop that we will consider Plato's version of the doctrine of transmigration, which he sees not as the symbol of kinship amidst the All, but instead as a maelstrom of punishment and suffering in the context of a program for the purification and escape of degenerate, fallen souls. This ascetic *praxis* is orchestrated so that mortal souls may be able to flee this realm of hate and conflict, of strife, so as to transcend toward that other realm, that other of true eternal love. A dark mirroring of Empedocles should be immediately seen in Platonic severance, as the sensible world, beyond the traces of beauty, is one of strife, while it is only the realm of the Good which is that of Love. Empedocles, as we will recall, held that the very unity of the individuated things and living beings was a marriage of heaven and hell, of love and strife. Yet, as in the case of Pythagoras and Anaxagoras, it is the *pathos* of the *nous* which holds the highest importance for Plato. In the context of our earlier discussion of the Pythagorean *bios*, it will be illuminating to consider the implications of such "morbid" ideas for the life of a community. For, as Nietzsche warns us,[5] those who speak of otherworldly hopes do not by that fact alone seek to leave the earth. Indeed, this call for self-denial is merely a strategy which seeks to seduce the mortal self to give away his own individual sovereignty of decision and power. We will see, in fact, that in Plato's scenario, the *topos* of decision for the self, the soul, lies beyond life and embodiment; the act is the *free choice*[6] prior to one's entrance into the entombment in the body. In this way, life amid the flux of existence is, for Plato, not free, which, we will recall, is distinct from the Pythagorean perspective which emphasized the free decision of the initiate to enter the *bios*. Indeed, during his career, Plato tried to convince Dionysius the Tyrant of Syracuse to implement his project of an "Ideal *Polis*." Yet, Plato was refused, and was placed in prison until he was allowed to return to Greece. Having failed as an advisor to a tyrant, Plato organized his Academy, which, while merely a microcosm of a *polis*, served for the dissemination of his doctrine, an organization whose final product was the release bestowed at death.

After all, this world is not any place for ideas such as his, as Augustine knew only too well, for, though he sought to have his political ideology implemented in *this* world, his ultimate affirmation, as Nietzsche contends, was that of *nihilation*, of the denial of the world as such. Instead of a *bios* in the Pythagorean sense, Plato erected an academy of reading, writing, and athletics, the propadeutic function of which was to train and discipline the disciple to turn away from the body and its pleasure, pain, and change, and turn to the divine, which for him is one of repose, stillness, an eternity which was not of the All, nor of this or any possible world. The ascetic orientation, as a denial of the self as a complete being of the All—as the selection of one aspect, the *nous*, and setting it to war against all other aspects, the "body," fighting on behalf of a Mind which did not merely steer all things, as with Anaxagoras, but instead contained the idea and truth of all that which is, and being more "true" and indeed "real" than anything that we may encounter in the world, this place of separation and mixture. Such an ascetic strategy excises much of the lifeworld that is not in accord with the ascetic "ideology" of the Mind, as the place of mortal existence is denigrated as ultimately an illusion and a place for the purification of the soul. Nietzsche writes, shortly after the quote at the head of this chapter:

> To be sure, to speak of spirit and the good as Plato did meant standing truth on her head and denying *perspective* itself, the basic condition of all life.[7]

These references to Nietzsche, although he considered Pythagoras a "melancholic," a mere "religious reformer"[8] and a "tyrant of the spirit,"[9] and also as a phenomenon of Orphic religiosity, serve to highlight some themes which we have already come across in our discussions of harmony, of the monochord, of the path of return as a magical *bios*, themes which seek to bestow full status of honor to the body. Nietzsche provides us, in his reference to Pythagoras in

The Birth of Tragedy with a possible portrait of the transformation of Greek philosophy from the Archaic Near Eastern thought to Athenian dialogical writing, a transition most readily symbolized, in the case of Pythagoras, in the displacement of the oral tradition by the written text.

We do not have a written text of Pythagoras to hand to prove the textual distinction between Pythagoras and Plato. Yet, the notions of an extended kinship and musical harmony, which is shown in the movements of the stars or exhibited in the tangible symbol of the monochord, are intimations of a way in which we can interpret the doctrine of transmigration without reference to the devaluation of the body or the need to escape from the physical *Kosmos*. Indeed, the very lack of written evidence may be an indirect clue if we remember the bodily space of the *bios*, which organized itself through the spoken word, in light of Plato's own *written* comments about the supremacy of the spoken word to written text. It will be the meaning of the Platonic doctrine of transmigration which we shall seek to conjure up in the following pages in which it will be made clear how and why he intends a scenario which differs from that of Pythagoras. Transmigration is a single word, but there are many ways to interpret its significance and meanings. We must remain vigilant to this truth as we seek to specify the meaning and the implications of the doctrine of transmigration for the early Pythagoreans. We must be able to draw fine lines betwixt its various advocates.

In the following, I will first investigate the "Myth of Er," in the *Republic*, which is the story of a "shamanic journey" of a fallen warrior to the underworld in which he learns the penitentiary truth of the doctrine of transmigration. I will next bring this punitive sense of the doctrine into relation with the "Myth of the Cave" and "The Divided Line" in which we will consider the isomorphism between the Platonic myth of escape and the organization of its philosophical itinerary. I will next turn to the dialogues, *Phaedo* and *Phaedrus*, so as to draw out a sketch of the eschatology of the soul, especially of that of the philosopher, and exhibit the specific meaning of the Platonic notion of transmigration. I will end with a brief exploration of the *Timaeus*, regarded as the most Pythagorean of all of Plato's dialogues, but one which is ironically the most forcefully opposed to the Pythagorean teachings of the cosmos, soul, and divine. At the end of the day, that which is significant is the *pathos* of the Platonic divine, one who, through his detachment as the voyeur of the demiurgical assembly-line—the Andy Warhol of gods—symbolizes the difference between Plato and Pythagoras.

The Myth of Er, a Warrior Bold: Transmigration and Judgment

This myth tells the story of a bold warrior who was killed in battle, but who came alive on the twelfth day just as his funeral pyre was to be set alight, telling wild tales of having gone over into the beyond. Plato writes (614b–d):

He said that when his soul went forth from his body he journeyed with a great company and that they came to a mysterious region where there were two openings side by side in the earth, and above and over against them in the heaven two others, and that judges were sitting between these, and that after every judgment they bade the righteous journey to the right and upward through the heaven with tokens attached to them in front of the judgment passed upon them, and the unjust to take the road to the left and downward, they too wearing behind signs of all that had befallen them.

As Er approached the place of judgment, he was "seen" as a messenger to humankind and told that he should be vigilant in remembering all that he was to witness in this alterior dimension. Amidst the plethora of souls here congregated, the judges sat directing each soul to its proper destination. Souls, "departing after judgment had been passed upon them" were beginning their descent into the earth for "what had befallen them," and others were going to their reward, having completed their cycles of purification. Other souls came out from one opening in the earth, "full of squalor and dust," having had been subjected to the cycles of punishment for the allotted duration of a thousand years. Still others, "clean and pure," were coming down from heaven to either begin the process once again or were descending there for the first time. These arrivals, who came "from time to time," gathered in the meadow and told each other of their respective experiences, those of suffering and those of delight. Since Plato, as we will see, articulates a conception of an ultimate *escape* from the world into the intelligible, we are left aback with respect to some elements of the story, such as the reason why a soul "clean and pure" would be subjected to the same torture once again, why they would mix with those covered in "dust and squalor," in their fall as wingless souls in a descent into inexorable cycles of punishment. One explanation would be that their very entry in this realm of impurity would be a prefiguration of the procedure of incarnation—driven perhaps, as with Mani, by the sexual lust of mortals who capture souls "clean and pure" in bodies. Plato does not allow us, however, to remain with such questions for his purpose lies in the *moral* interpretation of this mythopoetic symbol.

The narration of the myth is interrupted with a caution to the listener, Glaucon, that, due to its great length, only a summary will be given of the story. The summary consists of an account of the tenfold suffering for all transgressions against others, and rewards in the same measure for all acts of kindness and such like. Those singled out by Plato for great punishment, as witnessed and testified by those who came up from one of the openings in the earth, are, interestingly tyrants, most notably, Ardiaeus, and others of "private stations" who had committed great crimes. Plato gives us a taste of the punishment given to these transgressors by "savage men of fiery aspect":

But Ardiaeus and others they bound hand and foot and head and flung down and flagged them and dragged them by the wayside, carding them on thorns and signifying to those who from time to time passed by for what cause they were being borne away, and that they were to be hurled into Tartarus. (616a)

This "theatre of cruelty" was there for all in the place of the beyond. Those who were passing by hoped only that their name would not be called out by one of the judges—that they would be allowed to pass in silence and join the gathering in the meadow. Plato continues:

> But when seven days had elapsed for each group in the meadow, they were required to rise up on the eighth and journey on, and they came in four days to a spot whence they discerned, extended from above throughout the heaven and the earth, a straight light like a pillar, most nearly resembling the rainbow, but brighter and purer. (616b)

> They came to this band of light in another day, recalling that Er was dead for twelve days, and they saw there in the middle of the light the extremities of its fastenings stretched from heaven, for this light was the girdle of the heavens like the undergirders of triremes, holding together in like manner the entire revolving vault. And from the extremities was stretched the spindle of Necessity, through which all the orbits turned. (616b–c)

> The spindle of necessity has a hook and a staff which revolve in a "great whorl," which Plato describes: Its shape was that of those in our world, but from his description we must conceive it to be as if in one great whorl, hollow and scooped out, there lay enclosed, right through, another like it but smaller, fitting into it as boxes that fit into another, and in like manner another, a third, and a fourth, and four others, for there were eight of the whorls in all, lying within one another, showing their rims as circles from above and forming the continuous back of a single whorl about the shaft, which was driven home through the middle of the eighth. (616d–e)

Each of the whorls that made up the "great whorl" had a distinct orbit, color (along a white-yellow continuum) and its own speed (along a gradient of swiftness). Upon each whorl sat a Siren who sang a single note, and all of the notes together, as the great whorl, coalesced as a "concord of a single harmony" (617b). In unison with the songs of the Sirens, sang the Fates, daughters of Necessity, Lachesis, Clotho, and Atropos, symbolizing the ecstasies of the past, present, and future, respectively. Clotho helped turn the outer circles, Atropos, the inner, and Lachesis, with both of her hands, helped each of the others. As the throng were bidden to go before Lachesis, a prophet grasped lots from her lap, and spoke thus to the wanderers:

> Souls that live for a day, now is the beginning of another cycle of mortal generation where birth is the beacon of death. No divinity shall cast lots for you,

but you shall choose your own deity. Let him to whom falls the first lot first select a life to which he shall cleave of necessity. But virtue has no master over her, and each shall have more or less of her as he honors her or does her despite. The blame is his who chooses. God is blameless. (617c–e)

The prophet casts out the numbered lots and each takes that which falls nearest themselves. He next lays out myriad "patterns of lives" before those compelled to assemble. Good lives and bad, those of beauty and bodily strength and those who were ugly and weak, human and animal, or those beings of ill-repute. But, regardless of the quality of the choice, a life must be chosen, one which will determine the character of the soul. Beyond any consideration of the choice of life, Plato reveals:

> But all other things were commingled with one another
> and with wealth and poverty and sickness and health
> and the intermediate conditions. (618b)

In this way, Plato seems to suggest that, since all other things will remain the same, the key aspect of the situation of incarnation was the choice made of a life that would determine the character. At this point, the narrative of the myth is abruptly cut off, and a diatribe ensues asserting that all other studies are to be put aside in order to seek the Man who will teach the nexus of discipline required to make the "correct" choice, to instill into him a teaching amid the appropriate environmental conditions, guiding the self to choose the beautiful, the true, and the good. Socrates calls his students to have his "eyes fixed on the nature of the soul" and to choose the life "that is seated in the mean and shun the excess in either direction, both in this world so far as may be and in all the life to come, for this is the greatest happiness for man" (619a–b)

Plato returns to the narrative as Er relates the words of the prophet which suggest that this choice can be made at any time, even by the last, in other words, after many incarnations. It is even possible that those who are last are in the better position, for those who came from a well ordered polity, those who were inexperienced in suffering, chose their lots without appropriate examination. Those who had previously suffered, who had the truth burned into their souls, were more cautious and more reflective. Plato describes the significance of this *fallenness*:

> For which reason also there was an interchange of good and evil for most of
> the souls, as well as because of the chances of the lot. (619d)

Plato wishes to assure us however that we need not be deceived the first time around, and may, if we hold to a "sane faith" in wisdom, smoothly return to the divine, or at least, to avoid being the last to be released from these indefinite plunges into the maelstrom of the void. Plato writes that Er relates scornfully the various choices that have been made by many notable souls (such as Orpheus), "a strange, pitiful, and ridiculous spectacle" in which they chose to come back, for various reasons, as animals, such as lions and apes, or as birds, such as a swan, an eagle, a nightingale. Yet, Er denies his hearers such a vertiginous freedom as the choice to be made is limited by the trace of past incarnations, "as the choice was determined for the most part by the habits of their former lives" (619e). Of the notables, Odysseus is set forth as the last to draw his lot, last since he had undergone much turmoil, and, having "flung away ambition," he did not choose his lot with haste. Plato writes that Odysseus, in his wisdom of suffering amidst these grinding ordeals of purification,

> went about for a long time in quest of the life of an ordinary citizen who minded his own business, and with difficulty found it lying in some corner disregarded by the others, and upon seeing it said that it would have done the same had it drawn the first lot, and chose it gladly. (620c–d)

This process of choice by these various souls took place in the context of the broader event site of metempsychosis, from wild beasts to human beings, from human beings to wild beasts. When each had chosen its lot, they were "marshaled" to go before Lachesis, who sent for each a guardian genius who was the divinity of their own choice. The genius led the soul to Clotho, who ratified his lot and choice, to Atropo who made the choice irreversible, and next, each of the souls, "without a backward look," traversed "beneath the throne of Necessity." All of the souls wandered together toward the Plain of Oblivion, a place of heat and death, arid and without vegetation, through which flowed the River of Forgetfulness, Lethe, "whose waters no vessel can contain." They all drank the water, some drank too much, but all fell asleep and forgot all things. As they slept, the lightening event occurred, which with thunder, sent each to its chosen destination. Er himself returned to tell his tale, having drunk of the water, yet, for a reason he did not comprehend, he was able to be the messenger. Plato summarizes his account in one declaration:

> And so, Glaucon, the tale was saved, as the saying is, and was not lost. And it will save us if we believe it, and we shall safely cross the River of Lethe, and keep our soul unspotted from the world. But if we are guided by me we shall believe that the soul is immortal and capable of enduring all extremes of good and evil, and so we shall hold ever to the upward way and pursue righteousness with wisdom always and ever, that we may be dear to ourselves and to the gods both during our sojourn here and when we receive our reward, as the victors in the games go about to gather in theirs. And thus both here and in that journey of a thousand years, whereof I have told you, we shall fare well. (621c–d)

The Myth of Er casts into relief the narrative horizons for an interpretation of the Platonic ideation of metempsychosis as the process by which the soul becomes "unspotted from the world." Mortal life is merely a sojourn here; it is after a "journey of a thousand years" that we will receive our reward. In the Myth, Plato inscribes a narrative which contains both the threat of punishment, and the promise of a liberation from punishment, of redemption in the hope of an escape from the cycles of *samsara*. It is clear that, in distinction to the Pythagoreans, Plato is advocating the "one true path" and is operating within a mythopoetic infrastructure of impurity and purity, punishment and reward, one which seduces the self to acquiesce to an unchosen choice.

The Myth of the Cave and the Divided Line

This either/or of the previous scenario with its *forced* choice is further illuminated through a consideration of the Myth of the Cave (7.514), and the figure of the Divided Line (6.509) as concrete expressions of the path of liberation from the body and sensible perspective. These two "images," that of the myth and the figure, complement each other and belong together, as each is an analog of the other, the first as a mythopoetic symbol, the next, as a mathematical-theoretical sign, respectively.

The Myth of the Cave

Picture men dwelling in a sort of subterranean cavern with a long entrance open to the light on its entire width. Conceive them as having their legs and necks fettered from childhood, so that they remain in the same spot, able to look forward only, and prevented by the fetters from turning their heads. Picture further the light from a fire burning higher up and at a distance behind them, and between the fire and the prisoners and above them a road along which a low wall has been built, as the exhibitors of puppet shows have partitions before the men themselves, above which they show the puppets. (7.514a)

Then in every way such prisoners would deem reality to be nothing else than the shadows of artificial objects. (7.516c)

When one was freed from his fetters and compelled to stand up suddenly and turn his head around and walk and to lift up his eyes to the light, and in doing all this felt pain and, because of the dazzle and glitter of the light, was unable to discern the objects whose shadows he formerly saw, what do you suppose would be his answer if someone told him that what he had seen before was all a cheat and an illusion, but that now, being nearer to reality and turned toward more real things, he saw more truly? (7.515c–d)

Plato asserts that if questioned, this mortal would affirm only the shadows which surround and if he were forced to see the light, then he would turn away and seek out the images he had seen before, as he considers these *more clear* than this vision of truth of light. Plato seeks to find the proper method of transition from the cave to the sun, and he *officially* rejects the path of force, of compulsion—yet, he does not shy away from threatening the guardians of the night. He instead sets out a path of ascent which will train the wildness of man to look at that which is higher via habit. Plato writes:

> And at first he would most easily discern the shadows and, after that, the likenesses or reflection in water of men and other things, and later, the things themselves, and from these he would go on to contemplate the appearances in the heavens and heaven itself, more easily by night, looking at the light of the stars and the moon, than by day the sun and the sun's light. (7.516a–b)

Plato writes that eventually the mortal, who previously found his home in the cave, will

> be able to look upon the sun itself and see its true nature, not by reflections in water or phantasms of it in an alien setting, but in and by itself in its own place. (7.515b)

The traveler would be able to remember what he had thought he had known before, and thus, he will affirm the change, and have pity for those still chained deep within the cavern of shadows. With this knowledge, and supposing that he could return to the cave with such an insight, he would see through the superficial opinions and valuations of the Esteemed, as if the honors bestowed among themselves for the tricks of being the "quickest to make out the shadows as they pass and best able to remember their customary precedence, sequences, and coexistences" were worth more than an apprehension of the truth (7.516c–d). Plato asks if he may prefer to live the life of a landless man, to suffer "rather than opine with them and live like that?" (7.516d)

Continuing the supposition of a return from the ascent, Plato tells the story of one who comes back down and takes his old place in the cavern of shadows. Despite his ascension into the light, and the attainment of true vision, however, this wisdom is not only useless upon his descent, but is indeed a liability. His eyes are not accustomed to the play of light and darkness, his soul is not accustomed to the weight of the chains, of the body, and his intellect is not accustomed to this realm of perspective. Not only is he in no position to give to the chained hordes the "good news," but he cannot even keep up with these others who dance effortlessly amidst this opening of temporality. They laugh, jeer at him, and "if it were possible to lay hands on and kill the man who tried to release them and lead them up, would they not kill him?" (7.517a)

Plato conceives this myth as an allegory for the predicament of the self in the world, as an imprisonment of the soul, the truly divine spark of the self, within the matrice of the temporal body. Yet, in Plato's "drama," there must have already been at least one who had exited the cavern, who had seen the light, apprehended "the Good," and had returned to "his old place." Otherwise, there could be no suggestion that this world is an imprisonment of the soul, or that there is indeed an exit from the cavern. We could possibly take this as a reference to the divine sign of Socrates, or, perhaps, to the path of recollection, which however, must come to be known by the "liberator."

As we will consider more clearly below when we come to the *Phaedrus* and to the *Phaedo*, the references made to transmigration in the dialogues consistently emphasize, on the one hand, the radical difference betwixt *demas* and *psyche*, of the body and soul, as the body harbors at its core an unlimited excess of strife, and, on the other hand, the longing of Psyche who urgently seeks out *Eros* in her return to the love of the Divine. Plato posits the existence of a Divine spark, which has fallen from a greater fire, into the prison of the body, which is moist and cold. It is this spark which has value as it points to the source of value, a source outside and disconnected from the visible world of life and perspective, and which the target of his ascetic *praxis*. In this way, we can understand the doctrine of metempsychosis, within the methodological and aesthetic parameters of the text of Plato, as an allegory of incessant punishment, disciplining, or falling, again and again, to those who refused to be guided by the one who advertises his revelations in the cavern of shadows.

In this light, despite the laughter and the jeers, the hordes are being held back from laying their hands upon him by a peculiar spell. Plato keeps the prisoners back by enchanting them to opine that only he knows how each could be set free, that only he knows the secret of what is to be done. Plato specifies this project:

> But our present argument indicates, said I, that the true analogy for this indwelling power in the soul and the instrument whereby each of us apprehends is that of an eye that could not be converted to the light from the darkness except by turning the whole body. Even so this organ of knowledge must be turned around from the world of becoming together with the entire soul, like the scene-shifting periactus in the theater, until the soul is able to endure the contemplation of essence and the brightest region of being. And this we say is the good, do we not? (7.518c)

The eye must turn away from becoming toward the "brightest region of being." Yet, it cannot do this without turning the entire body to this region. In this way, under the direction of the eye, the body is to be turned away from the realm of Becoming, away from the sensible world of life. The conversion to the ideal can only take place via "turning the whole body," around a primary point of reference, or as Pliny the Elder writes in his *Natural History*, in the adoration of the "gods and doing reverence to their images, we use to kiss our right hand and turn about with our whole body."[10] In other words, the "true" self is distilled down to a metaphor of sight only, as an intelligible vision of radical interiority, ordered around the primary edifice of a devotional pedagogy. This prioritization of sight necessitates that the rest of the body, the ears, nose, mouth, and skin be first oriented to the placeless center of the interior eye, and second, in the denial of Becoming, these latter senses and the body will be denied. It is this denial of the body for the eye, one that equivocates light with intelligibility, that most clearly throws into relief the difference between the Platonic and Pythagorean philosophies.

We might suggest, moreover, that Plato, after considering his views on marriage and upon the illusion of personal choice, that is, of the Noble Lie, elsewhere in his *Republic*, did not consider the doctrine of transmigration as a symbol in the Pythagorean sense, but, instead as a fiction deployed in a rhetoric of enchantment, in a similar way to the criticism put forth by Dacier and Cornford. For, as we sense in the Myth of Er, the rhetoric of transmigration is propaganda, its deployment, a threat and intimidation, being a "medicine," a "cure by lies" for the ordinary, unenlightened subject of the realm.

Indeed, there is no assertion of universality for the doctrine, as this punishment is not meant for the philosopher, the man above even the higher man, who harbors the "good hope" of a swift, sweet release, possibly never being reincarnated at all. In this light, the highest eschatological pathway is one in which the notion of transmigration is only of secondary importance, and for those guardians of truth who proclaim it, a "noble fiction." Yet, this does not confirm Dacier's criticism with respect to the Pythagoreans, who via a symbolist appropriation of the word, saw transmigration as the magical core of the kinship of life and the attunement of the self and the world. In this different interpretation, not even Pythagoras would wish for a swift release, as this would subvert the event of being, this innocence of becoming. We can perhaps say that the fault of Dacier, Cornford and others in their criticism of the doctrine of transmigration is that of interpreting the doctrine and its advocates through the eyes of Plato. By so doing, we lose contact with the specificity of the Pythagorean interpretation of the doctrine.

Plato seems to have chosen the fable of a "judgment of the dead" with the express purpose of utilizing the narrative as a founding myth for the state, for the *polis*—and the conversion of the masses to this ideal. For Pythagoras, on the contrary, the body amid the *bios*, is a conduit of wisdom, and to achieve the wisdom of the All, one must become this All through myriad bodies and states of being. Plato does not have any time for this exploration of the self and the All, but seeks, instead, something distinct from the All, and pursues this "other" with the greatest urgency:

Of this very thing, then, I said, there might be an art of the speediest and most effective shifting or conversion of the soul, not an art of producing vision in it, but on the assumption that it possesses vision but does not rightly direct it and does not look where it should, an art of bringing this about. (7.518d)

Plato does not wish to instill vision, as one may have looking upon the shadows of incense smoke passing through the flame of a candle, but insists that this vision be directed toward that dimension of alterity, to that greater and higher source. He does not allow the self to have authentic insight, but instead gives to the initiate a docile habit brought about by the art of a speedy conversion. A quick and efficient release is wanted, one articulated as the metabolism of the *polis*, the repository of the secret and its dissemination, a state presided over by the arbiter of judgment, the philosopher-king. This solution is deemed necessary by Plato in that the higher men have become convinced that "they have been transported to the Islands of the Blessed," while still amid the earth and body, which, for Plato, are wastelands of punishment and of darkness. (7.519c)[11]

Plato concludes this region of his allegory, thus:

It is the duty of us, the founders . . . to compel the best natures to attain the knowledge which we pronounced the greatest, and to win to the vision of the good, to scale that ascent, and when they have reached the heights and taken an adequate view, we must not allow what is now permitted. (7.519c–d)

Only the philosopher, who is a *founder*, so says Plato, is capable of thinking in the interests of the whole since he is apart from the whole.

The Divided Line

Conceive then . . . that there are these two entities, and one of them is sovereign over the intelligible order and region and the other over the world of the eyeball, not to say the sky-ball, but let that pass. You surely apprehend the two types, the visible and the intelligible. (7.509d)

Represent them then . . . by a line divided into two unequal sections and cut each section again in the same ratio—the section, that is, of the visible and that of the intelligible order—and then as an expression of the ratio of their comparative clearness and obscurity you will have, as one of the sections of the visible world, images. By images I mean, first shadows, and then reflections in water and on surfaces of dense smooth, and bright texture, and everything of that kind, if you apprehend. (6.509–19)

As the second section assume that of which this is a likeness or an image, that is, the animals about us and all plants and the class of objects made by man. (6.510a)

By the distinction that there is one section of it which the soul is compelled to investigate by treating as images the things imitated in the former division, and by means of assumptions from which it proceeds not up to a first principle or down to a conclusion, while there is another section in which it advances from its assumptions to a beginning or principle that transcends assumption, and in which it makes no use of the images employed by the other section, relying on ideas only and progressing systematically through ideas. (6.510b)

There always seems to be a resemblance between Pythagorean and Platonic "ideas" in that each is alleged to harbor a desire for a return to the divine. But, we have already detected, in full force, the differing meanings of this desire for each philosophy. There is a clear difference between *bios* and *academos*, bodily *praxis* and ascetic discipline. These differences cannot be made more plain than through a juxtaposition of the radical division of the divided line and the Pythagorean notion of an extended kinship. In consolation to those who have the bad fortune of not being philosophers, Plato offers hope in the guise of a propaedeutic of virtue for the *demos*, organized and disseminated as the Ideal Polis, as an organization of education, of the recollection of that which in the self is pure, still, and silent. This method is the scaffolding to the sculpted medium, one projected in the image of the Good. It is the philosopher-king who is the ideal sculptor, his chisels being the guardians, who in concert with the artisans, effectuate the ideal operation of the *polis*, the happening of the sculpting itself, as the creative event of the philosopher. The sculptor chips away at the raw stone, conjuring his vision into life as an amulet which will allow the swift and efficient passing of each to their own insurmountable deaths. The *polis* heals the wound through the imposition of order.

If we look at the incarnations of Pythagoras, we can see no rhyme or reason to any significant extent and certainly there is never any great urgency for a disciplinary purification, or, of the ascent of a single aspect of the self. He remembers everything about his past lives, as memories of differing bodily and soular experiences, each reaffirmed as the All amidst this inevitability of recurrent death. Pythagoras lives various lives, explores myriad aspects of his greater self, which in the synergy of all his incarnations, running forever in a circle through all spheres of the *Kosmos*, sheer chance perhaps deciding on the reincarnation, his self, in all of its myriad depth and complexity, is unfolded as being actively the All, thus, returning to the All.

A notion of becoming the All, a pathway of enlightenment as the eternal quest of the self, differs from the path of release, which is coordinated by means of a hierarchy of value which seeks to flee the *topos* of the body, world, and music. In positing of a strict hierarchy of value betwixt the world of appearance and change, of becoming, and that of the eternal forms, of being, Plato had placed into precise theoretical practice, his maxim, "Only that which is intelligent has value". He adheres to the negative affirmation of his mentor, Socrates, reported by Xenophon, that that which is most valuable is not of this world. This pathway of thought, in its radical separation of value from things of this world, placing them into a detached beyond, denies to the world, to the body, and to any other phenomenon, such as carnal sexuality, an interpretation which would consider these as not only symbols of the divine, but as having divine status in and of themselves.

Of course, Plato can look at these various appearances from an intellectual perspective, he can read into these to confirm that which they are *not*—they are not one, silent, invisible, still. They are merely alive, and all life is ephemeral. He thus indicts these things after he has removed all the life from them with his speculative intellect. Once his purpose is fulfilled, once a phenomenon has been used as a metaphor, or a fable has been told to cast some point into relief, they are cast aside for they are not ultimately essential, they do not have any essential relationship with the dimension of eternal forms beyond. Plato attacks the value bestowed upon the body and world, and, in turn, gives them no value, or only a negative value, in his Idea. The myth of the cavern makes his position very clear: the body and world necessitate, with Empedocles, light *and* darkness, while Plato seeks only light in his pursuit of an exit from the cave, to leave behind darkness, to lose his perspective in a two dimensional *eidos*. Yet, once again, this tool, like that of the "Divided Line," is a mere pedagogical image, and is neither essential nor has it any kinship with that which is pointed to; it is a momentary, disposable tool of a pedagogical training of ascent, an example, which, as visible, will also be jettisoned throughout the program of purification and training.

The False Self and the True Self: Phaedo and Phaedrus

Phaedo: Death as the Profession of the Philosopher

In the *Phaedo*, the persistence of the visible stands as a symptom of illness, of the fall into a light tainted with shadow; however, in pure light, one is blind in his earthly eyes, and will see via an intelligible, divine sight and light. It is this insight which allows us to transcend this realm of only ephemeral and momentary enchantment and to perceive that other dimension of eternal truth, of Good, and Beauty. If one may apprehend those eternal things, moreover, there must be that which, as a divine spark amidst this self which apprehends, is of the same essence of those eternal things, as like is unto like. It is the immortal soul which resembles the divine, this resemblance which is not visible to terrestrial vision, but, making itself known only in deep contemplation, as an access to the invisible, the nowhere.

Socrates is portrayed as reclining comfortably upon his own deathbed, spurning the myriad suggestions and arguments of his admirers, who attempt to persuade him to relent from his path of suicide, as it is an unnecessary and wasteful death. It is significant that if he had wanted, he could have escaped the judgment of death, especially as the sentencing body had originally only sought an exile for this "corrupter of youth" and "worshipper of foreign deities," as reported by Xenophon in his *Memoirs of Socrates*. After much plotting and insistent, though idle, chatter among his disciples, Socrates discloses to Phaedo and to the others his reasons for possessing good courage in death, in that he has lived the life of a philosopher devoted to eternal truth. Socrates says furthermore,

> Ordinary people seem not to realize that those who really apply themselves in the right way to philosophy are directly and of their own accord preparing themselves for dying and death. If this is true, and they have actually been looking forward to death all their lives, it would of course be absurd to be troubled when the thing comes for which they have so long been preparing and looking forward. (*Phaedo*, 64a)

Simmias laughs, reluctantly, at the words of Socrates, saying that this is what the ordinary people have been saying all along, that the philosopher should die, that death will serve him right. Socrates grows impatient, however, with the opinions of ordinary *demos*, of the people, not to mention with the least attribution of "awareness" to them:

> They are not at all aware in what sense true philosophers are half dead, or in what sense they deserve death, or what sort of death they deserve. But let us dismiss them and talk among ourselves. (*Phaedo*, 64b)

Socrates, having dismissed the *doxai* of the people, then guides Simmias to assent that death is the separation of the soul from the body, and of the body from the soul. Since the philosopher, moreover, is making preparations for this separation, for death, it is also agreed that the philosopher will not only be unconcerned with the affairs of the body, but will also despise them. Socrates then asks Simmias:

> Then it is your opinion in general that a man of this kind is not concerned with the body, but keeps his attention directed as much as he can away from it and toward the soul?
>
> And most people think, do they not, Simmias, that a man who finds no pleasure and takes no part in these things does not deserve to live, and

that anyone who thinks nothing of physical pleasures has one foot in the grave? (64e)

To both of these questions, Simmias answers in the affirmative, and thus, begins a systematic revaluation of the status of the body, a revaluation which closely resembles the trajectory of the sections examined from the *Republic*. The body is, in the *Phaedo*, the veil which separates us from wisdom—there is no knowledge to be gained by it. The senses deceive us, the desires distract us, erupting as the din of worldly turmoil, of wars and revolutions, all of this is a nemesis thrown from the strife of the body. Socrates pleads:

> We are in fact convinced that if we are ever to have pure knowledge of anything, we must get rid of the body and contemplate things by themselves with the soul by itself.

And, he continues,

> If no pure knowledge is possible in the company of the body, then either it is totally impossible to acquire knowledge, or it is only possible after death, because it is only then that the soul will be separate and independent of the body. (66d–e)

With these insights in hand, Socrates reasons that if we are to be in a position to acquire any wisdom at all, or at least to approach such a path as to attain such wisdom, it will then be necessary for the true philosopher to disdain

> all contact and association with the body, except when they are absolutely necessary, and instead of allowing ourselves to become infected with its nature, purify ourselves from it until God himself gives us deliverance. (67a)

This deliverance, as it is believed, bestows a "happy prospect" to the one whose "mind has been prepared by purification." The latter process, as a preparation for separation, inaugurates, through its extreme ascetic *praxis*, a prefiguration of the end which is sought, a setting free of the soul from the body by means of a withdrawal of contact from the bodily and worldly. For Socrates, the true philosopher should guide the soul to abide "alone by itself, freed from the shackles of the body." (67d) As this separation of the soul from the body is the *raison d'etre* of the philosopher, this one must "live in a state as close as possible to death," making "dying their profession." (67e)

We will recall that the philosopher in the Pythagorean *bios* makes "living" his profession, as we would perhaps wish the philosopher-king to do as well, at least ideally. Yet, once again, the *polis* is just another means by which the soul is to be efficiently released, set free from the body, dispatched from this life—or, politically, be subject to control. The body becomes an appendage to an ascetic machine of purification. There is nothing to be learned from the body, as, in fact, it is the only barrier to a "pure" knowledge. Once again, it is plain to witness the stark difference of this teaching from that of the Pythagorean *bios* and its practical and symbolist approach to the body as the "seat" of possibility.

The Phaedrus: Good Versus Evil, Evil Versus Good

The *Phaedrus* picks upon these questions surrounding the status of the body and the meaning of the divine. The prior notion of a "separation of soul from body" is illustrated in the impending rupture in the "Myth of the Chariot." The soul shall not love the body, but must love the divine only. The body is not considered divine, but its enchantment has seduced the soul away from the divine.

Myth, says Socrates, is to be "our manner of discourse," so as to tell the tale in "briefer compass" via the substitution of a model or a game[12] that resembles that which we wish to describe, one more simple, as a "reduced form" which distills out and intimates the essence. The "Myth of the Chariot" seeks to indicate the "reason why the soul's wings fall from it, and are lost" (246d). This story tells of the "union of powers in a team of winged steeds and their winged charioteer," a symbol for the soul amidst the predicament of its *fallenness*. Socrates, saying that the chariot of the gods is one gathered into unity, portrays the contrary situation of mortals:

> With us men, in the first place, it is a pair of steeds that the charioteer con-
> trols; moreover one of them is noble and good, and of good stock, while the
> other has the opposite character, and his stock is opposite. Hence the task of
> our charioteer is difficult and troublesome. (246b)

The myth of the chariot displays an allegory of the complexity of the soul amid body, one disclosed as an assertion of a hierarchy of value betwixt myriad orders of being, each of which is placed with regard to their own respective distances, near or far, from the absolute position of the Good. Plato sets out to delineate this hierarchy of living beings, distinguished as mortal and immortal:

> All soul has the care of all that is inanimate, and traverses the whole universe,
> though in ever-changing forms. Thus when it is perfect and winged it journeys
> on high and controls the whole world, but one that has shed its wings sinks
> down until it can fasten on something solid, and settling there it takes to itself
> an earthy body which seems by reason of the soul's power to move itself. The
> composite structure of the soul and body is called a living being, and is fur-
> ther termed "mortal"; "immortal" is a term applied on no basis of reasoned
> argument at all, but our fancy pictures the god whom we have never seen, nor

fully conceived, as an immortal living being, possessed of a soul and a body united for all time. (246b–d)

The myth seeks to display the falling of the soul from the immortal dimension, how its wings are lost so that it becomes a living being that is mortal. The wings of the soul lift us up to god, if they are clean and healthy, good and beautiful. The soul is destroyed and wasted if its plumage is ugly and evil.

With these considerations, we are taken into the myth proper as Socrates calls each of those listening to behold the winged chariot of Zeus, the train of gods and demons, Hestia, who "abides alone in the gods' dwelling place," and the eleven other gods, each having its place in the order of rank, each commanding its legions. Socrates has projected our eyes into a realm in which each divinity with its wholesome chariot goes about doing its own work and flies easily to its destinations. This projection is contrasted with the situation of the mortal others with their bad steed, one which must be "schooled" if the driver is to have any hope at all of enduring the toil and struggle of this greatest weight. The immortals reach the summit easily and stand on the "back of the world," carried around by the "revolving heavens" allowing them to gaze upon the nether regions (247b–c). Socrates discloses the "truth" of this other "place" of the immortal beings:

> Of that place beyond the heavens none of our earthly poets has yet sung, and none shall sing worthily. But this is the manner of it, for assuredly we must be bold to speak what is true, above all when our discourse is upon truth. It is there that true being dwells, without color or shape, they cannot be touched; reason alone, the soul's pilot, can behold it, and all true knowledge is knowledge thereof. (247c)

The soul of the divinity, nourished with the "proper food" of reason and knowledge, when "she has beheld being and is well content," is turned upon a revolution of a circle, not in the neighborhood of *becoming*, but amidst that which veritably is, of *being*, to fathom and feast upon the truth itself, justice, temperance, and knowledge. Once the soul is full of wisdom, she once again comes back inside the heavens, "comes back home," and, "having so come, her charioteer sets his steeds at their manger, and puts ambrosia before them and draught of nectar to drink withal." (247e)

Even one of the "others," who must submit to a mimetic relation to the divinity, will have a difficult task constraining the steeds. Ambrosia and nectar will not come so easily, for this one sees only fragments of that which veritably is, but is luckier than the rest, who fall ever so quickly, travel and trample, hordes crashing down, with broken wings. Far from the bliss which once was, these "feed upon the food of semblance" (248b). *Tragedy abounds*, each is not blind enough, as vision is mixed betwixt the visible and invisible. Yet, these souls do share one common sentiment and nature, to return to these meadows which are the source. But, cycle after cycle, many will be trampled, the only chance given to those who are possessed and manic, who are mad with divine love. Socrates proclaims:

> Hear now the ordinance of Necessity. Whatsoever soul has followed in the train of a god, and discerned something of truth, shall be kept from sorrow until a new revolution shall begin, and if she can do this always, she shall remain always free from hurt. But when she is not able so to follow, and sees none of it, but meeting with some mischance comes to be burdened with a load of forgetfulness and wrongdoing, and because of that burden sheds her wings and falls to the earth, and thus runs the law. (248c)

There are nine ranks to which she may fall, from the philosopher to the tyrant, before she, if ever may be, is incarnated into a "brute beast." Any specific incarnation will depend upon the *anazetese* of the self in the past life, or, in other words, upon the level of wisdom attained. It is only the self which seeks after wisdom "unfeignedly," or "has conjoined his passion for a loved one with that seeking," (249a) will bypass ten thousand years of incarnations.

Once again, we apprehend the judicial handling of the notion of transmigration by Plato. The ordinary persons, well adjusted in the cave, ever ready to attack the stranger, who still has spots in front of his eyes, will be, ironically, trampled down since they live in a forgetfulness of Truth. This "other" soul, vigilant with respect to "truth," not having imbued the dimension of becoming, is set free in a timely way, as Socrates contemplates:

> Such a soul, if with three revolutions of a thousand years she has thrice chosen this philosophical life, regains thereby her wings, and speeds away after three thousand years; but the rest, when they have accomplished their first life, are brought to judgment, and after the judgment some are taken to be punished in places of chastisement beneath the earth, while others are borne aloft by Justice to a certain region of the heavens, there to live in such manner as is merited by their past life in the flesh. (249a)

These latter, "borne aloft by Justice," spend one thousand years in this circumstance, until they must choose their second life. Each is allowed his or her otherworldly choice, the allotments are there before them. It is indicated by the writer that the choice of the philosopher be the most expedient route, but, life upon life, one may choose to live as one of the "beasts." Only those may enter the human form which have beheld truth

> seeing that man must understand the language of forms, passing from a plurality of perceptions to a unity gathered together by reasoning—and such

understanding is a recollection of those things which our souls beheld afore-
time as they journeyed with their god, looking down upon the things which
now we suppose to be, and gazing up to that which truly is. (249c)

Socrates then proclaims that it is "meet and right" that only the soul of a philosopher should regain her wings in that she dwells in nearness to the divine.
He says:

Wherefore if a man makes right use of such means of remembrance, and ever
approaches to the full vision of the perfect mysteries, he and he alone
becomes truly perfect. Standing aside from the busy doings of mankind, and
drawing nigh to the divine, he is rebuked by the multitude as being out of his
wits, for they know not that he is possessed by a deity. (249c–d)

Socrates says that it is a madness to love the divine, to remember the divine in
all things, in which terrestrial beauty incites one to a remembrance of that
which is beyond earthly beauty, and, infinitely more valuable. This "mad love"
leads to visions for a few in which there is a total loss of self-mastery with no
apprehension of an agent of transfiguration. Our perception remains "dim,"
but we can still remember the "vision" of the splendid train of Zeus, gathered
into a unity, while we are incarcerated within a "prison house" of a body, "fast
bound therein as an oyster in its shell" (250c). Socrates closes the myth proper
with this summary, "There let it rest then, our tribute to a memory that has
stirred us to linger awhile on those former joys for which we yearn" (250c).

What this myth suggests to us is that the scenario presented in the *Phaedo*,
while accurate, is too simplistic, to the extent that the death that will attain
complete release of the soul from the body, as the proper death with a "quick
release," requires a distinction be posited in the soul itself, between, and, in
Cornford's borrowed words, the "higher" and "lower" soul. In this context, it is
not only the body and its indiscipline which harms the soul, but it is also that
this bodily activity is aided and abetted by a differing aspect of the soul itself.
The soul is *agonistic*, a *topos* in which its destiny is suspended in a war with itself,
a war that will be decided by the trajectory of its desire.

Interestingly, Plato closes his dialogue with a discussion of the nature of good
and bad speech and of the significance of good writing, as a remembrance
of the divine. The latter as semblance is an external mark, a reminder, but, not
memory. Plato, in a most Pythagorean way, instead, advocates the breath of living speech as that which is most near the divine. In that Plato is most readily
known as a writer, and not as a speaker (although he set forth stylized conversations), one could contend that Plato smacks of inauthenticity here, as if he may
wish to believe what he is speaking, but cannot since speech implies hot breath
and the movement of the limbs in gesture, all of the myriad signs that erupt
during discourse (one that includes all aspects of the body) and persists amidst

the totality of references which is the world. Once again, we can contend that Plato is only using a simulacrum of speech as a disposable metaphor for the divine *logos*, messenger of truth, but not really the speech of earthly life, of the *bios*, with its valorization of the body. These references to "living speech" must not deceive us into thinking that Plato is referring to the speech of *terra bios*, but instead, of the internal speech of the soul. Again, "living speech" is a disposable metaphor pointing to a detached divine dwelling "there," with *logos* as the guiding thread. Writing points to the divine, it allows one to remember the divine, but it is not the full effervescence of the Platonic divine. Yet, it is as yet a sign, and, for Plato, an advance over terrestrial speech, that "idle chatter" of the meandering *demos*.

Writing, for Plato, is a discipline, a craft, one which distills out the essence of the phenomenal, an orderly and measured activity, supplemented by occasional ecstatic "unions" with the alterity of his divine. Despite his occasional personal participation in the narrative of the dialogue, as a figure in the scene, Plato always remains aloof from the event, tracing descriptions, sculpting, and crafting his account, in detachment, his own practice mirroring that of the demiurge in the *Timaeus*. Writing is merely an aid to memory, but it is not memory itself, it is not the breath of living speech, the breath of that which is most "real." With this contention, however, we have clearly turned away from the body and its *topos* of becoming, for a destination that transcends all of our knowledge.

Timaeus: The Divine Craftsman and the Virtual Cosmos

Plato wishes us to divide our loyalties, to disperse "our" loyalties betwixt "opposed" aspects of existence. The Pythagoreans of the oral tradition, however, and perhaps some who lasted beyond the suppression of the *bios*, would apprehend that these allegedly "opposed" aspects of the phenomenon are "here" amidst an extended domain of kinship. For Plato, as with Zoroaster or Zarathustra, there are "good" thoughts, words, and deeds, and there are other phenomena, utterly apart from the divinity, that of the "bad" or "evil." These domains are strictly and exclusively separated, excepting, of course, the invisible thread which allows the philosopher to leap from one domain to the other in his escape from the labyrinth of everlasting purification and punishment. Plato selects those things, practices, and those thoughts which demonstrate, for him, a symbolic or indicative relationship with that which he designates as "divine." This process of selection is a displacement and a rejection, an erasing of that other domain of thoughts, words, and deeds, which does not entail a relationship to the divine. Yet, this reference to the specific judgment of Plato is not to suggest that he merely "opines" as there is a criteria from and by which he can undertake such decisions, an axiom of truth, a reference matrix of truth, a procedure of truth-deciding. The criteria would be plausible, however, only if there were someone who had already exited the cavern of shadows and had returned.

Plato does make his "philosophical actors" speak with great confidence, and it is Socrates who, even in his sublime ignorance, exhibits the greatest confidence. This posture of wisdom intimates the strategy of "essence" in the narrative of Plato, in his assertion of an axiom of truth. The axiom consists in the indubitable presence of the divine principle amidst the one who makes the judgment. Plato is a devotee to the axiom, who affirms the axiom, and also apprehends that which is not the axiom, that of the reference matrix which is set forth as a schematization of phenomenal, temporal life. However, as we have seen in the case of the divided line, this schema is coordinated with the asserted axiom of truth. The coordination is an act of "turning" of the temporal toward this axiom of truth, which sets forth that which is, upon reflection, designated as a procedure of truth. The procedure occurs before its formalization, as an *act* of selection guided by the axiom of truth.

The triple interplay of axiom, reference, and procedure, in the text of Plato, enacts a regimen of operation which posits the existential significance of thoughts, words, and deeds amidst the world, each of these being set against a value axiom, relative to which, many and much is not only deemed to have no value, but also to be false, ugly, and evil. Plato's assertion of antithetical values, and his advocacy of only one of the poles of the opposition, is the background for the decision which underlies his strategy of truth and the meaning of his philosophy.

One could, of course, contest, in light of our discussion of Philolaus, that the Pythagoreans set forth a "Table of Opposites," and that this must imply that they held differential values with respect to the oppositions. Again, these are "opposites," as they are not, each to each, alike, nor could they be. Yet, one must, in light of our previous discussions, recognize, if we open up our Pythagorean ears, that these are not only the primary constituents of this world, but are the constituents also of the soul, and indeed, of the divinity itself, conceived as the Divine All.[13] *Oppositions*, for example, 6th/12th, light and darkness, "good" and "bad," intimate differing aspects of a world in its "opening," each equally valuable in the constitution of the "real." Nothing is other than the All; each "opposite" acts amongst the All, and cannot be other than the All. That which is significant for the Pythagoreans is not the decision for or against any opposite, but the attunement of oppositions in the world.

In light of this foray into theories of truth and value, the fundamental difference between Plato and Pythagoras concerns their respective conceptions of and comportments with the "divine." In this way, it will be instructive to explore the *Timaeus*, which is considered to be the most Pythagorean of all his works. We have seen earlier in the chapter on Philolaus, that Plato had borrowed one of the works of Philolaus in order to write his *Timaeus*. Yet, in light of what we have learned from our discussion of Philolaus, and of Plato in the previous pages, it is clear that we must exercise due caution when we come to consider a work to be of "Pythagorean" character. It is precisely in that these philosophers are working within the parameters of the written tradition that each may have had an affinity to divinity of "externality," or with Nietzsche, of nihilism.

In the dialogue, the main speaker, Timaeus, the name of a noted Pythagorean of the "written" tradition, unfolds a narrative of the creation of the phenomenal universe, an account which we find to have marked similarities to that which has been called the "Path of the Event" above. In the following, I will examine the tale told by Timaeus of the generation of the world of becoming, with a specific focus upon the character of the demiurge, and upon the notion of time as a "moving image of Eternity." Each and both of these aspects of the problem will again cast into relief the severance of becoming and being and of the coordination of certain aspects of becoming to that of being, that is endemic throughout his works, as we have seen from our previous discussions.

Timaeus, calling upon the gods, begins his prelude:

> First then, in my judgment, we must make a distinction and ask, What is that which always is and has no becoming, and what is that which is always becoming and never is? That which is apprehended by intelligence and reason is always in the same state, but that which is conceived by opinion with the help of sensation and without reason is always a process of becoming and perishing, and never really is. (27d–28a)

This account resembles the Myth of the Cave and the other myths which we have detailed above. Yet, it seeks to tell us more, to provide a specific account of the generation of the universe by the creative artisanship of a demiurge who fashions the world of becoming as a simulacrum of the true reality of eternity. The demiurge fabricates this dimension of becoming, of time, a visibility that never truly is, but, one fashioned "after an unchangeable pattern," not one abiding amid or having origin in the world of sensation (28a). The world is created, has a beginning, since it is "visible and tangible and having a body . . ." (28b). Yet, the cause of this world is a divinity whom we need not know, of whom we can know nothing, except that it is not "us." Timaeus insists:

> But the father and maker of all this universe is past finding out, and even if we found him, to tell of him to all men would be impossible. (28c)

Instead, Timaeus asks his listeners a question:

> Which of the patterns had the artificer in view when he made it—the pattern of the unchangeable or of that which is created? If the world be indeed fair and the artificer good, it is manifest that he must have looked to that which is eternal, but if what cannot be said without blasphemy is true, then to the created pattern. (28c–29a)

Timaeus cajoles everyone by saying that the world must be fair and the artificer good, and that we must maintain a strict separation betwixt that which imitates the unchangeable pattern and that which attunes itself to the created phenomena. Timaeus claims that his narration, to his hearers, is a most plausible account, but only an account, for, as mortals, we will never possess wisdom. He closes his prelude to the main narrative:

> If then, Socrates, amidst the many opinions about the gods and the generation of the universe, we are not able to give notions which are altogether and in every respect exact and consistent with one another, do not be surprised. Enough if we adduce probabilities as likely as any others, for we must remember that I who am the speaker and you who are the judges are only mortal men, and we ought to accept the tale which is probable and inquire no further. (29c–d)

The residue of the dialogue unfolds as a likely story, one amongst the rest. Yet, this rest must also include the "magical" narrative which I have been articulating in this present work, of an account which is plausible amongst other narratives. But, plausibility is a slippery notion, one which depends upon the horizons of decidability for any person engaged in an event of decision. Moreover, we are discussing wide ranging issues, of Pythagoras, of Plato; these are different paths of knowing. Yet, this differing is glossed over in the respective treatments of the doctrine of transmigration by various scholars. Amidst this erasure, the Platonic version of transmigration is set comfortably near to that of the Pythagoreans, as if it were all of a piece. No one inquires further.

It would seem, on the basis of our current discussion, quite implausible to simply "graft" the Platonic stratagem of punishment and "liberation," upon the Pythagorean *bios*. These are differing philosophies, even if much of the narrative of the *Timaeus*, in its intricate description of the *Kosmos*, could be considered genuinely Pythagorean. That is why the focus upon the "artisan" god, one which persists strangely detached from his product, is significant: for Plato, there is no possible *explanation* of the event of One becoming Two; yet, Two is considered a fall from One. There erupts a parallel in the severing of the dimensions of sensible and the intelligible in the dialogues of Plato, as he not only asserts that only the latter is truly real, but also writes boldly that it is only the philosopher who will be liberated from the wheel. As we have seen, it is precisely the coincidence of dimensions which is the heart and soul of the Pythagorean affirmation; their horizon of decidability affirmed an extended kinship of the All, in the polemical context of the restricted economy of the Homeric pantheon. In this light, we can interpret Plato as one who reaffirmed the opposites, but cast into relief as deadly opposites, which harbored the necessity of an escape from the unsustainable conflict.

These are deadly since the soul no longer simply travels to Hades, sitting immersed forever in a cloud of nostalgia, remembering that which was most real in this nexus of decidability, the body. In the recipe of Plato, the soul is compelled through punishment and discipline to seek that which is higher, and this liberation takes place only under the sign of a death which fully cleanses the soul of the filth of the body. Plato inverts the Homeric valuation of body and soul through a revaluation of the specific character of each antithesis. With his revaluation of the distinction betwixt the mortal and immortal, instead of a descent of nostalgia a la Homer, he promises an ascent, but one plagued, except for the true philosopher, by a downward force of deviant desires of the body. It is these desires which are subjected to a comprehensive and ruthless punishment schedule in a project of bringing the realm of becoming into synchronicity with the divine "other." Through the containment of the body, the philosopher will obtain a life amidst that "beyond," which is, itself, only truly real. The divinity is an "artisan;" it has fabricated *this* which is here for "us." This is the "reason" we give to the question of why One becomes Two, the persistence of a question which intimates our paradoxical abandonment.

This is the cumulative message of Plato who writes that the cosmos is a "model" for the eternal: Time is a moving image of eternity, a simulacrum for the eternal. But, ultimately, such a body, even that of the All, is of no account, disposable, empty.

The Road Taken: Plato and the Ascetic Ideal of Purity

Plato advocates the scenario of transmigration, but, deploys it as the engine of a procedure of "moral" judgment, one cast down heavy and harsh via his ascetic God. The body amidst its ways and byways becomes the fodder for this ultimate goal of purification. That which is to be purified is the material upon which the artisan inscribed the traces of the divine form. This demiurge does not give birth to All through itself, but, as an artisan, fashions its inscription upon a material that is always already there as other than itself. There persists in this scenario a primary separation of the divine and matter, to the extent that only specifically divine "touched" aspects of phenomenal presence can be judged as affiliated with that divinity.

This casts into relief the distance which exists between Plato and Pythagoras, in that the latter is never known to have separated the divine from matter, nor, need he ever have done as he taught a philosophy of extended kinship. Plato's is clearly a much different scenario of transmigration than that of the Pythagoreans of the oral and biotic tradition. In the Homeric perspective, as we have said, such acts of transference seeking the divine, would constitute *hubris*, which is not to say, of course, that such a desire is impossible as such. In the Platonic perspective, this transference is possible and is indeed sought after betwixt similars, between the higher soul and the divine; but as an act of other worldly transference which does not depend upon an extended kinship of All. The transference that is enacted in Plato is a restricted kinship between the soul and the divine, which is an economy that is in opposition to the dimension of matter, together with those entities which have arisen through the corruption of the soul by an association of proximity to matter, the body and the world.

The Pythagoreans, in their turn, as Guthrie insists, held a notion of the extended kinship of All, a magical notion sheltered intact at the heart of the Pythagorean teaching, a continuation of "non-civilized" modes of thought. Such a notion is not constrained by the Platonic "bifurcation" of matter and the divine, for as it is a kinship of the All, and one that is "magical," that is, a "practical" philosophy. Contrary to the Platonic scenario, this *cosmic* philosophy comprehends that any path of return to the All requires neither a leap, nor, does it aspire to a liberation from the tomb of the body, as if the higher soul has been cast away from its home into a hostile expanse of darkness. A kinship of the All implies a "gathering" of alleged opposites, one that underlies the possibility of transference between similars amidst the All. In this perspective, the pathway of the soul is to be in harmony with the pathway of the body, if that is, one attunes oneself to the All. Similars, as those perspective-dependent points of reference on a trek, are not isolated from that which surrounds, the way of the path itself, no more than similar notes are separated from other notes or from the silences betwixt notes. These reflections, in the context of a notion of the extended kinship of All, can allow "us" to fathom the Pythagorean philosophy which could ascertain resemblances between the body and the divine, the monochord and the spirit of music, with an emphasis on the terrestrial activity that is implied by the notion of a pathway amidst All.

Plato, despite his scorn for the world, did not ignore this emphasis upon terrestrial *praxis*; but, as his conception was that of a restricted kinship for only the higher soul and the divine, for the some, and, not the All, his prescription for the body was that of asceticism and discipline, looking forward to the event of release from the world and the body. This conception, again, is a complete inversion of the Homeric scenario in which the life of the body was primary, and the soul, simply, a nostalgic "shadow" dwelling in Hades. However, in this inversion, Plato maintains a conception of kinship, and thus, of "identification," reminiscent of the Homeric separation of the realms, in the distance he places betwixt the higher soul and all that which is lower. This "method" of "segregation" is merely utilized for differing "ends."

Perhaps, it is Plato, who through this "turning" is the "true" revolutionary, and Nietzsche is correct to write that Pythagoras is merely a "religious reformer." From what "we" know of the teaching of Pythagoras, this is in many ways a fair assessment, except that, with the virtual deification of the body, it transgresses the Homeric taboo of a separation of mortal and immortal with the notion that the All can be obtained via a wandering throughout the All. In this way, the Pythagorean teaching affirms the Homeric appreciation of the body, but as the body is also the symbolic site of meeting for the Unlimited and Limit, a meeting which engenders soul and invokes a remembrance of the All, it is apprehended that there is no need for the soul to "descend" to Hades with death, but, that it could instead embark on a path of wandering throughout the "greater circles" of the body, as the plethora of other beings, terrestrial and celestial, each there amidst the All, always in a state of affirmation.

Pythagoras was a reformer to the extent that he played within the given horizons. Yet, he was a revolutionary in that his doctrine of radical friendship implied a subversion and transgression of the restricted economy of blood kinship. For Pythagoras, an extended kinship was the primary horizon for his alternative notion of the sublimation (not purification) of *ecstasis* through the *theoria* and *bios* of a "practical" philosophy (*metasomatosis*). His subversion invoked a breaking down of the Homeric separation of mortals and gods, as each strives to become attuned with the All.

Chapter 9

Plotinus: The Ascent of the Soul toward the One

We turn to another great advocate of the doctrine of transmigration, Plotinus, in order to examine the specific contours and textures of his interpretation, especially with respect to the status of the body and also to its commitment to a notion of an extended kinship of the All. This latter would imply that the living creature, the *Kosmos*, is not the model, but is the All itself, in its "visible" and "invisible" dimensions. We immediately detect when reading Plotinus that his notions are distinct from those of the Pythagoreans, although each of these philosophies do share various similarities. Yet, despite various resemblances, Plotinus presents a philosophy of the One of which the All is conceived in terms of an *emanational* architectonic, formalized by means of a vertical hierarchy and a matrix of antitheses, borrowed from the philosophies of Plato and Aristotle, and synthesized in the form of his own teaching. We will, in the following, investigate Plotinus' notion of the *ascent* to the One, an ascent which harbors within itself the memory of a violent fall, a fall conceived as a descent into a body conceived as a tomb, lost in a world where magic rules, and where there is no rest for the weary. These twin notions of fall and ascent come directly from Plato, and, as suggested in the previous chapter, these are very unlikely to be genuine Pythagorean notions for they imply a devaluation of the body and world.

The question, for Plotinus, of an ascent of the soul toward the One, and not the All, arises in the *Enneads*[1] with the presupposition of a primal distancing of the soul from the One. This original distancing is a descent, for Plotinus, and it can only be expressed in the form of myth of a Fall (III.5.9). Plotinus poetically narrates this opening of Reality, ". . . that huge illumination of the Supreme pouring outwards comes at last to the extreme bourne of its light and dwindles to darkness, now lying there beneath, the Soul sees and by seeing brings to shape . . ." (IV.3.9). Yet, in the wake of this opening, the One remains distinct in itself, ". . . the giver does not know of the gift but simply gives . . ." (IV.4.42). This poetic account of a beginning leads to a contemplation of the One and of its relationship to those various levels which have emanated from itself. Plotinus writes:

> The Soul of the higher extends across the entire material fabric, including in its spiritual membership the participation of the lower soul.

This lower soul, Plotinus writes, however, is

> [A] deserter from the totality; its differentiation has severed it; its vision is no longer set in the Intellectual; it is a partial thing, isolated, weakened, full of care intent upon the fragment; severed from the whole, it nestles in one form of being. (IV.8.4)

This soul seems to persist here amidst the physical dimension of body, of change and temporality. Yet, Plotinus writes, ". . . the void must be that in which body is placed; body (not soul) will be in the void" (IV.3.20). In a consideration of the presence of the soul to the body, Plotinus assents to the metaphor of light and air:

> [T]he light penetrates through and through, but nowhere coalesces; the light is the stable thing, the air flows in and out; when the air passes beyond the lit area it is dark; under the light it is lit . . . a true parallel to . . . body and soul, for the air is in the light rather than the light in the air. (IV.3.22)

The One is There as an alterior dimension of possible reality. It is eternal in its repose as the other-Same. The light of the soul disperses across the domain of body, fallen far away from the initial out flowing of divine light. It has touched the outer limit of void, without, however, being engulfed by it. The soul never touches absolute nothingness, and thus, has in itself the possible destiny of its return to the One.

In this way, there opens before our gaze the lattice-work relief of the All, and a beckoning intimation to the invisible-beyond. The All is the body of the *Kosmos* attuned with the higher Soul, a chiasmus extends throughout a gradient of presence toward the regions of lower soul and body. The circuit of All is kindredly administered by the All Soul, it is, Plotinus describes, the variety in unity of a perfect sympathetic organism. It is an eternal, total being to which there is neither proximity nor distance, but an intimacy in which the "far is near" (IV.4.32). Beyond the All, or, into the very depths of this All, there is the possibility for the nearing of the soul toward the One, that which is identified via its distance from the All. There is sought that invisible perfection beyond, or, in through, this visible dimension. The search arises here amidst this dimension of lower soul and body, yet, as we gaze out about the perfection of the movements of the stars, of the cosmic sympathy of the star souls, we fall into a state which intimates to ourselves the reality, but yet, the nowhere of a dimension of compact repose, of nearness toward the One.[2]

Even if that One is There, we can never find it amidst the here *and* there. It is beyond our sensibility, beyond even our reason. This question signals the destruction of our innocence in this tragedy of suffering, plagues of body, disease, death. This region of severance takes our innocence away from us. We no longer relish our joy amidst this here and now. We see in joy only an intimation of a beyond of this here and now. Plotinus writes,

> I am weary already of this prison-house, the body, and calmly await the day when the divine nature within me shall be set free from matter[3]

Life (and the body), here, is merely a necessary evil. The question is of a distance taken betwixt the soul and the One. This distance conjures a tension which craves a resolution. The resolution comes by way of the ascent of the soul toward the One. No one soul is the All-Soul, and thus, the departure of one will not disrupt the Circuit of All, or its Soul, Idea, or primal Reality. The departure is a traveling, not a wandering, on the way toward the One. This traveling soul toward the One resembles the ultimate separation of the soul from the body. Yet, the soul in death is distinct from that one wandering through the ascent toward the One, even though both move from here to there. The soul that has chosen this path seeks the One regardless of the reality of death. The ascent to the One is expressed as a pathway across many lives, a journey of incessant vigilance and preparation, unlike death, which may come as suddenly as the wind. Plotinus counsels that it is not wise to seek to force this departure, for as this journey concerns not just this single awakening, this one life, nevertheless, much of this life, much of this body, may remain imprinted, stained upon the soul. In this regard, he quotes the *Chaldean Oracles*: "You will not dismiss your Soul lest it go forth taking something with it" (I. 9.1). From this perspective, the soul which forces itself from the body will remain in these lower realms, for the proper preparation is that of a delicate cultivation. The one who forces this departure is cast to the winds of recurrence. The preparation and travel of the soul, seeking to cultivate perfection in itself, occurs amid these dimensions opened through the separation of soul and One. This dimension here is not the entirety of Reality, but is our site of departure, our only possible chance for awareness amidst this singular opening.

We depart amidst this architecture of Reality which has been strewn across our own situation of proximity and distance. This realm of the visible, of this soul-stretched body, this place, the prison of body, is at once caressed by the light of that other dimension, the other opening, the invisible. This light beckons our remembrance of the alterior dimension and calls for us to seek its repose (a god of sleep and dreams). This remembrance is only possible for the souls which have lost the vision of the One, who move amidst *this* rhythm.

Plotinus writes: "Memory . . . commences after the Soul has left the highest spheres; it is first known in the celestial period" (IV.4.6). This seeking of repose is a path, a single path amidst the sprawling ways and byways, toward the One. This single journey cultivates repose, a preparation of thought and practice which attunes to the gathering proper to the eternal. The path of the soul toward the One follows the trajectory of the original excession of the One toward the Many, yet, in the opposing direction, the soul retraces its flight, its falling, this soul flies, riding on this light which illuminates All. The necessity for a tracing out of this path underscores the distance through which the soul has fallen. For the life of the One has no sense of the ways and byways of measurement and movement. Plotinus writes, "There all is one day; series has no place; no yesterday, no last year" (IV.4.7). The nearness amid this excession of eternal light is however the path that must be chosen. Plotinus invites, "To those desiring to see, we point the path. Our teaching is of the road and the traveling; the seeing must be the very act of one who has made this choice" (VI.9.4). For the one who does not apprehend the call of the invisible, there is only ceaseless entrapment betwixt the rhythms and contours "proper" to the lower dimension, although from the Pythagorean perspective, this captivity is, in actuality, a sublime lattice of exploratory pathways. Through being each, the singular can fathom the All. Yet, as always, Plotinus, a child of his time, scorns the body and life, wishing escape,

> The sufferer, all unaware, is swept onward towards his due, hurried always by the restless driving of his errors, until at last wearied out by that against which he struggled, he falls into his fit place and, by self-chosen movement, is brought to the lot he never chose. (IV.3.24)

In this way, the one who does not aspire to nearness will nevertheless be lead with justice to its proper place amidst the circuit of the All. The magic will be performed in the end for the sake of the All. Yet, this one who does not seize upon this fate will fail to transcend. A proper destiny is not for the blind, apparently.

The path one takes is one of a specific style of practice, one leading to the stillness of contemplation, this higher aspect of the life of a soul. This style must attune with this destination toward the One. It must be a life work of attunement toward the One. What is tuned toward the one through this style of soul is the body, as well as that of the transfiguration of the lower to the higher soul. The body, this hindrance of a soul seeking perfection is made to conform to this project of transcendence, is thus made to serve the project of the soul. But, as the body is ultimately outside the grace of eternity, either of soul or of mind, it will not attune without the intervening of a power. This power is the openness of the soul to seek the One, to respond to this beckoning call, as a traveler who seeks to return home.

For this creature, there are two aspects of soul, one of which being the gateway through to the path toward the One, the other being a hole leading to the abyss of oblivion. There is a danger in this regard for the One is apprehended immediately as an alterity as such, not as one singular path. In this way, the lower phase of the soul can be overwhelmed by the calls from spiritual powers which remain in deference toward the One. The first step to the beyond is thus, for Plotinus, to embark upon the path which is properly attuned to the sending toward the One, that of contemplation.

The appropriate path toward the One exhibits itself through the project of unification which draws the soul toward the One. The soul is drawn toward the One via its attunement to That, it becomes akin to it, as like will know like. In its purposeful working—for attunement toward the One, amidst this exercise of remembrance of the One, that invisible, the soul must forget this dimension of the lower soul, of the visible, change, movement, and temporality. The soul remembers the visible in its being-amid, it senses the invisible as a desire for repose. Yet, this procession of memory confirms the embeddedness of this soul amidst the fallen realm of the visible, of the body, of evil.

Amidst the eternal dimension of One, there is no ecstatic fluctuation of temporality, there is thus no memory. One is to forget the visible vis-à-vis a deepening remembrance of that which has no memory, that One. Even an eruption of memory in the higher realms will not corrupt this assertion of distinction betwixt dimensions, if it be memory in the sense of regime and order, memory of events amidst design, and not of memory amidst temporality. What is truly at stake is the character of memory selected, of which dimension draws the soul into its sphere of power. In our remembrance of the one, we are to forget the dimension of memory as image, and embark toward the dimension of vision as intimate nearness, that intuition which apprehends only itself as One.

Yet, in the higher regions, the question of memory only has authentic relevance when the higher is compelled to turn toward the lower in its duty of administration. In this light, the path to be traversed is one from containment amidst this visible, implying the reproductive power of the imagination and its link to body, a gathering of impressions amidst persistent collocations, to the destination revealed in Remembrance, a dimension in which the path of return is finally eclipsed into irrelevance, redundancy, as what is *sought* and the *seeker* become one and the same. With this forgetting of the visible, our memory transfigures into the vision amidst the intimacy of the invisible.

What is sought is a trans-destination from time to eternity. For a soul to become near to the One, it must lose itself as soul, it must lose itself, and thus, become itself once more. This soul which hovers over this body is drawn into these many seductions across and throughout the visible dimension. Amid its magical bewitchment within the visible, the soul, hovering about this body, falls away from remembrance. The soul which is ruled by the dimension of the lower, of body, of change, of action, of temporality, at its eventual separation from this body, is influenced by this dimension to the extent that it recurs, throughout this circuit of transmigration, as a soul amidst body once more, either lower or higher on the scale of being. The desire to be drawn near toward the One traverses the sending of many lives of the soul. In this way, death is the passage by which the soul will recur or transcend recurrence. Yet, for a soul which merely hovers about and around the sphere of the visible, or, as this creature is ruled via the dimension of the physical, puppeted vicariously vis-à-vis the lower soul, there will be no transcendence of this everlasting circuit of life to life, of body to body, beyond, into the eternity of the One.

The pathway toward the One entails a delicate cultivation of the soul through a practice which prepares the soul for departure from the modified being of soul with body. This practice occurs amidst the visible field of actions. Yet, Plotinus warns (and in a manner which makes us prick up our ears), ". . . every action has magic at its source, and the entire life of the practical men is a bewitchment: we move to that only which has wrought a fascination upon us" (IV. 4.43). As it hovers amidst this differential nexus of powers and seductions, as it is implicated within the rhythm and circuit of All, the soul struggles for a turning toward a deeper reminiscence of the One.

Being amid this circuit itself, Plotinus counsels, departs a lesson to the soul with regard to its proper administration of the body, and ultimately, of the proper direction of the ascent toward the One. This lesson is the beginning of the journey to the One that it beyond the All. The justice of the All executes itself merely in the turning of the All. This justice is a physical criteria which unfolds as the workings of the eternal cosmos. Plotinus writes:

> The punishments are like the treatment of diseased parts of the body–here, medicines to knit sundered flesh; there amputations; elsewhere, change of environment . . . condition—and the penalties are planned to bring health to the All by setting every member in the fitting place; and this health of the All requires that one man be made over anew and another, sick here, be taken hence to where he shall be weakly no longer. (IV. 4.45)

The destiny of the modified body and soul is separation, death invokes the call for the departure and return of the soul. However, this separation itself entails no instigation of justice. Justice (*dike*) comes about with the resolution of the soul into its fate. Justice is the cultivation of a proper attunement of the soul with the One. This attunement is intimated through the display of the *Kosmos*. Yet, the desire for nearing of the soul toward the One cannot ultimately find its satisfaction amidst this circuit of the All. For even this realm of the Celestial participates within the dimension of temporality with its eternal movement. This is the life of the All-Soul and this is where memory initially emerges. With our path to the One, we not only seek to forget this dimension of restlessness through a deeper attunement near to the One, but in this seeking, we aspire to the repose of the eternal. The soul seeks to return to that from which it had originally fallen. It seeks to transcend the eternal recurrence of the paths of transmigration, to liberate itself beyond this dimension. Plotinus, as with Plato, illuminates this power of opposition to the circuit of the All through a distinction betwixt the higher and lower souls, "As for our being begotten children of the Cosmos, we answer that in motherhood the entrant soul is distinct, is not the mother's" (IV.3.7). This radical transcendence of the circuit can be compared to the escapist interpretation of the flight of Apollo, which we considered in Chapter 6.

This notion of transcendence has its source in various experiences of the soul amidst this realm of the lower soul. Initially, the experience of death itself serves to suggest that this dimension of body is not sufficiently real. There is additionally the gaze upon the region of the higher soul and the invisible order that it intimates. Lastly, there is the fleeting experience of Nearing that is achieved through meditative practice. In this light, there are indeed indications of that dimension we seek.

The apprehension of the higher has occasioned in the soul a desire for nearing toward the Beyond. The ascent to the One as a pathway requires the opening of a "magical" infrastructure of a specific character. Magic is the source of every action, it flows out as rhythm and contour, as this rhapsodic excession of presence, it is life itself amidst this visible dimension. Magic inhabits this dimension of visibility, in its sense, it is the truth of disclosure amidst concealment. Yet, this ascent toward the One transcends in its way beyond this containment amidst a visible dimension. The transcendence of this visible toward that invisible, in that the eyes are the windows of the soul, requires the magic of visibility, a "gateway" of access, toward those realms of invisible harmony of the divine. This is the capacity of the creative soul in its power of self-attention and dutiful apprehension of the intimate activities of the higher. Plotinus writes, "I think . . . that those ancient sages, who sought to secure the presence of divine beings by the erection of shrines and statues, showed insight into the nature of the All" (IV.3.11). Visible action in the service of nearing toward the One is necessary, yet, it must, as a cultivation of attunement with the invisible, have a specific henological character.

As this visible practice is seeking nearness to the One, this dimension of compact repose, this nowhere of overwhelming self-sufficiency, there must be the cultivation of a mastery of the self, of the modified soul and body, which prepares for the anticipated release of the divine from matter. This cultivation is a preparation for a death through which the knowing one "sets out to the place he must, understanding, even as he begins the journey, where he is to be housed at the end, and having the good hope that he will be with gods" (IV.4.44). This preparation is the act of self-mastery of soul in preparation for a "noiseless" departure from the visible dimension into and amid a *henosis*.

This character of self-mastery, this building of attunement resembles one ". . . playing the cithara for the sake of achieving the art, like practicing with a view to mastery, like any learning that aims at knowing" (VI.4.12). With respect to the cultivation of a selective forgetfulness, Plotinus writes, ". . . any special attention blurs every other" (IV.4.25). In this light, the path of forgetfulness is not a self-conscious scrutiny of various memories presented to the interior gaze, and the act of subsequent selection of these thought-images versus those. On the contrary, forgetfulness is attained through special attention to that which is of a different order to the visible, a practice of body and soul which aims, for Plotinus, toward the invisibles of form and order. Forgetfulness is attained through a vigilant practice whose inherent special attention, this activity, displaces the influencing powers and seductions of the lower regions.

Plotinus describes this process of vigilance,

> The creature will yield only to watchful, strenuous constancy of habit. Purify your soul from all undue hope and fear about earthly things, mortify the body, deny self, affections as well as appetites, and the inner eye will begin to exercise its clear and solemn vision. ("Letter to Flaccus," p. 291)

What is required in this specific practice is that the traveler "attune" with that which is higher in soul and body. One must chose to be integrated into the eternal sympathy of the enchained forces of the All. One must find the gateways whereby such a "linkage" may be fulfilled. Plotinus writes with respect to the initiation of the proper style of action, ". . . in the art of magic all looks to this enlinkment: prayer and its answer, magic and its success . . ." (IV.4.26). The action of the modified soul and body must resemble the graceful compliance of the dance:

> [T]he limbs of the dancer . . . adapt themselves to the plan, bending as it dictates, one lowered, another raised, one active, another resting as the set pattern changes. The dancer's mind is on his own purpose; his limbs are submissive to the dance-movement which they accomplish. (IV.4.33)

The choreography of the dance, in its unity with the patterns of music, displays the path nearing toward that invisible One. These visible actions intimate the invisible domain of unity, these fashion a dwelling appropriate to this glimpse toward the One, an orchestrated selection for the project of nearing the One. With the special attention being directed amidst these activities, the remembrance of the imagining faculty is displaced from the images of the visible toward the concealed directives of a divine which haunts the dwellings proper to itself. This is analogous to the conjuration of sanctimony via the rituals of prayer and meditation. In these activities, the will, through the cultivation of a space for remembrance, is surrendered to the opening of the invisible, and through such a surrender, the true essence of self-will emerges in its event of nearing to the One. Yet, music, prayer, and meditation (fasting, hygiene, etc.) each has its source in magic. As such, these still allow for the soul to be beguiled by the seductions of the lower. Although we have required these actions amidst the visible dimension, there must open for our gaze the dimension of the invisible, and hence, for the willful choice of the soul of wisdom. Plotinus writes, ". . . one, having penetrated the inner sanctuary, leaves the temple images beyond him . . ." (VI.9.11). We are, in this light, seeking the self intention of a transcendence of magic, of action, toward the contemplation of the One, of nearing the repose of the eternal. This repose is self-intent, and only "the self-intent go free of magic." This is the state of contemplation, which

> alone stands untouched by magic; no man self-gathered falls to a spell; for he is one, and that unity is all he perceives, so that his reason is not beguiled but holds the due course, fashioning its own career and accomplishing its task. (IV.4.44)

This contemplation is vision near toward the one; its gaze is that of rest, and ". . . we rest because we have come to wisdom" (IV.4.12). This contemplation is no mere thinking through the "faculty of reason," for even here there is multiplicity in a unity. Plotinus writes in *On the Nature and Source of Evil*, setting out the realm of mind which also must be transcended in the event:

> Our intelligence is nourished on the propositions of logic, is skilled in following discussions, works by reasonings, examines links of demonstration, and comes to know the world of Being also by the steps of logical process, having no prior grasp of Reality but remaining empty, all Intelligence though it be, until it has put itself to school. (I.8.2)

This is the pathway beyond all pathways, the ascent of the soul toward the One, the cultivation and fulfillment of the nearing of a return to the source and reality of All. This is a return to the One, a path which destroys itself in its accomplishment. Near the nowhere of liberation, the visible sign, as with the philosophy of Plato, is jettisoned. No one ever seems to question whether or not this intention, that of the transcendence of the All, of magic, is also the goal of the Pythagoreans. Can we, amidst this opening of movement and flux, of life, and perspective, be urged to desire a divine of repose, of only sleep and dream, and never true action and being? For if the Pythagorean divine All is the source of Limit and Unlimited, which exist in harmony, it certainly is not a god of repose, a god for the weary, the exhausted, who trade the world for death. It would seem to more clearly be attuned to the thought of Heraclitus and Empedocles, both of whom relished in the unity of opposites. We can think, in this context, that it is unfortunate that Plotinus fell under Plato's spell as it is certainly possible, as we have seen in the case of the Pythagorean *bios*, to seek out the divine without deprecating the body and the All and unduly falling under the spell of asceticism.

In the end, it comes back to the question of the meaning of transmigration and that of the divine. As we can see, Plotinus is perhaps closer to Pythagoras than Plato in his valorization of the choreography of the body, and not merely the intellectualism and training of the academy. However, at the same time, even with this family resemblance, the Plotinian affirmation of the One and his use, though, ultimate aversion to magic, as the life of the body and the All, is, in light of our exploration of the sympathetic character of magic in the Pythagorean *bios*, directly opposed to the way of life and destination of the Pythagoreans, whom never wished to transcend the All toward a One, and thus, never wished to leave magic behind. We will next turn, in our final chapter, to a brief consideration of the "Letter to Flaccus" so as to be clear with regard to the character of the philosophy of Plotinus as a *henological* mysticism, one at various with the *bios* of the Pythagoreans.

Chapter 10

Plotinus as Neoplatonic Mystic:
Letter to Flaccus[1]

This obscure text, written circa AD 260 is not included in the *Enneads*. It has been chosen since it offers indications of the specific practice of Plotinian Neoplatonism. I discovered this letter by chance, finding it quite revealing and unambiguous vis-à-vis the scattered comments of Plotinus which are inscribed concerning such contours as solitude, asceticism, and of the stern rejection of various magical notions, especially those linked with Egyptian *mythos* and his kindred condemnation of Gnosticism.[2] Yet, I would suggest that this letter is not only of anecdotal interest, but, casts important aspects of his philosophy into relief. It is well known that Plotinus was not simply a bookish thinker, but considered philosophy as a path of ascension by which the initiate could obtain nearness to That One. He himself testifies to several moments of compact repose, or ecstatic immanence amidst the One, experiences, however, which eventually subsided, his soul returning via a descent to the factical, everyday world. In this light, I feel that it is crucial to investigate this aspect of his philosophy in order to provide depth and sense to his sometimes cryptic references.

Plotinus commends Flaccus for his sincere devotion to this path of philosophy, this chosen pursuit cast into relief not only via a reference to the mythological homecoming of Ulysses, but also through the discipleship of Rogatianus, a Roman Senator, who had given up his Wealth and Station in order to allow his soul to set sail for "the only real country—the world of unseen truth." This advocation toward Alterity is underscored by his depiction of the turbulent times facing the soul amid the many threats to "our degenerate Rome." Plotinus testifies:

> In days like these, crowded with incessant calamities, the inducements to a life of contemplation are more than ever strong. Even my quiet existence seems now to grow somewhat sensible of the advance of years. Age alone I am unable to debar from my retirement. I am weary already of this prison-house, the body, and calmly await the day when the divine nature within me shall be set free from matter.[3]

In order to distinguish himself from other modes of thought which exalt a similar path of transcendence from the physical, Plotinus juxtaposes the ritual *praxis* of Egyptian priests to his own ascetic, visionary pathway.[4] Denying that one can merely engage sacred amulets and magical devices or invocation in order to still the heart, Plotinus sets out his path for the discipline of the wildness of *ipse*,[5] as a sacrifice of body and native instinct:

> The creature will yield only to watchful, strenuous constancy of habit. Purify your soul from all undue hope and fear about earthly things, mortify the body, deny self, affections as well as appetites, and the inner eye will begin to exercise its clear and solemn vision.[6]

After disclosing that he only decided to inscribe his philosophy at the insistence of Porphyry,[7] he answers a question of Flaccus with reference to his "criterion of certainty." His elaboration on this question elucidates not only the peculiarity of his pursuit, but also, implies an order of rank between the philosopher vis-à-vis "ordinary and practical men," far removed from kinship. Following Plato's demarcation of the Divided Line, Plotinus asserts that external objects provide only a glimpse, that of appearance, corresponding only to opinion, not to knowing. He thus turns the question:

> Our question lies within the ideal reality which exists behind appearance. How does the mind perceive these ideas? Are they without us, and is the reason, like sensation, occupied with objects external to itself? What certainty could we then have, what assurance that our perception was infallible? The object perceived would be a something different from the mind perceiving it. We should then have an image instead of reality.[8]

Plotinus at once finds this line of questioning objectionable, even "monstrous," as it may imply that there would be no effective criterion for certainty. For there persists a marked distinction that must be brought into the foreground, that is, this breach between worlds, that of the sensible and the ideal, or that which is *this* sensual flux and that which is, in truth, real, *that* intelligible. Plotinus attests that the intellect must apprehend ideal truth "exactly as it is" and that there must indeed be "certainty and real knowledge concerning the world of intelligence." In order to elude this monster of indeterminacy, Plotinus asserts that one cannot deploy this matrix of perception, of externals, the sensible of an imperfect world, for a model of intelligible vision. Plotinus inscribes:

> It is *within* us. Here the objects we contemplate and that which contemplates are identical—both are thought. The subject cannot surely *know* an object different from itself. The world of ideas lies within our intelligence. Truth, therefore, is not the agreement of our apprehension of an external object

with the object itself. It is the agreement of the mind with itself. Consciousness, therefore, is the sole basis of certainty. The mind is its own witness. Reason sees in itself that which is above itself as its source; and again, that which is below itself as still itself once more.[9]

With this projection of his criterion of certainty, Plotinus begins to delineate his order of rank, an architectonic which orchestrates and operationalizes this antithetical regime of Good versus Evil, and everything *in-between*. It flows like the river of Heraclitus, but, yet, with the former, this river flows down, vertically in one direction, as if it were a waterfall, through which, as the salmon perform, this soul strives to ascend beyond against the irrepressible power of the physical. The salmon struggles to ascend and with this becomes like the water ascending closer to the light, reflection, this shining gaze outward, as it becomes one life of myriad souls. It becomes intellect.

This path of crossing roads, these 3 degrees of knowing (1) opinion, sense, perception; (2) science, dialectic, understanding; and (3) illumination, intuition, reason, culminate with the latter in Absolute knowing, this utter "identity of the mind knowing with the object known." This tripartite tracing of these orders of knowledge adheres to a necessary ranking of priority vis-à-vis his portrayal of the configuration of these worlds, together amidst this precise intermingling of these domains, or, in other words, body, life, and rapture. This casts a relief for this sense of a unidirectional, vertical horizon of flow, one that is downward, a misty waterfall, but, yet, a strenuous pathway of ascension from dispersion to utter compactness, toward That One.

Before venturing on throughout this letter, there will be a brief reference to the *Enneads* in order to allege a propaedeutic for what is to follow. In the Third Ennead, Fifth Tractate, Division Nine, *On Love*, Plotinus issues this very revealing statement,

> "Our way of speaking"—for myths, if they are to serve their purpose, must necessarily import time-distinctions into their subject & will often present as separate, Powers which exist in unity but differ in rank & faculty; and does not philosophy itself relate the births of the unbegotten and discriminate where all is one substance. The truth is conveyed in the only possible manner; it is left to our good sense to bring all together again.

This reference is necessary for this letter moves into an extended metaphor which seeks to depict this vertical, unidirectional flow, cascading amidst this surge to That Beyond, in a language of this panoptic mythology of light, water, heat, and cold, all of these physical, even if, in this case, it is not cast as temporal projection.

This typology of expression cannot be lightly cast aside in the midst of thinkers who allege they have transcended this visible realm, in which, no less, there must be a shadow if there is to be any dimension, depth, relief. In that this rapture of ecstatic illumination must rely upon myth for its very expression, there opens up an horizon for this decisive contestation of this utterly pure, ideal world of perfect, unified intelligibility.

Yet, this persists as "Our way of speaking":

> There is a raying out of all orders of existence, an external emanation from the ineffable One. There is a returning impulse, drawing all upwards and inwards towards the centre from whence all came. Love, as Plato in the *Symposium* beautifully says, is the child of Poverty and Plenty. In the amorous quest of the soul after the Good, lies the painful sense of fall and deprivation. But that Love is blessing, is salvation, is our guardian genius; without it the centrifugal law would overpower us, and sweep our souls out far from their source toward the cold extremities of the Material and the Manifold. The wise man recognizes the idea of the Good within him. This he develops by withdrawal into the Holy Place in his own soul. He who does not understand how the soul contains the Beautiful within itself, seeks to realize beauty without, by laborious production. His aim should rather be to concentrate and simplify, and so to expand his being; instead of going into the Manifold, to forsake it for the One, and so to float upwards towards the divine fount of being whose stream flows within him.[10]

As with most of the statements of Plotinus, he entertains questions afterwards, and there is no exception in this case. The question beckons loudly in the midst of one who at once speaks of a realm beyond sense via this scattering relief of utter visual, physical metaphor. Plotinus shouts out, "You ask, how we can know the infinite? I answer, not by reason." It will obviously be grasped that it was written: "Reason sees in itself that which is above itself as its source; and again, that which is below itself as still itself once more."[11] Yet, this infinite is above, and beyond reason, mere intellect, and not illumination. This latter is this source, or, with Duns Scotus, the source of This. Reason cannot begin to grasp the ineffable, cast into relief via this mathematical metaphor of infinity. Plotinus provides a clue, a statement of ultrasense:

> You can only apprehend the Infinite by a faculty superior to reason, by entering into a state by which you are finite no longer, in which the Divine Essence is communicated to you. This is ecstasy. It is the liberation of your mind from its finite consciousness. Like only can apprehend like; when you thus cease to be finite, you become one with the Infinite. In the reduction of your soul to its simplest self, its divine essence, you realize this Union, this Identity.[12]

Yet, "we" at once return to this mundane world of finite beckoning. This ecstasy is over, subsides amidst these winds of mortality. It is so devastating, all of it, this utter plunge toward death. It is testified by Plotinus that this transcendence of finitude only comes and goes, even for these higher men. He departs, discloses to this poor seeker, Flaccus,

> I myself have realized it but three times as yet, and Porphyry hitherto not once. All that tends to purify and elevate the mind will assist you in this attainment, and facilitate the approach and the recurrence of these happy intervals. There are then, different roads by which this end may be reached.[13]

In this light, we can begin to fathom the sense of the Plotinian "grammar of ecstasy," as he seeks, with the use of extant language to communicate a sought-for experience to one who has not (yet) had this "rapture". Nevertheless, regardless of the contribution Plotinus makes toward our understanding of the use of mythic language, I hope that, with these discussions, we can better comprehend the clear and significant differences betwixt the various interpretations of the doctrine of transmigration. For instance, any scenario of guilt and expiation, which is shared by Plato and Plotinus, strikes one as quite foreign to the sense and spirit of the Pythagorean teaching. Moreover, the notions of ascent and descent could be questioned with respect to their compatibility with an extended kinship. Indeed, one of the most striking features of difference is the neo-Homeric affirmation of the body on the part of Pythagoras and of the contribution of memory (given to Pythagoras by the god Hermes) in the eternal recurrence of the greater self, a dysteleological state of being amidst the life of the All. It is clear that Pythagoras has no desire to forget the All, but seeks to remain true to that which *is*.

Epilog

The Fate of the Doctrine of Transmigration

The foregoing interpretation has attempted to grasp the status, role, and significance of the doctrine of transmigration for the Pythagoreans of the tragic sixth century. This reconstruction has been enacted in the manner of a phenomenological analysis and hermeneutical interpretation of this poetic doctrine. The latter, following Guthrie and Burkert, has been conceived as a *complex symbola* or, in the manner of the early Heidegger, a formal indication, of the theoretical and practical aspects of the Pythagorean teaching. A primary *critical* result of this study has been to establish a clear distinction between the Pythagorean philosophy and way of life and that of Plato and Plotinus, all of whom have been, for nearly two millennia, thrown together under the umbrella of "Orphism" as if they were variants of the same. In light of the foregoing study, it is clear that there are very good grounds to throw such an equivocation into question. As we will recall, a crucial element in this reinterpretation has been the role given to the body in the Pythagorean *bios*, and the magical, as opposed to mystical, interpretation given to the significance of *praxis*. In this light, the basic difference between the Platonic doctrine of metempsychosis and that of Pythagorean transmigration has been the latter's affirmation, following Homer, of the body as the exemplary *topos* of *praxis* for an attunement with the All, the latter having the indigenous meaning of a fulfillment of an immanent, *this-worldly* existence.

The distinction between magic and mysticism, mentioned earlier in discussions of Cornford, Guthrie, and Plotinus, has been elucidated with regard to not only the respective comportments of each of these conceptions to the phenomenal, visible world, but also, and related to this conception, of the notion of the divine and *either* its immanence *or* transcendence of the world. As we will recall, the way of the mystic is that of a rejection of the phenomenal world of the body, magic, and of a notion of a pantheistic divine manifested as the All. The pathway of magic, however, unites in its perspective the domains of the visible and invisible, each as necessary constituents of an ultimate and ongoing divine event. While this distinction may be lost upon a post-metaphysical generation which no longer remembers the significance of such questions, it is important to keep in mind that a failure to make this distinction played a significant role in the researches of Cornford in the 1920s with regard to the significance and unity of the Pythagorean philosophy, research which to a large extent determines our notions to this day. Cornford's work, moreover, was intimately related to the broader attempt by the Vienna Circle and its allies, such as Russell, to eliminate "metaphysics" from philosophy per se. Indeed, Russell used Cornford's research in his popular work, *History of Western Philosophy*. All in all, it is my contention that the lack of an *explicit* distinction between magic and mysticism—made only forty years later by W.K.C. Guthrie—served to undermine any attempt to give a *unified* interpretation of Pythagoreanism, with the result that, beyond a few historical surveys, there has been a near eclipse of the philosophical study of Pythagoras beyond his mathematical, scientific significance. However, not all of the blame for this catastrophe lies with the logical positivists.

A.E. Waite, a prominent Christian mystic of the early twentieth century and a contemporary (and perhaps the perfect "straw man") of Cornford, expresses, in a manner very similar to Plotinus and to the Neoplatonic tradition, a hostility toward magic, writing that it is a "path of illusion by which the psychic nature of man enters that other path which goes down into the abyss."[1] Magic is a path of illusion in that it affirms the phenomenal world, and it is this affirmation of the "outer" which leads to the abyss. Waite juxtaposes this path to that of a mystical theology in his discussion of the obscure work, *The Cloud of Unknowing*. He depicts the mystical path, to which he claims adherence:

> The path is a path of undoing . . . returning of the substantial creation into nothing; it is an entrance into darkness; an act of unknowing wherein the soul is wholly stripped and unclothed of all sensible realization of itself, that it may be reclothed in the realization of God.[2]

The path of mysticism, as in the case of the fourteenth-century mystic Marguerite Porete,[3] who sought *nihilation* and was burned at the stake for heresy, rejects and seeks to "dissolve" the phenomenal world as an illusion which separates the soul from God. It is a "work between the naked soul and God," one eschewing "doctrine and practice," and "symbol, rite and ceremony . . . " Waite writes that these visible references are "simply not there." The artifacts of the phenomenal world, while they may aid in leading one to a path of "the inward world, recollection, meditation, contemplation, the renunciation of all that is lower in the quest of all that is higher," must be thrown down as this work is "between God and the soul." Once this insight has been achieved, the true work begins and the visible, "outer" world is cast aside. Waite writes:

> Blessed and Holy are those who receive the experience of God in the dilucid contemplation, but sanctity and benediction and all in all is that state wherein contemplation is ineffably unified, by a super-eminent leap over of love, with

that which is its object; and in that love and in that joining together there is no passage any longer from subject to object. But this is the Godhead.[4]

In the language of Waite, we can detect a certain resemblance to the manner in which the Pythagorean teaching has been expressed (and rejected), especially by Cornford. This similarity is displayed in a parallel recognition of the transience of the body and of the affirmation of the reality of the divine. However, as suggested, even with these similitudes, these lines of inquiry remain distinct with respect to their respective comportments to the phenomenal world. The path of the mystic is an "undoing," an entrance into darkness, by which the naked soul may leap away from the world and get "lost in God." The phenomenal world is an abyss, an illusion to be rejected as soon as possible. One requires only the insight of the reality of God. We can see that the Pythagorean philosophy is at odds with such a path of negative theology. The Pythagoreans do not seek "undoing," or, an "entrance into darkness," or a "supereminent leap." We can see in the jest of Xenophanes that Pythagoras affirms the phenomenal world as the life of the divine All. In that the visible dimension is the point of departure for the life of the initiate in the *bios*, the pathway of magical kinship is not an "undoing," but an attunement, not an "entrance into darkness," but a "tending of the fire," and not a "supereminent leap," but a rigorous cultivation of the soul along a continuum which extends from the everyday to the divine. While the path of magic shares with the mystic an abandonment of the perspective of the immediate self for the divine, magic does not reject the *bios*, the phenomenal in its appropriate time, and thus, there is no conflict betwixt the visible and invisible dimensions.

From this perspective, it could be suggested that it is the distinction between gift and sacrifice which may shed some light upon the difference between Pythagoreanism and Platonism with respect to the meaning of the body and sensible world. Within the context of the Pythagorean *bios* and *ethos*, the body must be seen as a gift, as that which must be affirmed in the context of an exploration of the All. In this way, thinking would be similar to a state of thankfulness, as suggested by Heidegger's in his lecture, *What is Called Thinking?*[5] This trope of thankfulness is another way of intimating that *remembrance* was a fundamental aspect of the Pythagorean teaching. It must be said, though, that remembrance, as recollection, also plays a central role in Platonic philosophy. Nevertheless, that which is vital in this context is that which is being remembered. In the context of a Platonic discipline of utter purification, for instance, there is a total forgetfulness of the visible and the necessity for the sacrifice of the body, of that which is lower, *for* the soul, *for* that which is higher. In this way, Plato, as with Savinio in his short story *Psyche*, inscribes the sacrifice of the body, amidst a propaedeutic and political stratagem of a *polis* of Good, of Love. Yet, it is through the body and, via strife, of *bodies* that the soul can seek to return to the All, as the body is not only the seat of awareness, but is itself a *topos* amid the being of the All. It is in this way that the fate of the Pythagoreans, dismembered as they were midway through their unfinished tragedy, would be much better traced to Empedocles and to the Jena Romantics Hölderlin and Schelling, whose affirmation of Love *and Strife,* opened up the possibility of an affirmation of the body and of its aesthetic *praxis* under the aspect of the unity of the All. That which we are given is a *bios,* not a *polis*; sublimation, not purification; true enlightenment, not punishment. In this light, it is the body and world which allows us to *make sense* of the doctrine of transmigration as a poetic *symbola.* It tells us that we are always already in a state of intimacy with the divine All. It is the task of philosophy to allow us to remember and live this intimacy.

Notes

Introduction

[1] Arthur Rimbaud (1975) *Complete Works*, New York Harper & Row, p. 41. This quotation serves the argumentation of this chapter as it underlines the interpretation of the doctrine of transmigration as a philosophy of remembrance in the Greek context, one in which the "lyre" would intimate, though in an initially obscure fashion, the lyre of Apollo, the patron god of the Pythagoreans.

[2] K.S. Guthrie (1987) *The Pythagorean Sourcebook and Library*, Grand Rapids, MI: Phanes Press, pp. 272–274. This quotation serves the argumentation of this chapter as it underlines the contention that the doctrine of transmigration necessitates that there be a practical aspect to the Pythagorean philosophy, one grounded in the *bios* in which the protocols of the philosophy were fulfilled.

[3] Friedrich Hölderlin (2004) "The Death of Empedocles," *Friedrich Hölderlin: Poems and Fragments*, London: Anvil Press, p. 451. This quotation serves the argumentation of this chapter as it underlines the interpretation that the legacy of Pythagorean philosophy should be traced through Empedocles and Hölderlin and not through Plato and Neoplatonism.

[4] P.W. Buckham (1827) *Theatre of the Greeks*, Cambridge: W.P. Grant. Cicero writes: "*Veniat Aeschylus, non poeta solum, sed etiam Pythagoreus; sic eniam accepimus,*" which is translated as "Let us see what Aeschylus says, who was not only a poet but a Pythagorean philosopher also, for that is the account which you have received of him. . . ."(Book II.10)

[5] Friedrich Nietzsche (1967) *The Birth of Tragedy*, translated byWalter Kaufmann, London: Penguin. pp. 78–79. The reference to Pythagoras as a philosopher of tragedy not only will transfigure our conception of his and his follower's patronage of Apollo, but will also cast Nietzsche's 1886 "Attempt at Self-Criticism" into an entirely new light as to its attempt to explore the relationship between art and science in light of the affirmation of a tragic pessimism. For more on Nietzsche and Pythagoras, see James Porter (2005) "Nietzsche and Tragedy," *A Companion to Tragedy*, edited by Rebecca Bushnell, London: Blackwell.

[6] Benjamin Biebuyck et al., "Cults and Migrations: Nietzsche's Meditations on Orphism, Pythagoreanism, and the Greek Mysteries," *Nietzsche and Antiquity*, edited by Paul Bishop, Rochester, NY: Camden House, pp. 151–169. While this essay is vastly illuminating with respect to Nietzsche's positions on Pythagoreanism, it does not seek to challenge the basic traditional prejudices surrounding Pythagoras so as to *make sense* of Guthrie's claims, for instance, that the Pythagoreans were a "magical" as opposed to a "mystical" community.

7 Without undertaking a detailed interpretation of Nietzsche's tragic pessimism in *The Birth of Tragedy*, it is necessary to simply resist our own contemporary connotations for the terms "pessimism" and "optimism" in light of the revaluation of values undertaken through the "slave revolt of the masses," an event which is outlined by Nietzsche in *The Genealogy of Morals* (see Friedrich Nietzsche (2003) *The Genealogy of Morals*, translated by Horace Samuel, New York: Dover).

8 There are widespread claims (allegedly based in Porphyry and Iamblichus) that the *mathematikoi* were the true Pythagoreans while the *akousmatikoi* were lesser, mere listeners to the teaching, which was heard from behind a veil. However, this portrayal is challenged, among others such as Kirk and Burkert, by Charles Kahn (2001) in his *Pythagoras and Pythagoreans: A Brief History*, (Indianapolis, IN: Hackett Publishing) in which he describes the *akousmatikoi* as esoteric hearers who were permitted to listen to the teaching as a sound or music of truth. The diminishment of the *akousmatikoi* as those who listened to the teaching and whose medium was "tokens of remembrance" simply misunderstands the evidence and anachronistically misreads the hierarchy of initiation of ancient philosophy.

9 I refer in this context not to the "creationists" who seem to be the main target of those like Meillassoux and Dawkins, but to the Radical Orthodoxy which, like Badiou and Meillassoux, contest the Kantian and post-Kantian middle ground with respect to the delicate balance of modernism, but, unlike Meillassoux, are making use of Postmodernism in a strategy to subvert philosophy *as such*. In what appears to be an overt return to the dominance of theology in the Medieval era, this theological sect regards modernist philosophical critiques of theology as superficial and implicated in the metaphysics of subjectivity. For more, see Milbank and Oliver (2009) in the *Radical Orthodoxy Reader*, London: Routledge. It is troubling that "philosophy," so divided in itself, seems blind to this new threat, a blindness made worse by "speculative" realism.

10 Alain Badiou (2005a) *Being and Event*, translated by 0. Feltham, New York: Continuum; Quentin Meillassoux (2007) *After Finitude: An Essay on the Necessity of Contingency*, London: Continuum, for instance, clearly advocate a return to the pseudo-Platonic idol of infinity and the positivist methodology of mathematics so as to escape from that which they regard as the alleged subjectivisic impasse of the linguistic turn. It would seem that their rather selective interpretation of the history of modern philosophy rests upon an anachronistic and often inaccurate (cf. Meillassoux's preposterous trope of the "unthinkable" in his interpretation of Kant, for instance) interpretation of Kant and the post-Kantian tradition which they have set up as a straw man, much in the manner as did Analytic philosophers decades ago.

11 Alain Badiou (2005b) *Handbook of Inaesthetics*, translated by Alberto Toscano, Stanford, CA: Stanford University Press, makes himself very clear on the relationship of art, specifically poetry and philosophy in his *Handbook of Inaesthetics* where he contends, after delineating the three possible relationships of philosophy and poetry (didactic, romantic, and classical), that, at its best, poetry may serve philosophy as a seemingly unconscious producer, now and then, of "truths." That with which he has not come to grasp, however, is the possibility of a poetics of finitude that would be at once a poetics of truth, assuming, that is, that truth *is not* an infinite multiplicity. Indeed, the latter itself must be regarded as a poetic

figure and thus a dwelling for a singular and imminent truth. In this way, Badiou becomes just another poet of existence, along with the rest of us.

12 Quentin Meillassoux (2007) in his book *After Finitude: An Essay on the Necessity of Contingency*, London: Continuum, p. 12 writes, for instance: "In doing so, our physicist is defending a Cartesian thesis about matter, but not, it is important to note, a Pythagorean one: the claim that the being of accretion is inherently mathematical—that the numbers or equations deployed in the ancestral statements exist in themselves." This quotation clearly shows that this new variant of French philosophy, in its desire for literal "objectivity," remains deaf to the poetics and *praxis* of the Pythagorean philosophy, and is thus rightly regarded as a form of positivism.

13 It should be stated at the outset that Aristotle will not be a major source in the present study. This is due to several reasons. First, and as we will see in Chapters 4 and 8, his only acknowledged source for Pythagorean philosophy was Plato, who himself received his knowledge second hand from Philolaus. Second, he rejects the possibility of transmigration with the contention that the soul is uniquely suited to the body in which it abides, and that it could not enter into just any other body. Finally, Aristotle, in Book 1, Chapter 3 of his *De Anima* (see Aristotle (1987) *De Anima* (On the Soul), translated by Hugh Lawson-Tancred, New York: Penguin), discusses the significance of the soul in terms of *motion*, a position which occupied much of his time as he sought to sift through the complications of movement. Yet, the significance of the soul in the present study is that of *attunement*, or of a syndotic *ethos* of unity as the intersection of limit and unlimited in the body. It is in this way that the casual dismissals by Aristotle of basic elements of Pythagoreanism (and of the philosophies of other Presocratics), would not be warranted.

14 For a discussion of this doctrine in the philosophy of Leibniz, see James Luchte (2006) "Mathesis and Analysis: Finitude and the Infinite in the *Monadology* of Leibniz," *Heythrop Journal*, vol. 47, no. 4, pp. 519–543.

15 The use of an *indication* is meant to reflect the kinship of my analysis with that of the phenomenology of formal indication in the philosophy of Martin Heidegger, especially as articulated in his early lectures on theology and his use of myth as an indication in *Being and Time*, e.g. the myth of Cura. For an extended discussion of this myth, see James Luchte (2008) *Heidegger's Early Philosophy: The Phenomenology of Ecstatic Temporality*, London: Continuum.

16 This notion is taken from William Foxwell Albright (1957) *From the Stone Age to Christianity: Monotheism and the Historical Process*, New York: Doubleday Books in his description of the oral tradition.

17 Each of these symbols points in at least two directions, to a "face" and a "spirit," the symbol ties them together, as in the Greek "tally," in which parties in an exchange were tied together in negotiation. Dillon writes of the function of symbols in the Pythagorean curriculum, an education which enacted a protocol of transference from the exoteric narrative of the story through to the esoteric insight of the thinking sheltered in the narrative or verse. The "tally" of exoteric and esoteric resembles others we find in Pythagorean symbolism, such as Limit and Unlimited, the body and soul, and the 6th and 12th in the context of musical harmony. These "opposites" are analogous to the differing parts of the body, which if dead and dissected, could "render" isolated parts, but, as alive, the multifaceted "opposites" coalesce as

a happening of the All, as the play of the seen and unseen. These "opposites" are not in conflict, but are "distantiated" nodal aspects of a multidimensional and multisensory *Kosmos*, the All in All.

[18] Martin Heidegger (2003) "The Origin of the Work of Art," *Basic Writings*, translated by D.F. Krell, London: Routledge.

[19] In this respect, the function of transmigration as a symbol is one of a mnemotechnic character, as the Pythagoreans were among those sixth century Greeks who remained in the "oral" tradition. We can fathom the symbol of transmigration as an "aid" to memory in the context also of a consideration of the word and body as symbols for the divine, just as the monochord allows the spirit of music to unlock its voice, and herbs and medicines unlock the intimate relations of the body and world. Betwixt this affinity of the All, we are guided by the doctrine of signatures, the *theoria* of the symbolic affinities of plants and the body, such as the mandrake, which Pythagoras called a "little man."

[20] Much significance will be given to the fact that the Pythagoreans were practitioners of the spoken word despite the ubiquitousness of writing in the sixth century. The spoken word is a living excession of an active *ethos* which seeks, individually and associatively, a singular goal, a return to the source, to accomplish meaning amidst a sacred *physis*. This cathexis of interaction allows for an explication of not only the *theoria* of the teaching but also of synchronous *bios*, which together discharge an orientation characterized by practical and theoretical comportments with a common root in "magic."

[21] Margaret Wertheim's description of a magico-philosophical system in her *Pythagoras' Trousers* indicates that the insights of Burkert and Guthrie have finally been heard by at least some researchers (see Margaret Wertheim (1997) *Pythagoras' Trousers: God, Physics and the Gender Wars*, London: W. W. Norton & Company.). Yet, again, it would seem that, in the polemical context of late modernity and of faltering scientism, such a recognition of magico-philosophical symbolism in Pythagorean philosophy would no longer constitute its refutation.

[22] I have also considered the perspectives of Nietzsche, with respect to (1) his notion of the eternal recurrence of the same, (2) his vision of Apollo, the patron divinity of Pythagoras, (3) his Dionysian emphasis upon music and the body, and (4) to his interpretation of asceticism and the Platonic denial of perspective, body, life, and world. This contribution does not eclipse, but, instead allows for a "thinking through" of the doctrine of transmigration with a depth that is appropriate to the matter under discussion. After all, even Cornford read Nietzsche, a classical philologist, and approved of *The Birth of Tragedy*, a text which has much to say about Apollo, the patron of the Pythagoreans and in this connection, his notion of "sublimation," which is the term which I have used to described the relationship of the *bios* to *ecstasis*. Yet, the great gulf between Pythagoras and Nietzsche will be respected, for although both of these were exponents of "eternal recurrence," each lived amidst differing horizons, a differing most readily symbolized in the figure of the "death of god." But, there remains much to be learned from Nietzsche's views on Plato and the body which can aid us in a comprehension of the transformation that occurred betwixt Pythagoras and Plato et al. Moreover, in his invocation of the notion of a philosophical way of life, Nietzsche and his mythopoetic creature, Zarathustra, have a striking kinship with the personage of Pythagoras which has been handed down to us.

23 Christoph Riedweg (2005) *Pythagoras: His Life, Teaching and Influence,* Ithaca, NY: Cornell University Press. Although Riedweg gives what is to all accounts a balanced and inclusive interpretation of the mythical and historical significance, the doctrine of transmigration is treated in a rather peripheral way and for the most part merely in an ethical and political context (which merely repeats Dacier and Cornford in a different hue). It is the centrality of the doctrine of transmigration, however, and of its hermeneutical decipherment, which distinguishes the present work.

24 If the reader is uncomfortable with this notion of magic (although the philosophical meaning of this term is quite well-known after Guthrie, Burkert, and Wertheim), one could think of it as a "thinking practice" as in Johannes Hoff (2005) "Philosophie als performative Praktik. Spuren cusanischen Denkens bei Jacques Derrida und Michel de Certeau," *Cusanus-Rezeption in der Philosophie des 20. Jahrhunderts,* Regensburg: Roderer, pp. 93–120 (*Philosophy as Performative Practice. Traces of Nicholas of Cusa in Jacques Derrida and Michel de Certeau*).

25 Another excellent example is the heretical Christian mystic Marguerite Porete, whose work, *The Mirror of Simple Souls,* called for the *annihilation* of the soul in God. See Marguerite Porete (1993) *The Mirror of Simple Souls,* translated by Ellen Babinsky, Mahwah, NJ: Paulist Press.

Chapter 1

1 *Dwelling,* as in Martin Heidegger (1971) "Building Dwelling Thinking," *Poetry, Language, Thought,* translated by Albert Hofstadter, New York: Harper Torchbooks. It is in this essay that Heidegger explores Hölderlin's poetry, as with his other essay "Poetically Man Dwells," pp. 213–229, in which Heidegger elaborates upon his indication of language as a *house of Being.*

2 G.S. Kirk (1988) *The Presocratic Philosophers,* Cambridge: Cambridge University Press, p. 219. The actual background of this jest may have been Xenophanes neo-Homeric restriction of knowledge to the gods, or in the case of Xenophanes, to a "God" wholly other than ourselves, as suggested in Arnold Hermann (2004) *To Think Like God: Pythagoras and Parmenides, The Origins of Philosophy,* Las Vegas, NV: Parmenides Publishing. Such an implication of theological disagreement would allow an interpretation which would be quite different than the usual depiction of the jest by Xenophanes, who was himself deeply theological in his perspective.

3 F.M. Cornford (1922) "Mysticism and Science in the Pythagorean Tradition," *The Classical Quarterly,* Vol. 16, No. 3/4 (Jul.–Oct.), p. 142.

4 Kirk, *Presocratic Philosophers,* p. 216. As we will see in the following pages, especially Chapter 4, "Philolaus and the Character of Pythagorean Harmony," it will be necessary to question the usefulness and relevance of the testimonies of Philolaus and Archytas.

5 Ibid.

6 Guthrie (1987) *The Pythagorean Sourcebook and Library,* Grand Rapids, MI: Phanes Press, p. 112.

7 Ibid., p. 71.

8 Ibid., pp. 128, 132, n. 45.

9 Ibid., p. 126.

10 Ibid., p. 138.

11 Ibid., p. 142.

12 Ibid., p. 145. It would be useful to compare this account of transmigration with Leibniz in his correspondence with Arnauld.

13 Kirk, *Presocratic Philosophers*, pp. 346–347.

14 Guthrie, *Pythagorean Sourcebook*, p. 174.

15 Ibid., p. 180.

16 Ibid., p. 179.

17 Ibid., p. 190.

18 Kirk, *Presocratic Philosophers*, p. 215.

19 J. Soustelle (1971) *The Four Suns*, translated by E. Ross, London: Andre Deutsch, p. 234.

20 Marsilio Ficino (1996) *Book of Life*, Woodstock, CT: Spring Publications, p. 20.

21 Ibid., 106–107.

22 For an account of the return of Bruno to Italy and his subsequent trial and execution, see Francis Yates (1991) *Giordanao Bruno and the Hermetic Tradition,* Chicago, IL: University of Chicago Press, pp. 338–359.

23 Nietzsche counsels us against following in the pathway of Giordano Bruno in Friedrich Nietzsche (1988) *Beyond Good and Evil,* translated by R.J. Hollingdale, New York: Penguin, Part 1, "On the Prejudices of Philosophers."

24 Andre Dacier (1981) *The Life of Pythagoras* [1707], Wellingborough, Northamptonshire: Aquarian Press, p. 43.

25 Ibid.

26 Guthrie *The Pythagorean Sourcebook*, p. 287.

27 Dacier, *The Life of Pythagoras*, p. 44.

28 Ibid., pp. 44, 335. We should notice the kinship between this distinction and that of Cornford and the twentieth century discourse on Pythagoras.

29 Cornford (1922) "Mysticism and Science " , p. 141. Such a statement is astounding for many reasons, not the least of which is its clear departure from the dialectical philosophy of Hegel which dominated the academy in Britain before the eclipse of British Idealism. Ironically, the latter school fell not due to any philosophical inadequacy, but to the deaths of many of its adherents at tragically young ages.

30 F.M. Cornford (1987) "Divisions of the Soul," *Selected Papers*, Vol. 10, p. 243.

31 Ibid., p. 244.

32 Ibid.

33 Ibid.

34 Ibid.

35 Ibid.

36 Ibid.

37 Ibid.

38 Ibid., p. 245.

39 Ibid.

[40] F.M. Cornford (1980) *Plato and Parmenides*, London: Routledge & Kegan Paul, p. 4.

[41] Ibid., p. 5.

[42] Walter Burkert (1985) *Greek Religion: Archaic and Classical*, Oxford: Basil Blackwell, p. 300.

[43] He characterizes this emergence as the discovery of the individual and of its immortality. Cornford also refers to this birth of the individual and its conflict with the ties of kinship of the Homeric community.

[44] W.K.C. Guthrie (1962) *A History of Greek Philosophy, Vol. I: The Earlier Presocratics and the Pythagoreans*, Cambridge: Cambridge University Press, p. 181.

[45] Ibid., p. 306.

[46] Guthrie cites the various texts which are collectively known as the *Book of the Dead, or Going Forth By Day*, in which there is no reference to the doctrine of transmigration. It is possible that Herodotus is describing *lycanthropy*, or the metamorphosis into an animal form, similar to that described for humorous intent in *The Golden Ass*, by Lucius Apuleius (see Lucius Apuleius (2007) *The Golden Ass, or a Book of Changes*, translated by Joel Relihan, Indianapolis, IN: Hackett Publishing). But, this is distinct from the much broader implications of transmigration. This certainly renders the account by Dacier problematic, especially since, as he was writing in the early eighteenth century, he would have had no access to the Pyramid texts, deciphered only in 1822 by Champollian. (E. W. Budge (1966) *Egyptian Language*, London: Routledge & Kegan Paul, p. 18). However, there does seem to be a reference that may imply a transmigration for the divinity in a poem entitled "Hymn 80," but this does not mean that this would apply to everyone, or even to the Pharaoh. See John L. Foster (trs.) (1992) *Echoes of Egyptian Voices: An Anthology of Ancient Egyptian Poetry*, Norman, OK: University of Oklahoma Press.

[47] Guthrie, *History of Greek Philosophy*, p. 186.

[48] Ibid., p. 187.

[49] Ibid., p. 186.

[50] As the magical idea of kinship is central to the doctrine of Pythagoreanism, if only in a rationalized form, Guthrie comes in direct conflict with Cornford, with his statement that the doctrine of transmigration is "cut loose from it original roots." Cornford's position is similar to that of James Frazer in *The Golden Bough* which schematizes the transformations from magic to religion and finally to science. What is cut lose and left behind is magic, and what remains of the doctrine of transmigration has, thus, only a "religious" significance—of that which can satisfy some unsatisfied psychological need. It is thus merely a fable, whatever that is.

[51] Guthrie, *History of Greek Philosophy*, p. 165.

[52] Ibid., p. 167.

Chapter 2

[1] H.A. Frankfort et al., (1949) *Before Philosophy*, London: Pelican, pp. 24–25.

[2] Levi Eliphas [L.A. Constant] (1913) *History of Magic* (1860), translated by A.E. Waite, London: Rider, p. 29.

[3] W.K.C. Guthrie (1987) *The Greek Philosophers*, London: Methuen, pp. 12–15. Guthrie provides us in general with the implications of a *magical* philosophy through his

emphasis on the harmony of the *bios* and *theoria*. However, his endorsement of a "stages" theory of human mental development, in many ways reminiscent of Frazer's speculations, must remain problematic, that is, the magical, religious, and scientific.

4 Guthrie, *The Greek Philosophers*, p. 12.

5 In this context then, it will be helpful to quote Guthrie with respect to the significance of numbers as analogues, *The Greek Philosophers*, p. 15:

> Numbers in fact, like everything else—whether objects or what we should distinguish from objects as mere conventional symbols, words or names—are endowed with magical properties and affinities of their own. Some knowledge of these facts should help us to approach these early Pythagoreans a little more sympathetically.

6 Alfred Bertholet (1909) *The Transmigration of Souls*, London: Harper & Brothers.

7 W.K.C. Guthrie (1962) *A History of Greek Philosophy, Vol. I: The Earlier Presocratics and the Pythagoreans*, Cambridge: Cambridge University Press, p. 186. For somewhat more contemporary, and perhaps, less scholarly reflection upon the genealogy of taboo, see also Georges Bataille (1992) *Theory of Religion*, New York: Zone Books and Georges Bataille, (1986) *Erotism: Death and Sensuality*, translated by M. Dalwood, San Francisco, CA: City Lights Books.

8 For an in depth excavation of the premodern sense of resemblance, see Michel Foucault (2001) *The Order of Things*, New York: Routledge.

9 Jacques Soustelle (1971) *The Four Suns*, translated by E. Ross, London: Andre Deutsch, p. 134.

10 Ibid.

11 Wittgenstein, *Remarks on Frazer* in which he criticizes Frazer's condescension to those engaged in religious praxis which is "unimpeachable." For an extended analysis of Wittgenstein's treatment of Frazer, see Alastair Walter (2006) "Metaphysics, Magic and Frazer," (unpublished MA Thesis, University of Wales, Lampeter Library, Lampeter).

12 James Frazer (1993) *The Golden Bough: A Study in Magic and Religion*, Hertfordshire: Wordsworth Reference, p. 44.

13 Ibid.

14 Wittgenstein, L. (1987) *Remarks on Frazer's Golden Bough*, translated by A.C. Miles, Hereford: Brynmill Press.

15 For more on the relation of the "prophetic" and the philosophical *a priori*, see Husserl (1964) *Phenomenology of Internal Time-Consciousness*, Bloomington, IN: Indiana University Press.

16 Guthrie, *History of Greek Philosophy*, p. 186.

17 Ibid., p. 202.

18 I will, throughout the rest of this work, abandon this metaphor of purity, which seems to rely upon and to indicate Platonistic philosophy, in favor of the more appropriate "attunement." For an in depth exploration of the indication of "attunement" (Befindlichkeit) in terms of a diagnosis of the malady of modern philosophy, see Heidegger (2001) *The Fundamental Concepts of Metaphysics: World, Finitude, Solitude*, Bloomington, IN: Indiana University Press.

[19] Guthrie, *History of Greek Philosophy*, pp. 204–205.

[20] G.S. Kirk (1988) *The Presocratic Philosophers*, Cambridge: Cambridge University Press, p. 234.

[21] Ibid., p. 235.

[22] This conflict could give us some understanding of Cornford's interpretation of a division between mysticism and science, if that is, it could be shown that the *mathematikoi*, who are reputed to be concerned with scientific, or exoteric enquiries, were completely devoid of an esoteric interest. This is not shown by Cornford.

[23] This may shed light on Cornford's distinction between a religious and a scientific Pythagoreanism. Far from indicating a shift from religion to science, mysticism to rational inquiry, it would seem more likely that the inherent division between the esoteric and exoteric dimensions of the Pythagorean community fractured with the latter gaining preeminence. Cornford implies in his distinction an occurrence of progress, for like Frazer, he sees an order of rank ascending from magic, to religion, and finally to science. Yet, as stated, the order of rank for early Pythagoreanism gives preeminence to the esoteric dimension. Thus, we have to be cautious with regard to Cornford's ability to reveal this philosophy, at least from the standpoint of the whole. His specific analyses of number and cosmogony are important, yet his distinction between religion and science fails to provide us with an adequate interpretation of the doctrine of transmigration.

[24] John Dillon (1990) *The Golden Chain: Studies in the Development of Platonism and Christianity*, Farnham, Surrey: Variorum, p. 226.

[25] L. Wittgenstein (1958) *The Blue and Brown Books*, edited by Rush Rhys, Oxford: Basil Blackwell. For an in-depth consideration of Wittgenstein's use of the term "grammar" in relation to a radical phenomenology, see James Luchte (2009) "Under the Aspect of Time ('sub specie temporis'): Heidegger Wittgenstein and the Place of the Nothing," *Philosophy Today*, vol. 53, no. 1, pp. 70–84.

[26] Dillon, *The Golden Chain*, pp. 248–249.

[27] Ibid., p. 251.

[28] F.M. Cornford, (1922) "Mysticism and Science in the Pythagorean Tradition," *The Classical Quarterly*, vol. 16, no. 3/4 (Jul.–Oct.), p. 139.

[29] Considered for a moment as a temporal myth, keeping in mind Plato's designation of time as an "image of eternity" in his *Timaeus*, we could venture to write that the path of opening, for Plato, descent, mythically indicates the *ancestral* but one which incessantly recurs as the migrations of the soul into body after body. The path of life and closing represents an image of a possible future return, but this return is implied in both the past and present. The transmigration of souls then, conceived as a temporal myth, would intimate the comportment of the initiate in the present, as one *in-between* the descent and ascent, to use Plato's and Plotinus' terms.

[30] W.F. Albright (1957) *From the Stone Age to Christianity: Monotheism and the Historical Process*, New York: Doubleday Books, p. 335.

[31] Ibid., p. 64.

[32] For an example of the relationship of speaking and writing, and the contemporary significance of this question, please compare Heidegger's "Letter on Humanism" with Derrida's "Differance".

[33] There is a parallel here with the prohibition of eating flesh. For faced with the contradiction of a prohibition of flesh and the same with vegetables, Porphyry made the distinction of life and life with soul, the criteria of which was the presence of breath. It was held that plants did not breathe, these did not therefore possess a soul, and consequently, it was proper to consume them. In this way, the oral dissemination as a speaking, is synchronous with the notion of soul as breath. The kinship of the soul as breath with the divine and with other animals is expressed by the notion of the world as a living, breathing creature. In cosmogony, the origin of the world, as the path of opening or the event, was conceived as Limit breathing in the Unlimited.

[34] Albright, *From the Stone Age to Christianity*, pp. 65–66.

Chapter 3

[1] Walter Burkert (1985) *Greek Religion: Archaic and Classical*, Oxford: Basil Blackwell, p. 280.

[2] Ibid., p. 29.

[3] Ibid., p. 300.

[4] Ibid.

[5] Ibid., p. 303.

[6] F.M. Cornford (1922) "Mysticism and Science in the Pythagorean Tradition," *The Classical Quarterly*, vol. 16, no. 3/4 (Jul.–Oct.), pp. 139–140.

[7] Ibid., p. 142.

[8] Ibid., p. 140.

[9] Ibid., pp. 140–141.

[10] Ibid., p. 140.

[11] Ibid., p. 141.

[12] Ibid., p 149.

[13] G.S. Kirk (1988) *The Presocratic Philosophers*, Cambridge: Cambridge University Press, p. 221.

[14] Ibid., p. 21.

[15] W.K.C. Guthrie (1962) *A History of Greek Philosophy, Vol. I: The Earlier Presocratics and the Pythagoreans*, Cambridge: Cambridge University Press, p. 334.

[16] Cornford (1922) "Mysticism and Science," p. 146.

[17] Ibid., pp. 145–146.

[18] Ibid., p. 146. Although it will be discussed below, Cornford shows with his musical-mathematical conception of the soul an explicit connection between the spheres which he has so sternly sought to separate, the religious and scientific.

[19] Guthrie, *History of Greek Philosophy*, p. 308.

[20] Ibid., p. 309.

[21] Ibid., p. 354.

[22] Claudianus Mamertus, *De Statu Animae*, 2, p. 7: "The soul is introduced and associated with the body by Number, and by a harmony simultaneously immortal and incorporeal . . . the soul cherishes its body, because without it the soul cannot feel . . . " Quoted from K.S. Guthrie (1987) *The Pythagorean Sourcebook and Library*, Grand Rapids, MI: Phanes Press, p. 174.

²³ Soustelle (1971) *The Four Suns,* translated by E. Ross, London: Andre Deutsch, p. 162.

Chapter 4

¹ G.S. Kirk (1988) *The Presocratic Philosophers,* Cambridge: Cambridge University Press, p. 324.

² Ibid. Kirk, on p. 330, however, discounts this contention of Burkert by emphasizing the fact that Aristotle mentions Philolaus only once and that he relies upon a vague notion of "Pythagoreans" in his account that seems to be based upon anonymous sources. Such a wedge driven between Aristotle and Philolaus seems to further minimize Aristotle's account in its significance as it tells us nothing essentially new that is not already in Plato. Nevertheless, Kirk suggests that Aristotle must have turned to Philolaus' book when he wished to provide a more detailed account of various issues.

³ DK refers to the numbering system of Diels-Kranz (1961) *Die Fragmente der Vorsokratiker,* Weidmannsche Verlagsbuchhandlung.

⁴ Walter Burkert (1972) *Lore and Science in Ancient Pythagoreanism,* translated by E.L. Minar, Cambridge, MA: Harvard University Press.

⁵ Plato does not disparage all written texts, but was concerned that the writing may end up in the wrong hands. This, after all, informed his many layers of exposition. Yet, we must not forget that Plato was a writer at the end of the day, and that his highly detailed reports of the conversations of Socrates are in fact highly structured written fabrications. This detachment of Plato from immediate conversation together with his status as a scholar in an academy, that is, not a *bios,* is symptomatized in his writing and, we will see, is a recurring thematic in his philosophy as such, especially of his interpretation of the body and of its status. The detachment of the craftsman god in its turn symbolizes not only the detachment of the philosopher but also the violence of the hierarchical projection which establishes a rupture in the web of kinship.

⁶ Kirk, *Presocratic Philosophers,* p. 328.

⁷ Cf. Dillon, in that there is also the testimony that the early Pythagoreans held no supreme principle, which in this context seems highly unlikely. Moreover, Kirk writes, in his book *Presocratic Philosophers,* on p. 331 that it is possible the original Pythagoreans held the distinction betwixt odd and even to be more important that limit and unlimited. It is significant that such a distinction, of even and odd, more closely than the distinction between limit and unlimited, speaks of the terrestrial perspective and point of departure for migration in the body, which amidst the temporal world, is a life of harmony.

⁸ Ficino writes: "The astrologers say that Venus and Saturn are enemies of each other. Nonetheless, in heaven, where all things are moved by love, where there is no fault, we must interpret this as meaning that they differ in their effect." See Marsilio Ficino (1996) *Book of Life,* Woodstock, CT: Spring Publications, p. 69.

⁹ K.S. Guthrie (1987) *The Pythagorean Sourcebook and Library,* Grand Rapids, MI: Phanes Press, p. 168.

¹⁰ Ibid., p. 172 (Athenagoras, *Legat. Pro Christ.,* 6).

[11] Ibid., p. 433 (Clement of Alexandria, *Stromateis*, 3).

[12] Ibid., p. 169.

[13] Kirk, *Presocratic Philosophers*, p. 339.

[14] An interesting question is whether the souls were created at once and we only wait for the last ones to return to *end* the divine process, or, if the divine is continuously issuing forth *new* souls, which from our perspective, would give to this process a seemingly inevitable everlastingness.

[15] With some thought, it is not clear that this end-return is such an urgently desired demand (especially if the body turns out *not* to be a tomb of the soul); instead, it may be merely a secondary *effect* of a process which is seeking, as its goal, something else entirely, which may explain some of Socrates' caricatures, in the *Phaedrus*, of those, such as Orpheus, who expressed their desires to come back as birds and such. Surely, return is the *ultimate end* of this allegorical scenario, yet, the overall raison d'etre may be harbored *on the way* in a differing domain of purpose. For example, an *end* of sexual interaction may be procreation, yet, the goal or goals of this interaction may be many and varied, for instance, in the "communicative intimacy" with the "other," orgasm, recreation, etc. In this case, it is a sort of wisdom and experience which is sought through this interaction; this *end* becomes merely a symbol of "discovery," of saturation with this "other" self.

[16] Guthrie, *Pythagorean Sourcebook*, p. 174.

[17] Ibid.

Chapter 5

[1] F.M. Cornford, (1922) "Mysticism and Science in the Pythagorean Tradition," *The Classical Quarterly*, vol. 16, no. 3/4 (Jul.–Oct.), p. 137.

[2] Ibid.

[3] Ibid., p. 139.

[4] Ibid., p. 142.

[5] Ibid.

[6] It will be illuminating in this context Heidegger's contention in his lecture course *Schelling's The Essence of Human Freedom* that the concern, and indeed, the expressed need for a "system" is a phenomenon that arises only with *modern* philosophy, a need expressing the desire for a ground of knowledge in the wake of the collapse of theological justification.

[7] F.M. Cornford (1923) "Mysticism and Science in the Pythagorean Tradition (Continued)," *The Classical Quarterly*, vol. 17, no. 1 (Jan.), p. 5.

[8] Indeed, if he were correct, it would be difficult to account for the persistence of a network of resistance to the excesses of the doctrine of the One.

[9] To display the meaning of this charge of anachronism, an example is in order: it is written by the Roman philosopher Plutarch in his *On the Face of the Moon*, that in the fourth century, Cleanthes, an Epicurean philosopher, accused Aristarchus of impiety to Gaia for suggesting that the Earth moves around the Sun. Even Xenophanes believed in a nonanthropomorphic deity.

[10] Ibid., p. 10.

[11] John Dillon (1977) *The Middle Platonists: A Study of Platonism 80 BC to AD 200*, London: Duckworth, p. 127.
[12] R. Schürmann (1988) "Tragic Differing: The Law of the One and the Law of Contraries in Parmenides," *Graduate Faculty Philosophy Journal*, vol. 13, no. 1, p. 9.
[13] Ibid., p. 13.
[14] Ibid., p. 11.
[15] Ibid., p. 10.

Chapter 6

[1] In this way, the pantheon changes, like the others which preceded it, as a displacement of the father. Yet, in this case, Apollo does not become the successor, as did Zeus and Saturn, but is only the symbol amongst other symbols which intimate a harmony described as a kinship of the All, no longer in the image of man.
[2] John Dillon (1977) *The Middle Platonists: A Study of Platonism 80 BC to AD 200*, London: Duckworth. Moreover, it could be contended that from the perspective of an oral tradition, the writing of One may be a breach of the prohibition of representations of divinity.
[3] Georges Bataille (2002) *The Absence of Myth: Essays on Surrealism*, London: Verso.
[4] Robert Graves writes in his commentary to the fragments, "In Classical times, music, poetry, philosophy, astronomy, mathematics, medicine, and science came under Apollo's control." (Robert Graves (1964) *The Greek Myths,* vol. 1, Harmondsworth: Penguin Books, p. 82). This coincides distinctly with what we know of the Pythagorean All, in that the name, Apollo, symbolizes a participant amidst this All. But, once again, this does not exhaust wisdom. However, we must look at the myth more closely in order to comprehend the possibility of varying interpretations. The passages which relate to Apollo are: *Births of Hermes, Apollo, Artemis, and Dionysus* (vol. 1, p. 60), *Apollo's Nature and Deeds* (vol. 1, p. 79), and *Apollo receives the lyre from Hermes* (vol. 1, p. 69) (see Robert Graves (1960) *The Greek Myths*, vol. 1, New York: Penguin).
[5] Robert Graves (1964) *The Greek Myths*, pp. 27–30.
[6] Marsilio Ficino (1996) *Book of Life*, Woodstock, CT: Spring Publications, p. 174.
[7] H. Evelyn-White (trs.) (1959) *Hesiod, the Homeric Hymns and Homerica*, Loeb Library, Cambridge, MA: Harvard University Press.
[8] Jane Ellen Harrison (1957) *Prolegomena to the Study of Greek Religion*, New York: Meridian Books.
[9] Luce Irigaray (1993) *Sexes and Genealogies*, translated by Gillian Gill, New York: Columbia University Press.
[10] J.T. Sheppard (1912) "Greek Tragedy", *The Classical Journal*, vol. 8, no. 2 (Nov.), pp. 94–96; Rachel, Bowlby (1957) "Family Realisms: Freud and Greek Tragedy", *Essays in Criticism*, vol. 56, no. 2, April 2006, pp. 111–138; Michael, Zelenak (1998) *Gender and Politics in Greek Tragedy*, New York: Peter Lang Publishing, among others.
[11] We can also witness Jocasta who aids the fulfillment of prophetic destiny unknowingly in her disbelief by seducing Laius when he was drunk. He had refused to sleep with her in order to flee in the face of destiny. Therefore, with the collaboration of his half brother Dionysus, Apollo uses Jocasta in the fulfillment of his prophecy, which is simultaneously the supplanting of Jocasta and the maternal.

[12] F. Copleston (1975) *History of Philosophy*, vol. 1, London: Burns, Oates & Washbourne, p. 30.

[13] This distinction between the revelers of Dionysus and the Orphics is not meant to disregard the many commonalities and a common artwork by these groupings, but instead, to emphasize the *pathos* of each group through their event of communion, the former of ecstasis, the latter, of ritual *telete*.

[14] At a deeper level, it could be argued that music is only possible through an interpenetration of Dionysian raw tonal flux with Apollonian punctuating rhythms.

[15] Ficino, *Book of Life*, pp. 80–81.

[16] Ibid., p. 174.

[17] Ibid., p. 69.

[18] Narrow convictions in this regard, especially if these become operationalized as hegemonic cult formations, can through this narrow faith lead to senseless violence, intolerance, and arrogance, thus, poisoning life for all and everyone.

Chapter 7

[1] Walter Burkert (1985) *Greek Religion: Archaic and Classical*, Oxford: Basil Blackwell, p. 303.

[2] Michel Foucault (1987) *History of Sexuality*, New York: Vintage Books, vol. 1, p. 21.

[3] Burkert, *Greek Religion*, p. 301.

[4] Ibid., p. 302.

[5] W.K.C. Guthrie (1962), *A History of Greek Philosophy, vol. I: The Earlier Presocratics and the Pythagoreans*, Cambridge: Cambridge University Press., p. 203.

[6] Nietzsche, Friedrich (1989) *On Rhetoric and Language*, Oxford: Oxford University Press.

[7] Martin Heidegger (1985) *Early Greek Thinking*, New York: Harper Collins Publishing, p. 13.

[8] I am insisting on a path of *opening* in order to distinguish the Pythagorean teaching from that of Plato and Plotinus, in both of their metaphors of descent or fall.

[9] K.S. Guthrie (1987) *The Pythagorean Sourcebook and Library*, Grand Rapids, MI: Phanes Press, p. 319.

[10] Ibid.

[11] Ibid.

[12] F.M. Cornford (1923) "Mysticism and Science in the Pythagorean Tradition (Continued)," *The Classical Quarterly*, vol. 17, no. 1 (Jan.), p. 5.

[13] Guthrie, *Pythagorean Sourcebook*, p. 21.

[14] Ibid.

[15] Ibid., p. 28.

[16] Ibid.

[17] Ibid.

[18] F.M. Cornford (1922) "Mysticism and Science in the Pythagorean Tradition," *The Classical Quarterly*, vol. 16, no. 3/4 (Jul.–Oct.), pp. 137–140.

[19] Guthrie, *Pythagorean Sourcebook*, p. 27.

[20] Ibid.

21 The traditional depiction of the monochord is that of Robert Fludd in 1581. For a more recent mediation of the relation of art and philosophical magic, see Anselm Kiefer's lead and acrylic "bleibuch" *for Robert Fludd: The Secret Life of Plants* from Schirmer/Mosel Verlag Gm (30 April 2003).

22 Guthrie, *Pythagorean Sourcebook.*

23 Ibid., p. 28.

24 Ibid.

25 Ibid., p. 25.

26 Ibid.

27 Ibid., p. 327.

28 Ibid., p. 328.

29 Ibid.

30 Ibid. If one does not have a monochord on hand, one can use a guitar, in effect, six monochords. The presence of six strings presents the additional problem of tuning. It is interesting that in the process of tuning, one can hear the discordant distance of the tones of the strings as an oscillation of harmonics. As the two strings come into tune, the oscillation nears but never achieves a concordance of tone.

31 Ibid.

32 I am making use of the phrase a path of *return* to distinguish the Pythagorean perspective from that of Plato and Plotinus, in their metaphor of a path of ascent.

33 John Dillon (1990) *The Golden Chain: Studies in the Development of Platonism and Christianity*, Farnham, Surrey: Variorum, p. 215.

34 Ibid., p. 216.

35 Guthrie, *History of Greek Philosophy*, p. 206.

36 Cornford (1922) "Mysticism and Science," p. 150.

37 Dillon, *Middle Platonists*, pp. 37–38. It is significant that the next sentence reads: "We have seen evidence of Xenocrates' aversion to meat-eating."

38 I will deal with this issue of an architectonic hierarchy in the chapters on Plato and Plotinus, and elsewhere.

39 Guthrie, *Pythagorean Sourcebook*, p. 132.

40 There can be a significant discussion of the notion of magic as *bios* or magic as technique, way of life or incantation. Again, this notion of technique can be cast into relief through Foucault's work in the *History of Sexuality.*

41 Cornford (1922) "Mysticism and Science," p. 139.

42 Iamblichus writes that they partook of flesh from certain sanctioned animals, "lawful to immolate," yet, it is not certain that the Pythagoreans did eat flesh. There are differing accounts, ranging from the suggestion of flesh eating for athletes, eating of certain parts of animals for sacrifices, and the abstinence from flesh, as suggested by Porphyry, who does, however, seem to exempt "cocks and pigs," which were used in sacrifice to the gods. Yet, he does write that the sacrifice of the ox that took place when the Pythagorean theorem was discovered was "made of flour."

43 This reference to readings may be deemed problematic since the Pythagoreans were of the oral tradition. It may be suggested that certain memorized oratories were performed.

44 Guthrie, *Pythagorean Sourcebook*, p. 129.

45 Ibid., p. 130.

46 Ibid.

47 Nicholas Culpeper (1995) *Complete Herbal*, Wordsworth Reference, pp. 86, 203, 205.

48 John Lust (1974) *The Herb Book*, New York: Bantam Books, p. 262.

49 Rosetta Clarkson (1992) *Magic Gardens*, New York: Collier Books, p. 237. This black spot could be interpreted according to the doctrine of signatures prominent in the Middle Ages. This doctrine relied on the notions of kinship and sympathetic action, as for instance, Lungwort, its leaves shaped like a lung, was held to aid lung ailments. Modern herbalism has since verified this property.

50 Ibid.

51 Richard Evans Schultes et al., (2001) *Plants of the Gods*, Healing Arts Press, p. 89.

52 For a significant account of the influence of the *doctrine of signatures* of Jakob Boehme upon the Jena Romanticism of Hölderlin and Schelling, see Paola Mayer (2000) *Jena Romanticism and Its Appropriation of Jakob Böhme: Theosophy, Hagiography, Literature*, Montreal: McGill-Queen's University Press.

53 Guthrie, *Pythagorean Sourcebook*, p. 72.

54 Eric Maple (1974) *Magic of Perfume: Aromatics and their Esoteric Significance*, Wellingborough, Northamptonshire: Aquarian Press, p. 12.

55 Guthrie, *Pythagorean Sourcebook*, p. 112.

56 I borrow this phrase from Nietzsche's essay, "On Truth and Lying in the Extra-Moral Sense."

57 Guthrie, *Pythagorean Sourcebook*, p. 114.

Chapter 8

1 Friedrich Nietzsche (1988) *Beyond Good and Evil*, translated by R.J. Hollingdale, New York: Penguin, p. 14. This quotation serves the argumentation of this chapter as it underlines the interpretation of Plato that is being set forth in distinction from Pythagoras.

2 While I do not intend to rely too heavily upon Nietzsche's interpretation, especially since he merely repeats the time-honored prejudices regarding Pythagoreanism, I do insist that his perspective is relevant and significant, as Cornford himself is quoted as remarking on *The Birth of Tragedy*.

3 It could be suggested that the Pythagorean *bios* could be most closely approximated in the vision of a chorus without the tragic hero, without the stage, and without the audience.

4 Friedrich Nietzsche (1968) *The Will to Power*, translated by Walter Kaufmann, New York: Vintage, p. 822.

5 Friedrich Nietzsche (2005) *Thus Spoke Zarathustra*, translated by Graham Parkes, Oxford: Oxford University Press, pp. 30–34.

6 For a discussion of the paradox of a free choice to enter into the "Spindle of Necessity" Robert McGahey (1994) *The Orphic Moment: Shaman to Poet-Thinker in Plato, Nietzsche, and Mallarme*, Albany, NY: SUNY Press, p. 35.

7 Nietzsche, Beyond *Good and Evil*, p. 14.

⁸ Friedrich Nietzsche (1996b) *Philosophy in the Tragic Age of the Greeks*, Section 2, translated by Marianne Cowan, New York: Regnery.

⁹ Friedrich Nietzsche (1996a) *Human All Too Human*, Section 261, translated by R.J. Hollingdale, Cambridge: Cambridge University Press.

¹⁰ Pliny (1942) *Natural History*, translated by M. Rackham, Loeb Classical Library, Boston, MA: Harvard University Press, XXVIII, 2.

¹¹ It is interesting to note in this light that while still alive, Zarathustra does visit the Blessed Isles in Nietzsche's *Thus Spoke Zarathustra*.

¹² L. Wittgenstein (2003) *Philosophical Investigations*, translated by G.E.M. Anscombe, London: Blackwell.

¹³ This is similar to the Leibnizian notion that even god, himself, must follow the Laws of Logic.

Chapter 9

¹ Plotinus (1991) *Enneads*, edited by J. Dillon, translated by S. MacKenna, New York: Penguin. While Plotinus is a neo-Platonist, emphasizing the repose of the One, we can learn from him in that he did emphasize bodily *praxis* and did not forsake the oral tradition until late, under the influence of Porphyry. In this sense, his "One" can illuminate the "All."

² This compact repose which Plotinus indicates is not that of a reader or writer, but must be taken in a meditative sense, as it was only Porphyry, in the winter of the life of Plotinus, who urged him to write down his "memories."

³ Plotinus (1960) "Letter to Flaccus," *Encyclopedia of Occult Philosophy* (New Hyde Park, NY: University Books) quoted from Lewis Spence (1960) "Neoplatonism," *An Encyclopedia of Occultism*, New Hyde Park, NY: University Books.

Chapter 10

¹ Plotinus (1960) "Letter to Flaccus," *Encyclopedia of Occult Philosophy*, New Hyde Park, NY: University Books.

² A direct kinship can be suggested between these clear rejections and a scrawl by Plotinus of a criterion of certainty inhabiting consciousness, this being within and as itself. There would be a link betwixt the adequacy between representation and its external vis-à-vis divination by way of visible amulets. Yet, as Plotinus will assert in "On the Good, or the One," visible ritual-aesthetic objects may be witnessed as intimations, or signs of divinity. Yet, this is only secondary with respect to the approaching That One via ecstatic transgressions.

³ Lewis Spence (1960) *An Encyclopedia of Occultism*, New Hyde Park, NY: University Books, p. 291.

⁴ It must be noted that the Ancient Egyptian afterlife was achieved via a successful Ordeal which occurred only after death. The Egyptian, *Book of the Dead*, or more properly, *Coming Forth By Day*, is an amulet itself guiding the dead one, exemplified by Osiris, toward a state of bliss, amidst a new life which is embodied (there

will still be erotic ecstasy in the blessed dimension), yet, which has been purified of any mortal defect or defilement. This is why the Scarab is the activating principle of the world, it rolls it ball of excrement, but can only attain perfection through a purification of itself, and thus, to throw away the ball.

5 This is to borrow the phrasing of George Bataille in his book, *Inner Experience.*

6 Lewis Spence, *Encyclopedia of Occultism*, p. 291.

7 Ibid. "To write is always irksome to me. But for the continual solicitations of Porphyry, I should not have left a line to survive me."

8 Ibid.

9 Ibid.

10 Ibid.

11 Ibid., p. 292.

12 Ibid.

13 Ibid.

Epilog

1 A more recent example of the use of the term mysticism in relation to Parmenides and Empedocles comes from Peter Kingsley (1995) in which he sets forth a contrary sense of a pagan mysticism which used the body and the senses in the recognition of the divinity of the world. The present study would be open to such a possible understanding of the term, especially in light of the significance of Empedocles as the heir to the Pythagorean *bios*, but has refrained in the present study due to the influence of Cornford and his Neoplatonistic conception of mysticism.

2 A.E. Waite (1992) *Book of Spells* (*Book of Ceremonial Magic*), Wordsworth Reference, p. xviii.

3 Marguerite Porete (1993) *The Mirror of Simple Souls*, translated by Ellen Babinsky, Paulist Press, p. 82.

4 Waite, p. xx.

5 Martin Heidegger (1963) *What is called Thinking?*, translated by Fred Wieck, New York: Harper Perennial, p. 144.

References and Further Reading

Alastair, Walter (2006) "Metaphysics, Magic and Frazer," (unpublished MA Thesis, University of Wales, Lampeter Library, Lampeter).

Albright, William Foxwell (1957) *From the Stone Age to Christianity: Monotheism and the Historical Process*, New York: Doubleday Books.

Apuleius, Lucius (2007) *The Golden Ass, or a Book of Changes*, translated by Joel Relihan, Indianapolis, IN: Hackett Publishing.

Aristotle (1987) *De Anima* (On the Soul), translated by Hugh Lawson-Tancred, New York: Penguin.

Badiou, Alain (2005a) *Being and Event*, translated by O. Felthan, New York: Continuum.

—(2005b) *Handbook of Inaesthetics*, translated by Alberto Toscano, Stanford, CA: Stanford University Press.

Bataille, Georges (1986) *Erotism: Death and Sensuality*, translated by M. Dalwood, San Francisco, CA: City Lights Books.

—(1988) *Inner Experience*, Albany, NY: SUNY Press.

—(1992) *Theory of Religion*, New York: Zone Books.

—(2002) *The Absence of Myth: Essays on Surrealism*, London: Verso.

Bertholet, Alfred (1909) *The Transmigration of Souls*, London: Harper & Brothers.

Biebuyck, Benjamin, Danny Praet, and Isabelle Vanden Poel (2004) "Cults and Migrations: Nietzsche's Meditations on Orphism, Pythagoreanism, and the Greek Mysteries," in *Nietzsche and Antiquity*, edited by Paul Bishop, Rochester, NY: Camden House, pp. 151–169.

Bowlby, Rachel (1957) "Family Realisms: Freud and Greek Tragedy", *Essays in Criticism*, vol. 56, no. 2, (April, 2006), pp. 111–138.

Buckham, P.W. (1827) *Theatre of the Greeks*, Cambridge: W.P. Grant.

Budge, E.W. (1966) *Egyptian Language*, London: Routledge & Kegan Paul.

Burkert, Walter (1972) *Lore and Science in Ancient Pythagoreanism*, translated by E.L. Minar, Cambridge, MA: Harvard University Press.

—(1985) *Greek Religion: Archaic and Classical*, Oxford: Basil Blackwell.

Clarkson, Rosetta (1992) *Magic Gardens*, New York: Collier Books.

Copleston, F. (1975) *History of Philosophy*, vol. 1, London: Burns, Oates & Washbourne.

Cornford, F.M. (1922) "Mysticism and Science in the Pythagorean Tradition," *The Classical Quarterly*, vol. 16, no. 3/4 (Jul.–Oct.), pp. 137–150.

—(1923) "Mysticism and Science in the Pythagorean Tradition (Continued)," *The Classical Quarterly*, vol. 17, no. 1 (Jan.), pp. 1–12.

—(1980) *Plato and Parmenides*, London: Routledge & Kegan Paul.

—(1987) "Divisions of the Soul," *Selected Papers*, vol. 10, pp. 242–255.

Culpeper, Nicholas (1995) *Complete Herbal*, Wordsworth Reference.

Dacier, Andre (1981) *The Life of Pythagoras* [1707], Wellingborough, Northamptonshire: Aquarian Press.

Dillon, John (1977) *The Middle Platonists: A Study of Platonism 80 BC to AD 200*, London: Duckworth.

—(1990) *The Golden Chain: Studies in the Development of Platonism and Christianity*, Farnham, Surrey: Variorum.

Eliphas, Levi [L.A. Constant] (1913) *History of Magic* (1860), translated by A.E. Waite, London: Rider.

Evelyn-White, H. (trs.) (1959) *Hesiod, the Homeric Hymns and Homerica*, Loeb Library, Cambridge, MA: Harvard University Press.

Ficino, Marsilio (1996) *Book of Life*, Woodstock, CT: Spring Publications.

Foster, John L. (trs.) (1992) *Echoes of Egyptian Voices: An Anthology of Ancient Egyptian Poetry*, Norman, OK: University of Oklahoma Press.

Foucault, Michel (1987) *History of Sexuality*, vol. 1, New York: Vintage Books.

—(2001) *The Order of Things*, New York: Routledge.

Frankfort, H.A. John A. Wilson, and Thorkild Jacobsen (1949) *Before Philosophy*, London: Pelican.

Frazer, James (1993) *The Golden Bough: A Study in Magic and Religion*, Hertfordshire: Wordsworth Reference.

Graves, Robert (1960) *The Greek Myths*, vol. 1, New York: Penguin.

—(1964) *The Greek Myths*, vol. 1, Harmondsworth: Penguin Books.

Guthrie, Kenneth Sylvan (1987) *The Pythagorean Sourcebook and Library*, Grand Rapids, MI: Phanes Press.

Guthrie, W.K.C. (1962) *A History of Greek Philosophy, vol. I: The Earlier Presocratics and the Pythagoreans*, Cambridge: Cambridge University Press.

—(1987) *The Greek Philosophers*, London: Methuen.

Harrison, Jane Ellen (1957) *Prolegomena to the Study of Greek Religion*, New York: Meridian Books.

Heidegger, Martin (1963) *What is called Thinking?*, translated by Fred Wieck, New York: Harper Perennial.

—(1971) "Building Dwelling Thinking," in *Poetry, Language, Thought*, translated by Albert Hofstadter, New York: Harper Torchbooks, pp. 143–162.

—(1976) *Poetry, Language, Thought*, translated by Albert Hofstadter, New York: Harper Perennial.

—(1985) *Early Greek Thinking*, New York: Harper Collins Publishing.

—(2001) *The Fundamental Concepts of Metaphysics: World, Finitude, Solitude*, Bloomington, IN: Indiana University Press.

—(2003) "The Origin of the Work of Art," in *Basic Writings*, translated by D.F. Krell, London: Routledge, pp. 15–88.

Hermann, Arnold (2004) *To Think Like God: Pythagoras and Parmenides, the Origins of Philosophy*, Las Vegas, NV: Parmenides Publishing.

Hoff, Johannes (2005) "Philosophie als performative Praktik. Spuren cusanischen Denkens bei Jacques Derrida und Michel de Certeau," *Cusanus-Rezeption in der Philosophie des 20. Jahrhunderts*, Regensburg: Roderer, pp. 93–120. (*Philosophy as Performative Practice. Traces of Nicholas of Cusa in Jacques Derrida and Michel de Certeau.*)

Hölderlin, Friedrich (2004) *Friedrich Hölderlin: Poems and Fragments*, translated by Michael Hamburger, London: Anvil Press.

Husserl (1964) *Phenomenology of Internal Time-Consciousness*, Bloomington, IN: Indiana University Press.

Irigaray, Luce (1993) *Sexes and Genealogies*, translated by Gillian Gill, New York: Columbia University Press.

Kahn, Charles (2001) *Pythagoras and Pythagoreans: A Brief History*, Indianapolis, IN: Hackett Publishing.

Kingsley, Peter (1995) *Ancient Philosophy, Mystery and Magic: Empedocles and the Pythagorean Tradition*, Oxford: Oxford University Press.

Kirk, G.S. (1988) *The Presocratic Philosophers*, Cambridge: Cambridge University Press.

Long, H.S. (1948) *A Study of the Doctrine of Metempsychosis in Greece from Pythagoras to Plato*, dissertation, Princeton, NJ: Princeton University Press.

Luchte, James (2006) "Mathesis and Analysis: Finitude and the Infinite in the *Monadology* of Leibniz," *Heythrop Journal*, vol. 47, no. 4, pp. 519–543.

—(2008) *Heidegger's Early Philosophy: The Phenomenology of Ecstatic Temporality*, London: Continuum.

—(2009) "Under the Aspect of Time ('sub specie temporis'): Heidegger Wittgenstein and the Place of the Nothing," *Philosophy Today*, vol. 53, no.1, pp. 70–84.

Lust, John (1974) *The Herb Book*, New York: Bantam Books.

Maple, Eric (1974) *Magic of Perfume: Aromatics and their Esoteric Significance*, Wellingborough, Northamptonshire: Aquarian Press.

Mayer, Paola (2000) *Jena Romanticism and Its Appropriation of Jakob Böhme: Theosophy, Hagiography, Literature*, Montreal: McGill-Queen's University Press.

McGahey, Robert (1994) *The Orphic Moment: Shaman to Poet-Thinker in Plato, Nietzsche, and Mallarme*, Albany, NY: SUNY Press.

Meillassoux, Quentin (2007) *After Finitude: An Essay on the Necessity of Contingency*, London: Continuum.

Milbank and Oliver (2009) in the *Radical Orthodoxy Reader*, London: Routledge.

Nietzsche, Friedrich (1967) *The Birth of Tragedy*, translated by Walter Kaufmann, London: Penguin.

—(1968) *The Will to Power*, translated by Walter Kaufmann, New York: Vintage.

—(1988) *Beyond Good and Evil*, translated by R.J. Hollingdale, New York: Penguin.

—(1989) *On Rhetoric and Language*, Oxford: Oxford University Press.

—(1996a) *Human All Too Human*, translated by R.J. Hollingdale, Cambridge: Cambridge University Press.

—(1996b) *Philosophy in the Tragic Age of the Greeks*, translated by Marianne Cowan, New York: Regnery.

—(2003) *The Genealogy of Morals*, translated by Horace Samuel, New York: Dover.

—(2005) *Thus Spoke Zarathustra*, translated by Graham Parkes, Oxford: Oxford University Press.

O'Meara, Dominic (1991) *Pythagoras Revived*, Oxford: Oxford University Press.

Penglase, Charles (1997) *Greek Myths and Mesopotamia*, London: Routledge.

Plato (1989) *Collected Dialogues*, Princeton, NJ: Princeton University Press.

Pliny (1942) *Natural History*, translated by M. Rackham, Loeb Classical Library, Boston, MA: Harvard University Press.

Plotinus (1960) "Letter to Flaccus," *Encyclopedia of Occult Philosophy*, New Hyde Park, NY: University Books.

—(1991) *Enneads*, edited by J. Dillon, translated by S. MacKenna, New York: Penguin.

Porete, Marguerite (1993) *The Mirror of Simple Souls*, translated by Ellen Babinsky, Mahwah, NJ: Paulist Press.

Porter, J. (2005) "Nietzsche and Tragedy," in *A Companion to Tragedy*, edited by Rebecca Bushnell, London: Blackwell, pp. 68–87.

Raven, J.E. (1948) *Pythagoreans and Eleatics*, Cambridge: Cambridge University Press.

Riedweg, Christoph (2005) *Pythagoras: His Life, Teaching and Influence*, Ithaca, NY: Cornell University Press.

Rimbaud, Arthur (1975) *Complete Works*, New York: Harper & Row.

Savinio, Alberto (1992) "Psyche," in *Lives of the Gods*, edited by James Brook, New York: Atlas Press, p. 8–14.

Schultes, Richard Evans, Albert Hofmann, and Christian Rätsch (2001) *Plants of the Gods*, Rochester, VT: Healing Arts Press.

Schürmann, Reiner (1986) *Heidegger: Being and Acting, From Principles to Anarchy*, Bloomington, IN: Indiana University Press.

— (2003) *Broken Hegemonies*, Bloomington, IN: Indiana University Press.

— (1988) "Tragic Differing: The Law of the One and the Law of Contraries in Parmenides," *Graduate Faculty Philosophy Journal*, vol. 13, no. 1, pp. 9–13.

Sheppard, J.T. (1912) "Greek Tragedy," *The Classical Journal*, vol. 8, no. 2 (Nov.), pp. 94–96.

Soustelle, Jacques (1971) *The Four Suns*, translated by E. Ross, London: Andre Deutsch.

Spence, Lewis (1960) *An Encyclopaedia of Occultism*, New Hyde Park , NY: University Books.

Taylor, Thomas (1986) *Iamblichus' Life of Pythagoras*, Rochester, VT: Inner Traditions.

Waite, A.E. (1992) *Book of Spells* (*Book of Ceremonial Magic*), Wordsworth Reference.

Wertheim, Margaret (1997) *Pythagoras' Trousers: God, Physics and the Gender Wars*, London: W. W. Norton & Company.

West, M. L. (1996) *Greek Metre*, Oxford: Oxford University Press.

Wittgenstein, L. (1958) *The Blue and Brown Books*, edited by Rush Rhys, Oxford: Basil Blackwell.

—(1987) *Remarks on Frazer's Golden Bough*, translated by A.C. Miles, Hereford: Brynmill Press.

—(1993) "Remarks on Frazer's *Golden Bough*," in *Philosophical Occasions*, edited by James C. Klagge and Alfred Nordmann, Indianapolis, IN: Hackett Publishing, pp. 115–155.

—(2003) *Philosophical Investigations*, translated by G.E.M. Anscombe, London: Blackwell.

Xenophon (1990) *Memoirs of Socrates*, London: Penguin.

Yates, Fancis A. (1991) *Giordano Bruno and the Hermetic Tradition*, Chicago, IL: University of Chicago Press.

Zelenak, Michael (1998) *Gender and Politics in Greek Tragedy*, New York: Peter Lang Publishing.

Index

Printed in Great Britain
by Amazon